Classroom Communication and Diversity

Enhancing Instructional Practice
2nd Edition

Robert G. Powell and
Dana L. Powell

Routledge
Taylor & Francis Group

NEW YORK AND LONDON

First edition published 2004
by Lawrence Erlbaum Associates, Inc.

This edition published 2010
by Routledge
270 Madison Avenue, New York, NY 10016

Simultaneously published in the UK
by Routledge
2 Park Square, Milton Park, Abingdon, Oxon OX14 4RN

*Routledge is an imprint of the Taylor & Francis Group, an informa
business*

© 2010 Taylor & Francis

Typeset in Gill Sans and Sabon by Book Now Ltd, London
Printed and bound in the United States of America on acid-free
paper by Edwards Brothers, Inc.

Library of Congress Cataloging in Publication Data
Powell, Robert G.
Classroom communication and diversity / Robert G. Powell, Dana
L. Powell.—2nd ed.
        p. cm.
Includes index.
1. Multicultural education—United States. 2. Educational
equalization—United States. I. Powell, Dana L. II. Title.
LC1099.3.P694 2010
370.117—dc22   2009050480

ISBN13: 978–0–415–87718–3 (hbk)
ISBN13: 978–0–415–87719–0 (pbk)
ISBN13: 978–0–203–85606–2 (ebk)

Contents

Classroom Communication and Diversity

Teachers face myriad communication challenges in today's classroom, reflecting the growing diversity of the student body; the ever-increasing number of students; gender issues; and students' learning disabilities. This volume provides a useful framework for helping new and experienced teachers manage the diverse communication challenges they encounter. It also encourages teachers to reflect on how their personal cultures influence their expectations about appropriate classroom communication and ways to demonstrate learning.

This textbook is distinctive in its integration of information from a variety of sources to establish a viewpoint that focuses on the needs of the individual learner. Drawing on the research in the communication and education disciplines, authors Robert G. Powell and Dana L. Powell provide theoretical models and useful strategies for improving instructional practices. They address the ways in which culture influences communication in the classroom, and assist teachers in developing the skills necessary to meet the needs of the students in their classrooms.

Much of the information shared in this text derives from the authors' research and experience in schools and from the experiences of others, including teachers, parents, and children. Their experiences, combined with the cross-disciplinary approach, produce a volume of unique perspectives and considerable insight. Teachers and scholars in the communication and education disciplines will find this text to be a practical and valuable tool for classroom teaching, and it is appropriate for instructional communication courses in the areas of communication and education.

Robert G. Powell (PhD, University of Nebraska) is Director of the Assistant Lecturer Program at California State University, Fresno. He is currently investigating alternative instructional strategies for teaching and measuring critical thinking. He is also interested in the role of student culture on instructional practices and better understanding processes which influence learning in the classroom. He has been selected as a Master Teacher by WSCA and was Chair of the Instructional Development Division of ICA. He is an Associate Editor of the *Journal of Applied Communication*.

Dana L. Powell is Assistant Professor of special education at California State University, Fresno. She has over 20 years' experience, as a teacher, administrator, and therapist, working with students who have learning, emotional, and/or behavioral problems. Her research interests include programming for students at risk, parent involvement, behavior management, social skills training, and inclusion of special needs students in the mainstream.

Communication Series
Edited by Jennings Bryant/Dolf Zillman, General Editors

Figures

Tables

Preface

The first edition of *Classroom Communication and Diversity: Enhancing Instructional Practice* was designed to provide a framework for helping new and experienced teachers manage the challenges they face in the classroom. The feedback that we received from our colleagues and students who used the book indicated that it was theoretically grounded and pedagogically useful. We were particularly gratified to learn that many students choose not to sell the text back to the bookstore after completing the class. However, as we advise our students, learning does not end with one project or one classroom experience. Rather, learning involves a process of thoughtful reflection that leads to more clarity, insight, and work. After using the first edition and learning about new research on instructional practice, we decided to write a new edition.

There are several changes to the 2nd edition that we believe improve it considerably. Diversity is discussed throughout the textbook. We consider diversity to include but not be limited to race, ethnicity, gender, and ability. Moreover, we also believe that diversity is fluid and multidimensional. Different facets of diversity emerge in different contexts. Consequently, an aspect of diversity is discussed in each chapter.

We updated and extended the content throughout the text. In Chapter 1, we added a discussion of the ways in which language, power, and privilege are contested in classrooms. Chapter 2 contains a focused discussion of four theories of motivation that have been used to explain student interest and academic engagement. An extended discussion of identity and academic performance has been added to Chapter 3. We also offered strategies for teaching in dialectically diverse classrooms.

Chapter 4 contains content on the brain research that has been used to explain behavioral differences between males and females. We continue to explain that classrooms are "gendering spaces" that constrain academic and social performance. We have also added data on the performance of males and females in language and math. Similarly, in Chapter 5, we added information on Universal Design for Learning, a strategy for increasing the academic success of all students.

A discussion on the theories explaining the positive effects of teacher–student relationships has been added to Chapter 6. We also discuss how different relationship theories apply at different developmental stages. Chapter 7 includes an extended discussion of strategies for building learning communities.

Chapter 8, which focuses on behavioral management, includes an extended discussion of natural and logical consequences. New information on differentiated instruction and culturally responsive teaching has been added to Chapter 9. This chapter provides the reader with a template for planning and implementing effective teaching strategies for teaching students with a range of abilities. Finally, in Chapter 10, we updated the data on how students use technology and included recommendations for the meaningful use of technology in the classroom.

Finally, at the end of each chapter, we have provided the reader with learning activities on the concepts discussed and web sites for additional supporting materials. As a whole, we believe that this edition promotes our belief that learning is a complex social endeavor and the goals of learning are best served by promoting positive and respectful teacher–student relationships.

Acknowledgments

There are several people that we would like to acknowledge. First, we would like to thank the professionals at Routledge, Linda Bathgate, Katherine Ghezzi, for their support and help in the preparation of this edition. Second, we would like to thank Jacqueline Williams and P. Rudy Mattai whose thoughtful and insightful reviews helped us sharpen the focus of this revision. Third, we thank Barbara Aston and David Lennon who collectively have more than 60 years of classroom experience. They used the first edition of the text in their classes and offered excellent suggestions on how to make the content relevant and meaningful for classroom teachers. Fourth, we would like to thank Linda Caffegian, who has dedicated more than 30 years to being a special education teacher and to supervising special education teachers. Her feedback was extremely helpful. Finally, we would like to thank the students who, through their responses to the text, inspired us to write a second edition.

Introduction

The aim of this edition of *Classroom Communication and Diversity*: *Enhancing Instructional Practice* is to provide a useful framework for teaching in today's diverse classroom. We believe that effective communication is at the heart of the teaching process. Lesson plans, state standards, textbooks, and technologies do not stand on their own but are put into action through communication. Good teachers are effective communicators.

One of the challenges to effective communication is diversity. There are many approaches to studying and teaching about diversity. Some theorists equate this term with multicultural education (e.g. Banks, 1999). Banks and Banks (1984), for example, defined multicultural education as "a field of study and an emerging discipline whose major aim is to create equal educational opportunities from diverse racial, ethnic, social-class, and cultural groups" (p. xi). Wlodkowski and Ginsberg (1995) acknowledged the different interpretations of diversity and for the purposes of their research argued that it "conveys a need to respect similarities and differences among human beings and to go beyond 'sensitivity' to active and effective responsiveness" (pp. 8–9). Nieto (2002) described diversity as "[the] range of differences that encompass race, ethnicity, gender, social class, ability and language" (p. 183). We build on these definitions but also consider diversity to be a fluid and multidimensional concept. Culture, ethnicity, gender, class, and exceptionality emerge and converge in a number of communication spaces. Consider, for example, a crystal. It is multifaceted and complex. Depending on the way light reflects through it, certain features become prominent while learning styles. We conclude the chapter with a discussion of ways to cultivate culturally responsive teaching.

There are four units in this volume. Unit I focuses on the foundations of communication in the learning context. In Chapter 1 we explain the components of the communication process that are discussed throughout the text. This volume contains an extended discussion on language, and class and clarifies the relationship between culture, class, language and learning. Chapter 2 explores the relationship between communication and learning outcomes. This chapter discusses three major areas: student abilities (the competencies that students bring to the classroom), student motivation, and communication processes. Four major theories of motivation are reviewed): self-efficacy theory, attribution theory, self-worth theory and achievement goal theory. We conclude Chapter 2 with the discussion of the communication processes that impact learning outcome.

Unit II explores diversity. Chapter 3 examines cultural diversity. We introduce the reader to the value dimensions of culture and the way they impact classroom behavior. Culture, language and identity are examined in detail. Specifically, we challenge the reader to consider attitudes about language, how it varies from situation to situation, what it means for academic connection, and learning. Chapter 3 also discusses the impact of culture on relationship. This chapter also discusses ways in the teacher–student relationship develops and changes over time. We conclude the chapter by discussing specific constructs that predidt academic engagement.

Chapter 4 examines studies on sex and gender. Researchers and teachers frequently use gender and sex interchangeably but they are different and lead to very different conclusions about females and males. One of our goals, then, is to understand the differences between sex, which is biological, and gender, which is social psychological. This chapter begins with a brief discussion of brain research on males and females. The second section examines the way in which schools serve to shape and reinforce gender identities. The chapter reviews studies on male and female academic performance and discusses classroom interaction patterns. One of our goals is to challenge teachers not to tie academic and social expectations to attitudes about sex differences.

The final chapter in Unit II provides an overview of students with exceptionalities. Students who are culturally and linguistically diverse and have disabilities present some unique challenges for educators. The characteristics of students qualifying for special education are presented in detail as well as teaching techniques and strategies to help students succeed both academically and socially. We discuss the importance of collaboration in this process. Finally, we introduce two initiatives which support the use of research-based practices for individualizing instruction for all learners. As we argued previously, students with special needs also are a resource to be cultivated in the classroom.

In Unit III, we examine research on ways to build, sustain, and manage teacher–student relationships. Instructional goals are more easily accomplished when teachers have positive relationships with their students. We begin Chapter 6 with a discussion of theories explaining the way in which academic engagement is influenced by a positive teacher–student others stay in the background. Similarly, people are multidimensional; different features of identity are enacted and negotiated in different contexts. In our experience, too many teachers view diversity as something a student must overcome if they are to be academically successful. We would like educators to view diversity as a valuable resource that will help them forge positive relationships that will in turn promote positive student learning outcomes.

Chapter 7 focuses on ways to build a community of learners. We outline the defining features of community and explain how to foster it in a classroom setting. Among the topics examined are teacher support, peer-mediated learning, cooperative learning, peer mediation, classroom meetings, and service learning.

Behavioral management is the focus of Chapter 8 Educators' perceptions of the underlying causes of behavior will inform the way they attempt to manage it. Chapter 8 covers several theoretical perspectives on behavior including etiology and application. We also consider the way culture influences the perception of behavior. In this chapter we discuss punishment and the use of proactive strategies. New information has been added on ways to use natural and logical consequences.

The goal of Unit IV is to provide insight on strategies for presenting instructional material. Planning is a key to effective teaching. We provide information on lesson plans and differentiated instruction. Differentiated instruction is especially designed to help teachers design curriculum for diverse learners. Following this discussion, we offer communication strategies for presenting and managing academic content. Specifically, we discuss lecturing, small groups, cooperative learning, ways to enhance explanations and the use of questions.

We conclude the text with a discussion on the role of technology in the classroom. In addition to providing the reader with ways to use technology in the classroom, we have added a section on the attributes of meaningful learning using technology. Another addition is on ways in which mobile phones can be used to accomplish instructional tasks. This chapter also identifies changes in access and the different strategies for implementing technologies into instructional practice.

We believe that learning is best served when students and teachers have an on-going conversation about concepts and ideas. As in the first edition, we have provided reflection questions to promote discussion. At the end of each chapter we have also provided examples of learning activities to enhance understanding. Finally, internet resources are included for further information.

Unit 1

Foundations of Classroom Communication and Diversity

This unit lays the groundwork for effective instructional communication in diverse classrooms. Chapter 1 focuses on the communication process and its role in learning. First, we review three models of communication. Second, we discuss verbal symbols and their role in learning. Third, we discuss nonverbal communication. We conclude Chapter 1 with a discussion of listening.

The major factors influencing instructional outcomes are discussed in Chapter 2. We outline three major predictors of academic performance: individual ability, motivation, and communication. First, we review the literature on multiple intelligences and emotional intelligence. Second, we overview four major theories of motivation. Finally, we discuss the communication processes that are used to manage instructional processes.

Chapter 1

Communication in the Classroom

John, a first-year second-grade teacher, is about to begin his reading group. Desmond, a Native American, sits at the table with his arms crossed, looking down. When it is his turn to read, Desmond remains silent. The teacher calls him by name: "Desmond, why aren't you reading, are you tired? Did you stay up late last night?" The more the teacher implores, the more Desmond resists. The teacher threatens Desmond and says, "If you don't read, you will lose recess time." Finally, Desmond gets up from the table and leaves the classroom. The teacher follows yelling for Desmond to go to vice principal.

This scenario reveals the complex relationship between communication and culture. Desmond is a Native-American child who has been taught that silence is appropriate and revealing private feelings and emotions is inappropriate. The teacher, a white male, expects the student to engage in a learning task when called on. These different orientations are underneath the surface, but they can result in conflict, misunderstanding, and alienation. These types of events occur every day in America's schools, as teachers and students navigate their interpersonal relationships, instructional goals and objectives. The aim of this book is to inform teachers and potential teachers about the central role of communication in today's classroom. We are particularly interested in helping teachers understand the ways in which diversity influences classroom communication and orientations to learning.

Communication

Human communication is ubiquitous. It exists everywhere and has profound impact on what unfolds in a communication setting. All that happens in the classroom is created and sustained through communication processes. Lesson plans, teaching methods, discipline strategies, explanations, and critiques of student work occur through the communication exchanges between teachers and learners. Communication is dynamic and complex, but it can be learned and understood if we carefully examine it in "chunks" and apply what we learn to real-world circumstances.

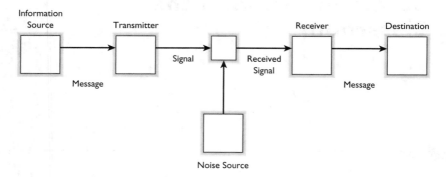

Figure 1.1 Message-Centered Model of Communication: the Shannon and Weaver Model.

To begin our examination of classroom communication, we will first describe how our understanding of communication has evolved. The way in which we approach and manage communication is related to our definition of it. The early theorists focused on the message. Communication was considered a one-way phenomenon. Different occasions called for different types or forms of speech. Campaign speeches required one kind of communication, funeral orations another. Thus, the early theorists contributed to our understanding of communication by suggesting that messages were connected to the setting. An effective communicator needed to master these different forms of discourse. A message-centered approach to human communication continued for many years. Shannon and Weaver (1949) refined the message-centered approach by describing the processes that influenced the clarity of messages (see Figure 1.1).

Communication was considered a linear process, with the initiation of a message at one point (information source) and the termination of it at another (destination). The key to effective communication was the clarity of communication exchanges. Clarity was achieved when the message sent was the message received. Noise, both external and internal, distorted a message and interfered with clarity.

Consider, for example, a lecture. The instructor (information source) presents the information in front of a class (transmits through speech). As the instructor presents the information a lawnmower is roaring outside the classroom (external noise). Some of the students are focusing on the lawnmower noise and others on a tiny white piece of tissue that is stuck on the chin of the teacher (internal noise). The students receive the information in light of the processes that influence its reception.

David Berlo (1960) dramatically influenced our thinking about human communication. His book, *The Process of Human Communication,* built

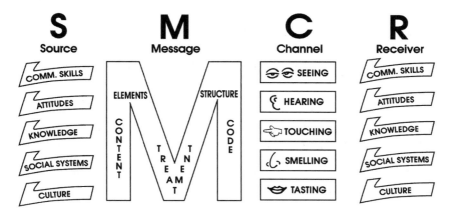

Figure 1.2 The SMCR Model of Communication.

upon previous thinking but also introduced a number of new ideas. He continued to maintain a focus on the message but he addressed the factors influencing the production of and reception of messages (see Figure 1.2).

Berlo's (1960) model is important for a number of reasons. It introduced the complexity of the human communicator. Notice that any message is influenced by a number of individual difference variables. Let's focus on teachers for a moment. They come to the classroom with a variety of communication skills. Some are good listeners, some are organized, and some are funny. They also have different attitudes. Some like athletics, some like math. Teachers have different levels of knowledge. Some seem to know a great deal about the subjects they teach, others seem to struggle. Teachers come from different social systems and cultures. Culture and social system influence perceptions, language use and rules for appropriate behavior. Taken together, these factors shape the way in which a message is structured, what is emphasized, and how it is coded.

Messages are sent through a variety of channels. The senses—seeing, hearing, touching, smelling, and tasting—can be part of a communication exchange. The reception of a message is also influenced by the receiver's communication skills, attitudes, knowledge, social system and culture. The farther apart the sender and receiver are on these variables, the more problematic the communication becomes.

Berlo went on to introduce other principles of communication that previously had not been discussed. One principle is that communication is a process. Berlo drew from Heraclitus, an ancient scholar, who posited that people could never step in the same river twice. Over time, the people and the river are different. Berlo explains the importance of process when he states:

If we accept the concept of process, we view events and relationships as dynamic, on going, ever changing, continuous. When we label something as a process we also mean that it does not have a beginning, an end, a fixed sequence of events. It is not static, at rest. It is moving. The ingredients within a process interact; each affects all of the others.

(p. 24)

Consider an apology. When you have done something to hurt someone, saying "I'm sorry" does not erase the action that caused the hurt. In communication we are constantly building and responding to actions that have occurred. We build and rebuild but we never start from scratch. Every communication has a consequence and each exchange builds upon previous ones. Even though we might like to start each day anew, the reality is that we build upon the residue of previous events.

Another principle Berlo introduced is interdependence. He contended that any source (speaker) is dependent on a receiver to carry the communication forward. Consider the way interdependence plays out between students and teachers. A student needs a teacher to do "teacher things," such as constructing lesson plans, assigning homework, correcting student projects and imparting information. Teachers in turn need students to do "student things," such as asking questions, completing homework, and listening attentively to the teacher. This interdependence helps shape an educational context with expectations about appropriate behavior.

Berlo made significant contributions to our understanding of communication behavior, his model continued to emphasize the message. In 1970, Dean Barnlund produced a transactional model of communication (see Figure 1.3), which focused on the way that communicators act upon the meanings they construct.

Barnlund's model reintroduces the importance of the setting or context of communication. In the Barnlund model, communicators respond to a number of internal and external cues. A communicator is simultaneously a sender and receiver. In a communication event, senders and receivers may focus on public cues such as the type of setting. A cramped classroom is different from a roomy comfortable one. A church provides different guidelines from a mosque. Senders and receivers also act on private cues. Teachers may say to themselves as they give a lecture, "These students have no idea what I am talking about." Senders and receivers also respond to nonverbal behavioral cues. One teacher used to spit so much when he lectured that the students stopped sitting in the front row. Students may focus on the way a male teacher tugs at his mustache while answering questions or the way he uses his hands to emphasize important points. Finally, there are verbal cues. The words and language styles that senders and receivers use impact communication. One philosophy

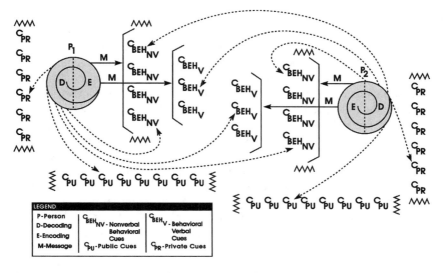

Figure 1.3 Barnlund's Meaning-Centered Model of Communication.

teacher used to spice his lectures with Latin phrases and then say, "which need no translation." Needless to say, several of the students were very confused.

Barnlund's transactional model stresses the fact that communication is complex and individuals ultimately act on the meanings they construct. Some receivers may get their meanings from private cues and others may focus on the verbal message. All the elements of the context interact to help shape understanding. The nonverbal style of the teacher (gestures, mannerisms), the verbal style (sentence structure, vocabulary), the physical environment (a warm and inviting room or a cold and unappealing setting), all influence the meanings constructed by students.

The Barnlund model also notes that meanings are negotiated between communication participants. Teachers and students work through course content and teacher–student relationships through the process of communication. Frymier and Houser (2000) examined the communication skills associated with this process. The authors extended Burleson and Sampter's (1990) research on the skills necessary for friendship to the classroom setting. Eight communication skills were assessed: conversational skills (the ability to initiate, maintain, and terminate conversations), referential skill (the ability to convey information), ego-supportive skill (the ability to make others feel good about themselves), comforting skills (the ability to make others feel better when depressed), conflict management (the ability to reach mutually satisfying solutions to conflicts), persuasive skill (the ability to get people to modify their thoughts or behaviors), narrative skill (the ability to entertain through jokes and stories), and regulation (the ability to help someone who has violated a norm to fix the mistake effectively). Although each of the skills were considered important, referential skill, ego support and conflict management were particularly significant. In addition, the authors found that communication skills positively correlated with student learning and motivation.

A meaning-centered view helps us understand the differences in the way teachers respond to classroom activities. Expert teachers, those with a great deal of experience in the classroom, see classroom events differently from novice teachers (Bransford, Brown, & Cocking, 2000). In addition to being more knowledgeable, experts are better able to contextualize learning material. That is, because they are well versed on the information, they can adapt it to the world-views of different students.

So where are we today? Contemporary theorists do not believe that communication rests in the production and presentation of a single message. Rather, any communication event involves a context in which a number of factors play roles in the way the communication unfolds. Among the issues that are important are the physical setting, the relationship between the participants, and the goals of participants. In summary, our concept of communication has evolved from a linear notion that focused exclusively on the message to a "transactional one" in which participants share in the construction and management of meanings.

Several factors are related to the way in which these meanings are managed. Each individual enters a communication exchange with a set of experiences, values, and beliefs. In addition, each person has a wide range of competencies that also influence the production and reception of messages. At the center of these processes is the individual's symbol system.

Verbal Symbols

Verbal messages, the symbols we use to communicate, play a dramatic role in the classroom. Symbol making and symbol using are fundamental to human communicative behavior. A symbol is something that stands for something else. Words, icons, and some gestures are symbols. Symbols are contextually flexible. Meanings for symbols vary from situation to situation. In Milwaukee, a drinking fountain is called a bubbler. The machine used to harvest wheat is called a combine in Nebraska and a harvester in the San Joaquin Valley. We drink a soda in California and pop in Cleveland.

Symbols are also arbitrary. We make up words to represent something. Think about the nicknames people have. How did they get them? What do they signify? Educators are notorious for creating new labels for students. Labels such as jock, shy, gifted, bilingual, ADD, prep, skater, and nerd have specific meanings and imply expectations about academic performance and classroom communication. Although labels might be efficient, they can also be problematic. We can lock people into an expectation based on the words we use to describe them. Words and situations change, but if individuals do not have an understanding of the context in which the symbol is being used, then misunderstanding and sometimes embarrassment can result.

Reflection

♦ **What are some of the labels used to describe students?**
♦ **What do these labels imply or suggest about these students?**

Finally, symbols are abstract. Some words are quite concrete and are easily understood. Words such as basketball, notebook, and desk have a limited range of interpretation, but words such as love, democracy, and racism are more difficult to understand.

We cannot underestimate the role that language plays in the instructional setting. Our model of communication presupposes that individuals act upon the meanings they construct. These constructions are inextricably tied to the symbol system individuals possess. Teachers are constrained by the symbols they use to impart information and students are constrained by the symbols they use to understand the teacher. A young Latina tried to explain a quinceanera to her Anglo teacher. The young woman struggled to find ways to explain this cultural tradition in a way that her teacher would understand. She grew frustrated and closed off the exchange by saying—"Oh, never mind." How many times have teachers grown so frustrated over trying to explain a concept that they have given up and moved on to a new or different idea?

Human symbolic behavior influences not only the content of messages but also the way we organize and structure interaction. For example, students must understand the difference between a question and a directive. A teacher may say to students, who are talking during a lesson, "Are you finished with your work?" The teacher is really saying, "Get to work and stop talking," but for that utterance to be effective, the student must also understand that this utterance is a directive. The student who says, "Yes" and continues to talk, seeing the comment as a question, may be chastised for being disrespectful.

Language and Learning

Theorists also argue that there is a relationship between language and knowledge. Dance (1982) contended that human capacity to use speech, to talk and listen, leads to the development of human conceptualization, which is necessary for the development of intellect, understanding, and knowledge. Language does more than package or represent something, it embodies an individual's understanding of the world (Langer, 1942; Stewart, 1986). Knowledge, then, is socially constructed rather than individually received. Sprague (1992) argued that individuals interested in instructional communication have focused too much on the role of teacher talk in the classroom. She contended that student talk facilitates learning of all subjects and should therefore, be understood by teachers and researchers as well.

Vygotsky (1981), a prominent Russian scholar, contended that mental processes and communication are inextricably intertwined. That is, the ability to learn and think is connected to communication processes. One of Vygotsky's major contributions was the zone of proximal development (Vygotsky, 1978). The zone of proximal development is the distance between independent problem solving ability and the potential development that can be accomplished through adult guidance or in collaboration with more skilled peers. Communication, therefore, is the mechanism through which these developmental processes occur.

According to Forman and Cazden (1998), communication with more competent peers, teachers, and tutors requires individuals to reconcile different perspectives on an issue or problem and as a consequence experience cognitive growth. Negotiation is one of the communication activities that influences cognition. (Azmitia, 1998; Miller, 1987). As individuals move from childhood to adulthood, they must learn to manage situations involving alternative viewpoints. Negotiation requires individuals to engage in arguments that reveal strengths and weaknesses of a perspective. Think about the way in which students deliberate on classroom projects. The tension fueled from these exchanges must be resolved. Learning a new perspective or developing a new insight is one way the tension is resolved (Piaget, 1965). Knowledge, then, is not passively received, but emerges through interaction with peers and teachers.

The relationship between learning and language is at the core of constructivist approaches to education. Constructivism is predicated on the belief that learners construct their own meaning from interaction with texts, problems, materials, students, teachers, and other features of the learning environment (Arends, Winitzky, & Tannenbaum, 2001). Students are not empty vessels to be filled with some type of intellectual fluid. Each student comes to the educational environment, steeped in experiences, competencies, and beliefs. Communication processes play a significant role in the way instructional processes are managed.

Language Diversity

American classrooms are linguistically diverse spaces (Nieto, 2002). One of the more challenging tasks students face is learning the language of the classroom. Reagan (2002) observed that participation in classroom discourse practices requires students to learn a linguistic system different from the one they are used to. This language tends to utilize formal grammar and syntax. A number of factors influence student use of Standard English such as culture, social class, and gender. Some teachers and administrators have negative attitudes about language diversity and believe that some students enter the class with language deficits that must be fixed if they are going to be successful. Numerous theorists challenge this belief and contend that it creates a power differential that not only privileges a style of discourse but also the person who speaks it. (e.g. Bernstein, 1990; Bourdieu & Passeron, 1990; Cazden, 1988; Reagan, 2002). Nieto (2002) argued:

> It is evident that issues of status and power must be taken into account in reconceptualizing language diversity. This means developing an awareness that privilege, ethnocentrism, and racism are at the core of policies and practices that limit the use of languages other than officially recognized high status languages allowed in schools and in the society in general. When particular languages are prohibited or denigrated, the voices of those who speak them are silenced and rejected as well.
>
> (pp. 81–82)

It should not be surprising then that bilingual students also face challenges. Bilingual education is one of the more controversial topics in education today. Gollnick and Chinn (1994) observed that rather than valuing children who speak more than one language, we expect them to give up their home language as soon as possible. There is a prevailing belief that bilingual children are educationally disadvantaged. The data supporting these educational attitudes are not clear. Yeung, Marsh, and Suliman (2000) conducted an extensive investigation of the effects of home language on academic performance. The results indicated that proficiency in a language other than English as home language had a positive effect on objective tests of English proficiency. Vang (2005) reported that Hmong youth, who could read their native language, were more proficient in learning English than Hmong youth who could not read in their native language.

The child who is competent in a home language and regularly uses a language other than English may over time reap some important educational advantages. The child who does not have proficiency in a home language, however, is in a precarious position. Some students speak linguistic blends such as "Spanglish," which is a casual form of discourse. Yeung, Marsh, and Suliman (2000) acknowledged that if the learner's first language was not established, there would not be positive effects of home language on second-language acquisition. Many students who sit in linguistic limbo may be the students at most risk.

Nonverbal Communication

In addition to verbal language, nonverbal cues affect meaning (see the Barnlund model). Literally hundreds of studies have been conducted on this area of communication (e.g. Burgoon, 1985; Knapp, Cody, & Reardon, 1987; Knapp, Wiemann, & Daly; 1978; Smith 1984).

Lustig and Koester (1999) suggested that nonverbal communication serves to accent, complement, contradict, regulate, and substitute for verbal messages. We can use a nonverbal message to emphasize a point, to say Donny got it right! Nonverbal messages can be contradictory. Think about the teacher who looks at his watch while saying, "Come in and see me; I always have time for my students." Nonverbal communication can be used to substitute for verbal messages. For example, a teacher might put an index finger over the mouth to ask for silence.

These general functions of nonverbal communication become problematic when we introduce culture. Students from different cultural backgrounds have different interpretations for nonverbal communication. White students often "grin and nod," when they agree with a teacher, and Asian students may "grin and nod" even if they don't understand the teacher.

Knapp and Hall (1992) provided a useful typology for examining non-verbal communication in the classroom. Their classification consists of: (1) environmental factors; (2) physical appearance; (3) proxemics; (4) kinesics; and (5) paralanguage.

Environmental Factors

The physical setting is an environmental factor that influences communication in a number of ways. We cannot identify a direct relationship between a physical setting and learning, but we can conclude that the physical setting establishes a set of expectations and constraints that influence attitudes and communication. We may have a very aesthetically pleasing classroom with tasteful artwork, well-organized workstations, and moveable desks designed to facilitate learning tasks and communication, but we cannot be sure that learning will occur in that setting. Similarly, we cannot conclude that learning will not occur in classrooms with tiles falling from the ceiling, faded paint on the walls, and outdated equipment. Ultimately, educational outcomes are most directly related to the activities occurring in the context of instruction.

Physical Appearance

Knapp and Hall (1992) noted that the physical characteristics of students and teachers influence communication in a number of ways. We live in a culture obsessed with physical looks so it is not surprising that attraction plays a substantial role in the classroom. Research indicates that attraction correlates with grades and that teachers interact more with students considered attractive

(Gibson, 1982; Richmond McCroskey, & Payne, 1987). Attractiveness is also related to popularity (Boyatzis, Baloff, & Durieux, 1998).

One feature of physical appearance discussed by Knapp is artifacts. Artifacts are clothing and other materials worn or displayed by individuals. These symbols are significant because they play a central role in identity management. Skaters, preps, and jocks dress in ways to signify who they are. Students may have tattoos, wear jewelry, or fix their hair in ways that reflects their identity. More and more students are getting tattoos and piercings to express their individuality. In some school systems, students are not allowed to wear clothing that can be construed as gang related.

A growing body of research has examined the effects of attire on judgments of teachers. Morris, Gorham, Cohen, and Huffman (1996) examined the effects of the attire of teaching assistants on their credibility. Three conditions of attire—formal professional, casual professional, and casual—were tested. The study found that perceptions of competence were directly affected by dress. The more casual the dress, the less competent the teaching assistant was perceived to be. The results also indicated that a casual dress style was related to sociability.

Roach (1997) examined the effects of graduate teaching assistant attire on student learning, misbehaviors, and rating of instruction. The research found correlations between teaching assistant attire and student learning (affective and cognitive). Learning increased with professional attire. Interestingly, teaching assistants who dressed more professionally also encountered less student misbehavior. Professional dress helped the instructor establish and maintain appropriate distance and boundaries. In addition, teachers who dressed professionally received higher teacher evaluations. Students seem to expect professionalism from an instructor, and dress style helps the teacher fulfill this expectation.

The research reported above is consistent with a wide range of studies that have examined the effects of attire (Davis, et al, 1992; Gorham, Cohen, & Morris, 1997; Hensley, 1981; Kleinke, 1977; Lang, 1986; Lukavsky, Butler, & Harden, 1995; Molloy, 1975; Newhouse, 1984; Schneider, 1974). Individuals in professional contexts, such as teaching, positively influence their credibility by dressing in a professional fashion. Simmons (1996), a long time supervisory teacher summed up the issue of dress in the following way: "Without a question, dress sends a strong message about who teachers are as individuals and as professionals. The message is clear—those who want respect for themselves and their profession must dress accordingly" (p. 293).

Proxemics

This area of non-verbal communication is concerned with the management of space. Research has been rather consistent in this area. The proximity of the teacher influences the participation of the student (Smith, 1984). In traditional classrooms, there is a zone of classroom participation (see Figure 1.4).

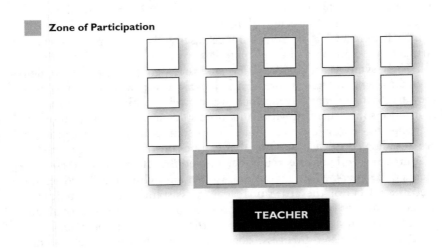

Figure 1.4 Zone of Participation.

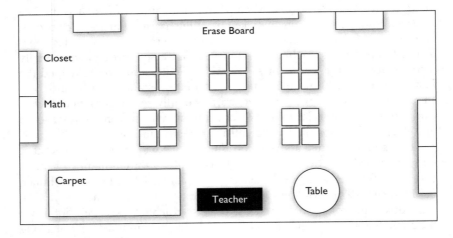

Figure 1.5 Classroom Arrangement.

The shaded area shows where most of the interaction occurs. Students sitting on the sides and in back do not receive as much attention and do not engage in as much interaction.

Teachers must remember that no single seating arrangement is ideal for all classes, learning situations, or individuals (Williams, Alley, & Hensen, 1999). The classroom shown in Figure 1.5 reflects the instruction goals of one fourth-grade class.

> *Reflection*
>
> ◆ **What are the advantages and disadvantages of placing the student desks in the center of the room?**
> ◆ **What is the purpose of placing the computer station in the front of the room?**
> ◆ **How would you arrange this classroom?**

In this class, the instructor has created several different "classrooms," each is designed to accomplish a different goal. At the center are cooperative teams. Four students are placed in the center where group activity and direct instruction occurs.

The carpet is a place where students can go for free reading, work on puzzles, or do other tasks. There is a table where reading groups can work without distracting other groups. In this classroom, students can work on several instructional activities simultaneously. Notice that the teacher's desk is not at the center of the room.

Given the choice, students will seek out areas in the classroom that accommodate their orientation to communication. Those who do not like to participate generally seek out areas where there is a lower probability of being called on by the teacher. Teachers, therefore, must think about ways to organize their classrooms to accomplish their goals. Teachers might experiment with different arrangements through out the school year.

Kinesics

Kinesics, according to Knapp and Hall (1992), refers to gestures, posture, touching behavior, facial expressions and eye behavior. Ekman and Friesen (1969) studied body movement and contend that there are five primary categories of movement: emblems, illustrators, affect displays, regulators, and adaptors. Emblems have a direct verbal translation. Americans wave to say hello while Eastern Indians clasp their hands together in front of the face. Illustrators are used to highlight or explain a verbal message. We can pretend that we are holding a fork and move it to our mouth to show, or illustrate, something about eating. Affect displays are those gestures that reveal emotion. These are primarily seen in the face. A smile is one way we show we are happy. Regulators are used to manage the give and take of conversation. People raise their voice when they do not want to give up the floor; they shift their posture when they wish to give the floor to someone else. Postural shifts occur as individuals participate in conversations. Finally, individuals use adaptors to manage stress or arousal. Some students tap their feet when they are anxious. Other people play with pens, tug at their hair, or snap gum to manage tension.

The way in which teachers carry themselves has a great impact on the attitudes of students. A great deal of research has been conducted on teacher immediacy, a concept developed by Mehrabian (1970a, 1981). According to Mehrabian, immediacy behaviors signal approach. The behaviors considered immediate are smiling, eye contact, forward body lean, proximity, and a relaxed posture. A number of studies have shown that immediate teachers are perceived positively regardless of student cultural identity (Collier & Powell, 1990; Powell & Harville, 1990; Sanders & Wiseman, 1990). Teachers using immediacy behavior indicate that they are open and they like their students.

One of the most controversial non-verbal behaviors is touch. Although touch is considered an essential component of human development, it can be problematic in the classroom. Touch can be used to comfort, discipline, and focus attention. When appropriate, it can send powerful messages of affirmation and care. When used inappropriately, the results can be devastating. Behaviors that appear nurturing in one situation can be litigious in another. Hugging a third grader who falls from the swing may be appropriate while hugging a student in an empty classroom for being a "good student" may have a very different implication. Mongeau and Blalock (1994) found that, of all the teacher immediacy behaviors they studied, touch was the only one perceived to be inappropriate.

Paralanguage

The final area discussed by Knapp and Hall (1992) is concerned with the nonlinguistic features of speech, such as voice volume, tempo, pitch, and intensity as well as intruding sounds. Accent is certainly a paralinguistic feature that influences communication in the classroom. Research reveals that accent influences speaker credibility. Powell and Avila (1986) compared Anglo, Latino, Asian, and African-American students on the Communication Competency Assessment Instrument (CCAI) and found that students from Latin and Asian cultural backgrounds were considered less competent than individuals from the other groups. One of the variables accounting for this difference was pronunciation, which is influenced by accent.

Gill (1994) investigated the effects of accent on comprehension. The results indicated that listeners had more favorable responses to teachers with standard North American accents than to those with British or Malaysian accents. Further, the students were able to comprehend more information from North American teachers than from foreign teachers.

Student attitudes may influence how they perceive a teacher who has an accent. Students who do not do well in a course may use the teacher's accent as a reason for their poor performance. The accent of the teacher may be less significant to the students who do well in the course. Students accepting of culture may be more tolerant of a non-mainstream accent while students less accepting may be much more critical of a non-mainstream accent. Similarly, teachers may develop expectations about students based on stylized features. Students with a non-dominant style of speech may not be perceived as bright, motivated, or interesting as a student with a dominant style of speech. Some teachers feel that it is the obligation of education to create a homogenized community that uses the same code. Students with accents, regardless of their intellect, may be inappropriately pushed to the margins. Teachers need to be very aware of the attributions they make about students who have accents.

Listening

The final aspect of the communication process that we wish to discuss is listening. Meanings are intimately tied to listening ability. Students who are distracted do not focus on main ideas and have difficulty following instructional messages. Wolvin and Coakley (1993) provided a useful typology of listening consisting of five major functions.

According to Wolvin and Coakley, *discriminative* listening is distinguishing among auditory and visual stimuli. This type of listening undergirds all other forms of listening. In the classroom, teachers and students must sort through a wide range of auditory stimuli. Students talking, shuffling papers, snapping gum, the squeak of chalk, are among the sounds that are processed in the classroom context.

Discriminative ability is fundamental to musicians, auto mechanics, parents and teachers. Each must determine the significance of certain sounds and how to respond to them. The musician learns how to coordinate certain tones and blend them into melodies. The mechanic listens to the "ping" in an engine to determine why it isn't running smoothly. Parents learn to differentiate cries for attention from cries of fatigue. Students and teachers must sort out a multitude of stimuli as they negotiate the meanings of instructional material.

Listening for *comprehension* builds on discrimination of stimuli to an understanding of the message. Many of the educational processes engage this listening function. Students listen to lectures, student reports, classroom discussions, announcements, and the admonitions of teachers. Successful comprehension requires that listeners avoid an evaluative attitude about the topic being discussed or the speaker. A student, who does not like history, may have difficulty attending to a lecture on the Revolutionary War. Listening is made particularly difficult then the listener does not like the speaker. It is easier to attend to messages from people we like and tune out messages from people we dislike.

Listening is facilitated when the listener can identify the speaker's main ideas. As we have observed, in any instructional context, a multitude of messages are shared. Listeners must learn to discard extraneous information and focus on that which is most relevant to the instructional task. Comprehension is difficult in diverse classrooms where there may be vast differences in vocabulary. Students may hear many words but not know what they mean. Finally, comprehension requires listeners to store information in short-term memory, rehearse it, and move it into long-term memory so that it can be retrieved later.

Therapeutic listening, according to Wolvin and Coakley (1993) requires that the listener help the speaker solve problems. To fulfill this function, the listener serves as a "sounding board" so that the speaker can identify ways to define and solve a problem. Teachers often play this role when they listen to the difficulties students have at home, or the struggles they have with friends at school. In these contexts, the teacher attempts to empathize with the speaker and show understanding. However, when students are experiencing more serious emotional difficulties, they should be advised to consult with professionals who are trained in counseling.

Critical listening requires the listener to render a judgment about the information received. This skill is invoked in several ways. When a speaker's purpose is to persuade, a listener must make a judgment about the validity and strength of evidence. Effectiveness in this situation requires listeners to understand the way in which persuasive arguments are structured and supported. Teachers put on their "critical" listening hats when they listen to student accounts for late work or a problematic pattern of behavior. They also model good listening when they help students process good arguments from more problematic ones. Students must learn that criticizing an argument does not mean criticizing the person.

The final function that Wolvin and Coakley (1993) discussed is *appreciative* listening. Listening to music, the sounds of a mountain stream, or a favorite television program are examples of appreciative listening. This type of listening is subject to individual tastes and standards. Conduct a survey of your class and identify the different music forms that students like.

There are numerous circumstances that make effective listening difficult. One is that listening is always part of an interpersonal relationship. I have frequently heard teachers ask students, "Are you listening?" What they are really saying is that the students are not doing what the teachers want them to do. It is easier for participants to listen to individuals they respect and like and tune out and counter-argue with individuals they do not like. In addition to these relational features, there are other blocks to effective listening worth mentioning:

- *Preoccupation*: Listeners feign attention while they think about other things. Students may grin and nod, exhibiting attentive behaviors, while thinking about what they want for lunch.
- *Noise*: As we noted earlier in this chapter, internal and external noise can distort instructional messages and interfere with the creation of meaning.
- *Information overload*: Listeners process information better in manageable chunks. When students receive too much information, too quickly, they may tune the teacher out.
- *Boredom*: Listeners easily tune out a speaker who is monotone, slow paced, and uses no vocal variety.
- *Selection*: Listeners will tune into information they perceive is relevant and tune out information they believe is irrelevant. These choices are based on personal tastes and attitudes.
- *Counter-argument*: Listeners listen to those features they can refute. As a consequence, they may miss other important features of communication.
- *Language competency*: Listening is difficult when listeners do not understand the language being spoken. This is especially true when speakers are continually translating the messages they hear.

Listening is often treated as an independent category of the communication process. We believe that listening is part of a host of behaviors that are used to make sense out of instructional material. Cooper and Simmonds (1999) contended that effective listeners are actively involved in the communication process. One effective strategy is to paraphrase another person's message. The goal of paraphrasing is to capture the content and feelings of the other's response. A student who feels that an assignment is too difficult may blurt out, "I don't get it, this isn't clear." A teacher might paraphrase this statement by saying, "You seem anxious about this assignment."

Another strategy that Cooper and Simmonds discussed is *perception checking*. The purpose of this technique is to assess another's thoughts, feelings, or perceptions. According to Cooper and Simmonds, perception checking involves three ideas: (1) referencing the sensory data leading to a conclusion; (2) the conclusion that has been drawn; and (3) a question asking the other if your conclusion is accurate. For example, a teacher may have a student athlete who has been late with homework and inattentive in class. The teacher may be concerned that the student is spending too much time on the athletic field and not enough time studying. In probing this situation, a teacher may ask this student if she understood the assignment that was due. The student may look down and say, "I understood it but I had so much to do that I couldn't get it done." This perception can be assessed in the following way: "Julie, I know that the playoffs are coming up this week and you do not seem as focused on your studies. Are you spending so much time practicing that you are not attending to your schoolwork?"

There are other ways to facilitate effective listening, however. We want to emphasize that listening is part of an on-going interpersonal relationship that is established and maintained. Effective listening involves more than implementing a few 'techniques. Good listeners and good communicators are sensitive to a host of behaviors that are involved in the communication process. As your knowledge of this process increases, so will your communication ability.

Summary

Over the years, researchers have come to appreciate the complexity of human communication. Early theoretical approaches were linear and simplistic. Contemporary orientations are complex and circular. Communication processes are negotiated among participants as they act upon the meanings they construct and share. Verbal and nonverbal behaviors are the mechanisms through which instructional sense making is achieved. Contemporary theorists also emphasize the powerful relationship between learning and communication. How we come to understand instructional material is a function of communication. After reading this chapter, our hope is that you recognize that understanding communication is an exciting and difficult challenge.

Learning Activities

- The Ideal Teacher
  Pair up with another student and go for a learning walk. On this walk discuss the defining characteristics of the ideal teacher. When you return to class, list the characteristics on a wallboard or flip chart. Note the similarities and differences among the descriptions.
- Nonverbal assessment
  Analyze the way that nonverbal communication influences the meanings you construct. Specifically, contrast the communication differences in two or three different physical settings. How do people dress and how does it influence the impressions you formed? What types of gestures did you observe? How does

space impact communication? Finally, what different accents, languages, or styles of speech did you hear and how did you react to them?
- Build a communication model using the concepts discussed in the chapter.

Resources

- Communication activities
www.essortment.com/all/communicationte_rqmd.htm
- The essentials of language teaching
www.nclrc.org/essentials/listening/liindex.htm

Chapter 2

Factors Influencing Learning and Communication

Enrique and Danielle are in the teachers' lounge savoring the last drops of their coffee before scurrying off to their first period class. Rosa Parks Middle School, where Enrique and Danielle teach, is located in a low-income ethnically diverse community. For many students, English is not their first language and the verbal skills of many other students are below grade level. The test scores at Rosa Parks have been low and the Principal has made it very clear that she expects substantial improvement. Teachers like Enrique and Danielle face a daunting task—they must meet state standards, raise test scores, and excite the students about learning. It is in this context that teachers can easily forget their fundamental charge—to help students learn.

Learning is a complex process entailing a number of interrelated factors. Enrique and Danielle will be more effective in the classroom when they have a deep understanding of these factors, then they can develop teaching strategies to meet their instructional goals and address the needs of students. In this chapter we will define the learning context and examine three areas that are related to the teaching learning process: student abilities, student motivation and classroom communication.

Reflection

◆ **What role does communication play in the learning process?**
◆ **How can a teacher motivate a student to learn?**

The Learning Context

Our definition of communication states that people act upon the meanings they construct. Our view of learning follows from our definition of communication. It is not fruitful to believe that students are empty vessels to be filled with intellectual fluid. Rather, students are active agents in the creation and management of educational material. Constructivism, a perspective that has been studied in communication and education, resonates with our view. Kelly's (1955) Personal Construct Theory, Piaget's (1955) Developmental Theory, and Mead's (1934) Theory of Symbolic Interactionism provide the conceptual basis for this perspective. Brooks and Brooks (1993) summarized constructivist processes when they stated:

> Each of us makes sense of our world by synthesizing new experiences into what we have previously come to understand. Often we encounter an object, an idea, a relationship, or a phenomenon that doesn't quite make sense to us. When confronted with such initially discrepant data or perceptions, we either interpret what we see to conform to our present set of rules for explaining or ordering the world, or we generate a new set of rules that better accounts for what we perceive is occurring. Either way our perceptions and rules are constantly engaged in a grand dance that shapes our understandings.
> (p. 4)

Thus, learning occurs through the continuous building, integration, organization, and rebuilding of material. At the core of this perspective is the recognition that language, culture, home, and community play important roles in the knowledge structures students possess. Consider, for example, the way that a class discussion on music would be impacted by culture. One family may listen to *rancheras, corridos, cumbias*, and *marriachi* music. Another may listen to country western, bluegrass, and gospel. The discussion of music will be intimately tied to the students' experiences.

Culture also influences the constructs that students have for managing social situations. An Iranian student new to America went shopping for clothes at a department store. After selecting the shirt he wished to purchase, he haggled with the clerk over the price. The Iranian student equated buying a shirt in a department store with buying a shirt in the open marketplace in Tehran where negotiating the price is the common practice.

Constructivist approaches recognize that students come to the instructional context with different levels of competencies, interests, and experiences. Unfortunately, much of our educational curriculum is based on a "one size fits all" metaphor. As students move through the system, little effort is spent on tailoring instructional cloth to better fit each student. Unfortunately learning does not follow this pattern. Students come to class in many different shapes and sizes.

Indeed, students draw upon a range of interpersonal and educational constructs to learn instructional material and manage classroom relationships. Garcia (1999) stated that meaningful instruction accounts for the socio-cultural, linguistic, and experiential background of students. While an instructor may have jurisdiction over curriculum, ultimately the student has jurisdiction over what it means (Wenger, 1998). In other words, students use their experiences and abilities to make sense out of the instructional material.

Because learning entails the negotiation of instructional material, it is difficult to isolate the specific ways that teaching influences learning. Some theorists go as far to contend that teaching plays a rather minor role in learning (e.g. the Coleman Report, 1966; Heath & Nielson, 1974; Mosteller & Moynihan, 1972). The findings of this early research indicated that family socio-economic status, ethnicity, and family background are more important predictors of achievement than teaching. Think about arguments teachers like Enrique and Danielle make when they try to explain the low scores of their students on state achievement tests. These teachers recognize that there are significant factors outside of the school that influence learning. At the same time, we do not want to argue that teachers do little to influence learning process. Friedrich (1982) argued that three sets of interrelated variables account for classroom learning: student ability, student motivation, and the quality of classroom communication are the primary factors influencing achievement. These three areas provide a useful starting point for our discussion of the relationship between teaching and learning.

Student Ability

We argued earlier that students enter the classroom with a wide range of abilities and competencies. Friedrich (1982) contended that these abilities account for a substantial amount of variance on a range of cognitive outcome assessments (i.e. achievement tests, aptitude tests, general intelligence measures, unit measures). The scores that students receive on standardized assessments, such as multiple choice tests, may have more to do with the intellectual predilections of the student than with the classroom instruction.

Recent developments in cognitive psychology give insight into the intellectual capacities that students possess and bring to the instructional scene. Gardner (1983, 1993, 1999) proposed a provocative framework that has dramatically influenced educational practices. In his original work, *Frames of Mind*, Gardner outlined seven intelligences and in *The Disciplined Mind*, he added an eighth intelligence. Following is a brief discussion of these intelligences:

- *Linguistic Intelligence* entails the ability to use words effectively in both oral and written modes for a variety of purposes such as debate, poetry, prose writing, story telling, and persuasion. Individuals with highly developed linguistic intelligence enjoy verbal jousting, puns, and other forms of word play. These individuals achieve best when they can speak, listen, read, or write.

- *Logical-Mathematical Intelligence* involves the capacity to reason, to think atomistically, and linearly. People who employ logical-mathematical intelligence are effective at finding patterns, establishing causal relationships, and working through formulas. Among the processes that emerge with this intelligence are categorization, classification, hypothesis testing and generalization.
- *Spatial Intelligence* addresses the ability to perceive, create, and re-create visual images and pictures. Individuals who are strong in spatial intelligence, perceive small details, and are sensitive to color, tone, composition, shape, and form. This intelligence entails the capacity to visualize and represent ideas graphically or spatially.
- *Bodily-Kinesthetic Intelligence* involves the ability to use one's body to express ideas and feelings. Among the defining features of this intelligence is heightened tactile competence, coordination, balance, dexterity, and flexibility.
- *Musical Intelligence* is the ability to understand, create, interpret and discriminate among musical forms. Musically intelligent people have the ability to sing in key, keep tempo, and are sensitive to rhythm, pitch, and melody.
- *Interpersonal Intelligence* requires individuals to be socially and personally perceptive. These individuals are able to perceive the moods and feelings of others and adapt messages to the demands of social situations. Interpersonally intelligent people enjoy social settings and work well with other people.
- *Intrapersonal Intelligence* entails the ability to be in touch with one's emotional state and predispositions. Individuals who are aware of their inner moods, intentions, motivations, temperaments, and desires and have the capacity for self-discipline are intra personally intelligent. This intelligence helps individuals create a "realistic" view of their strengths and weaknesses.
- *Naturalist Intelligence* is the capacity to be attuned to natural world of plants and animals. Individuals who possess this intelligence enjoy the outdoors, are aware of patterns in nature and have a deep appreciation for the environment.

It should not be surprising that students will be drawn to academic tasks where they feel most competent. Students with logical-mathematical intelligence will enjoy and perform well in math and science and students with linguistic competence will enjoy and perform well in language arts.

Gardner cautioned against viewing these intelligences as fixed and discrete. Individuals possess each of the intelligences to a degree but one or two may be particularly dominant.

Reflection

♦ **What are your strongest intelligences?**
♦ **How are these intelligences manifested?**
♦ **How can teachers build on student intelligences?**

A number of recent educational textbooks discuss ways to integrate multiple intelligences into educational practice (Armstrong, 2000; Carrozza, 1996; Silver, Strong, & Perini, 2000). Silver, Strong, and Perini (2000), for example, outlined strategies for realigning the curriculum to account for learning style and multiple intelligences (MI). The authors also provided guidelines for developing authentic assessments. Armstrong (2000) discussed ways to develop a MI portfolio. He identifies what should be included in such a portfolio and ways to evaluate it. The instructional approaches using multiple intelligences are concerned with measuring student growth and development, not with indexing student deficit. Building and extending student strength is one way to create more engaged and enthused learners.

Emotional Intelligence

Goleman (1995) extended Gardner's work into the area of emotional ability. Individuals who are emotionally intelligent are tuned into their affective states. There is growing interest in the area of emotion and learning. Goleman identified five dimensions of emotional intelligence:

- *Knowing one's emotions*: Recognizing a feeling as it happens. The ability to monitor feelings is crucial to psychological insight and self-understanding.
- *Managing emotions*: Appropriately handling feelings. The ability to work through anxiety or gloom is central to success.
- *Motivating oneself*: Marshalling emotions in service of a goal is essential to paying attention, for self-motivation and mastery.
- *Recognizing emotions in others*: Empathy is a fundamental social skill. People who are empathic are attuned to subtle social signals indicating how people feel.
- *Handling relationships*: Skill in managing relationships, popularity, leadership and interpersonal effectiveness.

Emotional intelligence plays an important role in the classroom. The way in which students manage their emotions influences their approach to academic tasks and their ability to work with other students. Healy

(1998) argued that social-emotional factors are important predictors of academic and lifetime success. She described a study that investigated preschoolers' ability to delay immediate gratification. The preschoolers were given one marshmallow and told that if they could wait 15–20 minutes, they would get two marshmallows. These students were evaluated 14 years later. The results indicated that the students who could delay gratification scored higher on the SAT, were better liked by teachers and peers, and were more emotionally stable.

The research on emotional intelligence is compelling. Encouraging students to work before play, to be diligent in the face of adversity, to be respectful and caring, helps foster an attitude of self-efficacy, which in turn positively impacts academic achievement.

Perspectives on Motivation

Student interests, attitudes, and self-views relate to how motivated and engaged they are in the learning material. Maehr and Meyer (1997) argued, "motivation is at the heart of teaching and learning" (p. 372). Adolescents spend tremendous amounts of time e-mailing friends, connecting on networks such as My Space, and talking on the telephone. Redirecting these energies to academic tasks is more challenging. To better understand the role of motivation it is helpful to review the perspectives that have been used to explain how motivation works in educational settings. In the next section we will examine some of the contemporary perspectives on motivation in education.

Seifert (2004) argues that four major theories—self-efficacy, attribution theory—self-worth theory, and achievement goal theory are prominent in education. Each of these perspectives offers important insight into the factors that influence students' academic investments.

Self-Efficacy Theory

The key theorist of self-efficacy theory is Albert Bandura (1981, 1986, 1991, 1997). He argued that individuals develop judgments about their personal effectiveness which he labeled self-efficacy. Individuals who believe that they can successfully complete a task will expend the necessary effort to accomplish it. When individuals have low expectations, they are less likely to expend the time and effort on the task.

Bandura (1997) discussed four factors that influence a person's judgments of self-efficacy. The first factor is enactive influences. These judgments result from the way in which a person performs certain tasks. According to Bandura (1997), enactive experiences are the most powerful because they provide the most authentic evidence of whether the individual can access what it takes to succeed. Success leads to a strong belief in one's personal efficacy. However, efficacy does not always follow from success. Individuals who only succeed at easy tasks may come to lose patience and not persist when the tasks become more troublesome.

A second factor influencing self-efficacy is vicarious experience. Individuals continually compare their own competencies with others. Modeling, then, serves as another way to achieve personal efficacy. The most powerful effect is based on peer comparisons. An individual's self-efficacy is not affected by comparisons with substantially younger, older, or substantially more talented others.

Miller (2000) examined the effects of internal and external comparisons on self-regulated learning. Self-comparisons (internal) occur when students compare their ability in one area, such as English, with their ability in another area such as math. External comparison occurs when students compare their performance in an academic area with that of their peers. The results indicated that students gave more weight to external comparisons than self-evaluations. This tendency, although understandable, is also problematic. Individuals do not always have information to make accurate comparisons. Skill levels, the amount of time on task, and interest can vary from student to student and are frequently ignored when comparisons are made. Miller (2000) suggested that educators should help students develop more balanced constructs of their abilities.

The third way that individuals develop self-efficacy is through persuasion. Bandura (1997) argued that persuasion has its greatest impact on those who have some reason to believe that they can achieve their goals. Persuasive information focusing on the target's ability and effort seems to positively influence efficacy. Persuasive messages focusing only on effort, however, can be counterproductive to the development of efficacy. If an individual does not have the necessary skills, no amount of effort will impact self-efficacy. Simply telling a student to work harder will not be an effective strategy.

Two additional features play an important role in the effects of persuasion. One involves the credibility of the source and the second entails the discrepancy between what individuals are told and their view of themselves. Research in persuasion clearly indicates that source credibility is one of the most powerful features of persuasive communication (Bostrom, 1983). Information from a low credible source, even when it is accurate, may be distorted or discounted. The persuasive effects on self-efficacy are directly related to the credibility of the sender.

Self-efficacy is also related to the degree of disparity between the information received and the individual's view of self. Bandura (1977b) noted that information might differ minimally, moderately, or markedly from a person's view of self (p. 105). For example, one high school baseball player had a successful season in his senior year in high school and received an offer to play baseball at a major university. The youngster's coach encouraged him to consider taking this opportunity, but the young man did not believe that he had enough talent, regardless of the statistics and the arguments from his coach. Rather than going to the large school, he decided to attend a local community college where he believed that there was a better fit for his talent.

The final factor influencing self-efficacy involves physiological and affective states. Arousal states can vary from falling asleep in class to suffering panic attacks. Some tasks create great anxiety for students, which influences their ability to complete the task. For example, many students have tremendous fear of public speaking (communication apprehension) and the anxiety attached to this activity negatively affects performance. High apprehensive students break out in hives, their voice quivers, and their stomach aches in anticipation of a five-minute presentation. Other students enjoy public speaking and channel their energy and excitement into dramatic delivery.

Self-efficacy is impacted by the way individuals work through these affective states. Bandura (1997) stated that an understanding of emotional states is developed through a process of social labeling that is coordinated with lived events. Children may experience an internal state (anger) and behave in a way that is connected to the emotion. Parents, teachers, and peers help identify the emotional state (e.g. "You're mad because you didn't get your way," "Are you too embarrassed to read?"). The effects on self-efficacy relate to the way in which individuals learn to label and manage these emotional states. The manifestation of these emotions and the way they are processed, explained, negotiated, and managed has a great deal to do with the development of efficacy. Students with higher levels of emotional intelligence are better able to stay focused on a task and persist through difficult situations.

Attribution Theory

Attribution theory builds on many of the assumptions of self-efficacy theory and also provides important insight into the factors influencing motivation. The conceptual foundation of attribution theory comes from Heider (1958), Jones and Davis (1965), and Kelley (1967). These theorists proposed that individuals are "naïve scientists" who search for causal reasons that explain behavior. Heider (1958) contended that a task outcome might be attributed to four attributional variables: the degree of ability possessed by the actor, the amount of effort expended, the difficulty of the task, and chance factors in the environment.

Weiner (1984, 1985) contended that attributions invoke emotions which influence task engagement. For example, an outcome such as failing or passing a test may result in an emotional reaction. To assess this emotional response, the individual turns to three primary characteristics:

locus of causality (the cause resides in the individual or the situation), stability (the cause is always present, or the cause varies), and controllability (the agent can affect the cause or the outcome is out of the agent's control). Research on attribution theory suggests that individuals who are successful tend to attribute success to internal cause (ability, effort) and individuals who are unsuccessful tend to attribute failure to external causes (unclear instructions, lack of time).

Seifert (2004) stated that students who attribute success and failure to internal, controllable causes have higher self-esteem, will engage in more difficult tasks, and will persist in the face of adversity. On the other hand, students who attribute success to external forces (luck, the task was easy) are less likely to experience positive emotions such as pride or confidence. And learned helplessness, the most problematic attribution, occurs when students feel that no amount of effort will make a difference because they do not have the ability to control or influence an outcome.

Heidi and Harackiewicz (2000) argued that interest also influences attributional processes. Interest was conceptualized as the "interactive relation" between individuals and certain aspects of their environment (Heidi & Harackiewicz, 2000). Some individuals are interested in social studies, some soccer, others fashion. Interest can be considered a state and a disposition of the individual and has cognitive and affective features. Research suggests that interest plays an important role in academic performance. It stands to reason that students will be more attentive to and expend more effort in subject areas that interest them.

Researchers differentiate between two types of interest. Individual interest is a stable internal disposition that develops over time in relation to a particular topic or subject area. A student, therefore, may develop an interest in history that lasts throughout his or her educational experience. Situational interest, on the other hand is generated by certain features of the environment that draw attention and focus to a particular area. The interest fostered in this context, may or may not last. For example, a dramatic lecture or a novel experiential activity may activate student interest in a topic that was previously considered boring.

Heidi and Harackiewicz (2000) noted that individual and situational interests may be distinct but they are not bi-polar. Individual interest can serve as a filter for situational interest and situational interest may feed individual interest. The authors contended:

> … individual interest in a particular topic may help students persevere through boring presentations or text about that topic, and situational interest elicited by presentations or texts may maintain motivation and performance when individuals have no personal interest in particular topics.
>
> (p. 155)

We can see how interest is also related to intrinsic motivation. Intrinsic motivation is defined as the motivation to engage in activities for their own sake (ibid.). This definition incorporates both individual and situational interest. Some students may inhale the Harry Potter novels because they are positively disposed to reading. Interest in reading may also be promoted for situational reasons. Individuals may be assigned a Harry Potter novel for a class assignment and become so interested in it that they read the entire series.

Self-Worth Theory

Covington (2000) argued that that academic goals embraced by students represent an attempt to create and maintain self-worth in a culture that values competency and success. He contended that grades play a dominant role in the way a student judges self-worth. He further argued that while grades are important, they are only one measure of success. Some students attempt to be the best they can be and do not compare their performance to others. These students are likely to take on difficult tasks and feel comfortable with academic challenges. Other students see ability as a function of status and thus compare their performances with others. These students are more likely to avoid failure rather than strive for success. Students who are driven to avoid failure employ several self-protective mechanisms, according to Covington (2000).

Self-worth protection involves withholding the effort when risking failure. When this strategy is invoked, the self-concept appears to be protected because the cause of failure remains ambiguous. Students who are reprimanded by friends, teachers or parents for not trying are receiving an external message that they are incompetent. They failed because they did not try.

A second strategy is self-handicapping. Here the student creates a real or imagined barrier which provides a convenient excuse. According to Covington, procrastination and setting unrealistic goals are typical tactics that failure-avoiding students employ. The student who studies at the last minute and fails cannot be criticized for not having the ability. And the student who succeeds is perceived to be especially talented. Another tactic is to establish unrealistic goals. A student cannot be blamed for failing at a difficult task. Finally, a student may state a worthy goal, such as claiming he or she will do better on the next exam without a reasonable analysis of how to achieve it.

According to Covington (2000), the third strategy is defensive pessimism. Students using this defensive strategy maintain low expectations of ever succeeding or trivialize the importance of the assignment. Defensive pessimism helps the student manage the anxiety that may occur when the student takes an assignment seriously but knows they do not have the ability to fulfill it.

Effort is a key feature of self-worth theory. Failure-avoidant students link effort with ability. Because successful students are bright, they don't have to work hard. People who work hard are not considered to be bright. Seifert (2004) stated that success that comes from ability results in pride. Success that comes from low effort implies ability and also results in pride. Failure that is a function of low effort results in guilt but failure that results from low ability results in humiliation. Covington (2000) contended that students would rather experience guilt than humiliation. Thus, rather than work hard and fail (leading to humiliation), they will not work hard and fail (guilt). Self-worth theory helps teachers understand the choices students make. According to Covington (2000), the central issue for students is to protect their sense of self-worth.

Achievement Goal Theory

Dweck (1986) contended that motivation is related to the way students conceptualize their learning goals. He specified two sets of goals. Learning goals refer to increasing an individual's competence, understanding, and insight. Intelligence and learning for these individuals is malleable. Success or failure does not have a substantial effect on the learner's identity or sense of self-worth. Performance goals, in contrast, are those in which individuals seek a favorable evaluation of their competence. Intelligence following from a performance goal orientation is considered fixed and static. According to Dweck (1986), these different cognitive sets take students in vastly different directions. The individual who is competency oriented is more likely to attribute success to persistence and effort. Failure is not viewed as a reflection on personal identity. The individual who is performance oriented and sees intelligence as fixed does not see that effort and ability lead to success and, therefore, may take on academic tasks that are less challenging. They ask for a great deal of guidance on assignments, may avoid certain classes or teachers and may be more inclined to cheat.

Each of the perspectives reviewed above offer important insights into the processes influencing motivation. Each perspective addresses the role of perceived competence. That is, a student is likely to invest in an academic task when they feel they can successfully accomplish it. When they do not feel that they can be successful, they use strategies to protect their personal identities. The other common thread is the important role that emotions play in motivation. How students feel about their abilities and the meaningfulness of the task they are performing are what Weiner (1984, 1985) labeled motivational catalysts. The affective orientation can serve to bolster or constrain effort and learning.

Seifert (2004) identified five major patterns that are reflected in the perspectives used to study motivation. The first pattern is concerned with mastery. Students who have learning goals or who are internally motivated, will have positive affect, will persist in tasks, are resilient and learn from their mistakes (e.g. Dweck, 1986; Weiner, 1984, 1985).

A second pattern is failure avoidance. These students have performance goals, are externally motivated, and are driven to protect their individual identities. According to Seifert (2004), these students believe that outcomes are beyond their control and as tasks grow in difficulty, they are likely to engage in failure-avoiding behaviors to reduce threat to self.

The third pattern is learned helplessness. These students will not expend the effort because they believe it will result in success. Such students make internal, stable and controllable attributions for failure but make external attributions for success. In other words, this student will say, "I failed because I am incompetent" or "I succeeded because I was lucky." Students with this orientation are particularly challenging for teachers.

The fourth pattern involves students who are bright but bored. These students do not see meaning or value in the task and spend only the necessary effort to fulfill minimal expectations. Seifert contended that the student with learning goals would seek out meaning in the task while the bored student expects the teacher to make the task meaningful.

The fifth is the hostile work avoidant pattern. Seifert stated that the hostile student does not engage in academic tasks as a way to punish the teacher. This strategy may be another way the student protects self-worth. They may resent the work required and therefore refuse to do it. Several years ago one of the authors had an athlete in class who refused to complete a required assignment. When asked why, he stated, "I don't have to do this crap, I'm on the basketball team." This response is typical of hostile students.

What then can teachers do with this information on motivation? This is a difficult question but the literature reviewed above suggests that student motivation is enhanced when they develop mastery over the tasks they are required to perform. Gettinger and Stoiber (1999) provided recommendations that may enhance motivation. They suggested that teachers should assign tasks that are moderately challenging but within the students' ability. Second, teachers should link student success to the effort they put forth. When this occurs, students are more likely to take control of their academic engagement. Third, teachers should create opportunities for students to be successful.

Consider the following example. George is struggling with algebra. He studies but continues to fail the examinations at the end of the week. He questions his ability and spends less time studying. For George, it is too painful to work hard only to fail. One day, while grading the tests, the teacher discovers that George transposes numbers when he is writing the algebra formulas. Rather than writing down the number 23 in a formula he writes the number 32. The teacher reviews all of George's previous quizzes and finds that this is a consistent pattern. The teacher has a conference with George and carefully explains this error. In the next quiz, the teacher continues to remind George to make sure that he has not transposed any numbers. After George turns in the quiz, the teacher checks his answers and tells him that his scores have improved significantly. After this intervention, George continues to show improvement in algebra and his spending more and more time in this subject.

In this example, the teacher used a strategy that would directly influence George's mastery over the content. He is frustrated with his math scores and wants to understand why he is having a problem. His interest is piqued when the teacher explains why his answers have been incorrect. She encourages George and states, "Hey bud, you can do this, but make sure you don't flop your numbers. I will watch to see if you make this mistake during the quiz."

George now understands his error and corrects it, and as a result his test scores improve. When he corrected the problem and improved his quiz scores, his feelings of competence increased because he felt more control over the outcome. This scenario is designed to illustrate the subtle ways that teachers can help students increase their competence which will also increase their motivation.

So far we have examined two areas that are related to academic performance, student ability and motivation. In the next section we will turn our attention to the communication processes that occur in the classroom context. First, we will describe the dominant features of instructional communication and then we will explore the communication behaviors that have been linked to academic performance.

Reflection

- ♦ Identify and discuss teaching strategies that increase student interest.
- ♦ What are your academic goals and how do they influence your motivation in a class?
- ♦ Which perspective on motivation best explains your approach to academic tasks?
- ♦ Identify and discuss your favorite academic subjects.

Communication Processes

Thus far, we have discussed the effects of student ability and motivation on learning. We will shift our focus to the third factor component of the learning model explicated by Friedrich (1982)—the quality of classroom communication. The effects of classroom communication are circular and their impact on learning and achievement are difficult to determine. Further, differences in contexts and the methodological variations used to study communication make comparisons problematic. Nevertheless, there are some trends that have been identified and in the next section we will review the dominant communication patterns occurring in instructional contexts.

Instructional Patterns

Belleck, Kliebard, Hyman, and Smith (1966) characterized classroom interaction as a "game" with rules that teachers and students follow. Four communication moves are used in the game. Structuring moves are used to establish the context for appropriate student behavior. Teachers might say, "This morning we are going to discuss the reading assignment I made yesterday." Soliciting moves seek to elicit a verbal response from the students. "Did you bring your cultural artifacts for today's discussion?" Responding moves follow from soliciting moves. They consist of the responses to student answers. Reacting moves are statements used to modify, or evaluate what students have said. When classroom communication is defined in this fashion, the teacher is expected to do most of the talking. In most classrooms, teachers talk approximately 70% of the time.

Haslett (1987) stated that instructional communication entails three language functions. One function involves directing students. This type of communication is concerned with giving students the information necessary to complete an instructional task. A second language function, informing, involves giving students new content. The third language function, eliciting, involves soliciting student responses. Asking students if they understand a task is an example of eliciting.

Cazden (1988) stated that the fundamental pattern of classroom interaction is the three-turn unit called the IRE. In this pattern, the teacher initiates a communication exchange, (I) a student responds, (r) and then the teacher comments on the response (E). Cazden stated that the initiation usually comes in the form of a question. Teacher questioning, then, is one of the dominant forms of communication used in the classroom.

The research cited above suggests that teachers engage in a limited range of behaviors. They give information, they ask for information, and direct student behavior. These descriptions, while informative, do not provide insight into the effects of these communication patterns on student learning and achievement. Research shows that the use of questions, and teacher clarity, impact learning (Brophy & Good, 2000; Kindsvatter, Wilen, & Ishler, 1996).

Questions

Questions are used by teachers to invite student participation and engage them in learning. Brophy and Good (2000) stated that research spanning 30 years shows that frequent questioning by teachers correlates positively with student achievement. Maximum effects on learning, however, are related to the clarity of the question and the way it is managed. Kindsvatter, Wilen, and Ishler (1996) stated that student achievement is enhanced when teachers ask clearly phrased questions, probe student responses, redirect questions to non-participating students, wait for student responses, and provide feedback on the accuracy of student responses. Learning is not linked to the difficulty of the question. Teachers can ask a series of lower order questions and then build to higher level ones. Asking only one type of cognitive question (all low or all high) does not appear to promote learning. We discuss the use of questions in more detail in Chapter 9.

Clarity

Teacher clarity has also been linked to academic achievement. Clarity is facilitated when the teacher uses communication strategies to enhance understanding of instructional material. Bush (1977) conceptualized teacher clarity in terms of seven behaviors: (1) gives examples and explains them; (2) explains the work to be done, and how to do it; (3) gives written examples; (4) uses common examples; (5) gives explanations that the students understand; (6) speaks so that all the students can hear; and (7) takes time when explaining. Behaviors that detract from clarity include ambiguity, vagueness, hedging, bluffing, insufficient examples, and mazes (false starts, halts in speech, redundancy in spoken words). Bush, Kennedy, and Cruickshank (1977) used factor analysis to identify the underlying dimensions of teacher clarity. They found that clear teachers: (1) explained ideas; and (2) used ample illustrations while explaining ideas; and giving directions.

Hines, Cruickshank, and Kennedy (1985) examined teacher clarity and its effects on student achievement and satisfaction. Three types of clarity behaviors were examined: (1) teacher stresses important aspects of content; (2) teacher explains content by use of examples; and (3) teacher assesses and responds to perceived deficiencies in understanding. The results indicated that cognitive achievement and satisfaction with the instruction was positively related to teacher clarity.

After a systematic review of the literature Brophy and Good (1986) stated that achievement is maximized when teachers actively present material, structure it with overviews, provide internal summaries, and signal important main ideas. These communication strategies require teachers to use examples that connect with the experiences of students.

Although the behaviors reviewed above may facilitate understanding, we want to emphasize that clarity is unlikely to occur when a teacher uses low inference clarity behaviors. Students process information in terms of their own frames of reference and signal their understanding or lack of understanding of the material to the teacher. Ultimately, clarity is the result of these negotiated processes. Think for a moment of the teacher who uses an example the students do not understand. According to research by Darling (1989), students signal their lack of understanding in one of three ways. They provide specific information on what they do not understand and request clarification (focused/directive strategy). Here the student is very direct ("How is self-efficacy different from internal locus of control?"). A second strategy (focused non-directive) signals a lack of understanding but the student does not ask for clarification ("I don't understand what you mean by multiple intelligence"). The third strategy (personally qualified) entails a series of questions or mazes that the teacher must work through to provide clarification ("Why am I wrong, I said the same thing that Lindsey said?").

The research by Darling (1989) and Kendrick and Darling (1990) suggests that clarity is relational. These findings resonate with Civikly (1992a) and Eisenberg (1984) who argued that clarity is embedded in a relational context. Understanding is negotiated between teachers and students in instructional episodes. Teachers or students introduce concepts which are discussed, critiqued, and clarified. Clarity is compromised when closure is not brought to these episodes. The nature of the student–teacher relationship also plays a role in the way these episodes unfold. Some teachers can read the nonverbal behavior of students and recognize that an example does not make sense. From this feedback a new example is introduced and the information continues to be negotiated. In our judgment, then, it is best to consider clarity an episodic and relational process.

Teacher Immediacy

An extensive body of literature has examined the effects of teacher immediacy on learning. After summarizing the literature Rodriguez, Plax, and Kearney (1996) claimed: "No other teacher communication variable has been so consistently associated with increases in both students' affective and cognitive learning in the classroom" (p. 293). This claim, while compelling, may be overstated. The role of immediacy in learning is a bit cloudy.

Teacher immediacy is anchored in the research of Mehrabian (1969a, 1969b, 1970a, 1970b, 1971) who argued that people move toward those they like and away from those they dislike. It is important to emphasize that Mehrabian believed that immediacy was communicated through implicit nonverbal codes. Immediacy is primarily signaled through non-verbal behavior. Andersen (1979) extended the immediacy construct to the instructional setting. She reasoned that the nonverbal behaviors that reduce physical and psychological distance between teachers and students would positively impact learning. Behaviors such as smiling, eye contact, a relaxed body posture, and movement toward students, signal immediacy. Andersen found that nonverbal immediacy positively influenced student affect or their feelings about the teacher and the course but did not influence how well students did on a standardized measure of cognitive learning.

After the publication of Andersen's original article, a number of studies explored the effects of immediacy on learning. These studies have consistently reported positive correlations between measures of immediacy (nonverbal and verbal) and affective learning (e.g. Christensen & Menzel, 1998; Gorham, 1988; Kearney, Plax, Smith, & Sorensen, 1988; Kearney, Plax, & Wendt-Wasco, 1985; Kelly & Gorham, 1988; Moore, Masterson, Christophel, & Shea, 1996; Powell & Harville, 1990; Sanders & Wiseman, 1990). However, this program of research has not been successful in explaining the effects of immediacy on cognitive learning. At best, these studies reveal that students believe they learn more from immediate teachers. However, no study demonstrates that test scores or other cognitive measures are impacted by immediacy in any clear and consistent way.

Hess and Smythe (2001) contended that four models have been used to explain the relationship between immediacy and cognitive learning. The learning model was initially advanced by Andersen (1979) and proposed that immediacy directly influences learning. The teacher who engages in positive immediacy will engender positive student outcomes. Studies testing this assertion have found no association between immediacy and test scores. Andersen's seminal investigation found positive associations between immediacy and affective orientations to the class and teacher but there was no impact on test scores.

The motivation model, hypothesized that immediacy facilitates an indirect affect on learning (Christophel, 1990; Richmond, 1990). Immediacy engenders state motivation (how students feel about a particular class and teacher) and as a consequence students study harder, go to class, increase their study time and learn more.

Rodriguez, Plax, and Kearney (1996) advanced the affective learning model which also hypothesized an indirect relationship between immediacy and cognitive learning. In this model, affective learning serves as a trigger or mediator for cognitive learning. Immediacy primes affective learning which is a precursor to cognitive learning.

The arousal model twists the previous explanations and argues that immediacy creates arousal which increases attention and learning. Comstock, Rowell, and Bowers, (1995) proposed that the relationship between immediacy and cognitive learning is curvilinear. They found that moderate amounts of teacher immediacy had the greatest impact on cognitive learning. The teacher who displays no immediacy puts students to sleep and the teacher who has too much immediacy may create anxiety or tension.

According to Hess and Smythe (2001), the studies testing these models have several flaws. First, the studies have not provided cognitive explanations of immediacy. The studies show patterns of association between immediacy and a number of outcomes such as affective learning, but they do not explain why these associations exist.

The measure of immediacy is the second flaw identified by Hess and Smythe (2001). The authors contend that too many studies have relied on self-reports rather than actual teacher behavior. The danger with self-report is that student judgments of immediacy might be confounded with other factors. For example, teachers might be considered immediate because they are an easy grader, bring food to class, or meet student needs. What is driving the student evaluation of immediacy is difficult to determine. In addition, extant instrumentation has departed from the original conception of immediacy. Gorham's (1988) measure of verbal immediacy, for example, is predicated on a presumed relationship between teaching effectiveness and immediacy. Immediacy and teaching effectiveness may be correlated but they are different constructs.

The third flaw concerns the measures of cognitive learning. A number of studies have used student reports of learning. In a typical study, students are asked to estimate what they have learned rather than to specifically measure what they learned. Hess and Smythe (2001) argued that students are not able to accurately measure what they learned. Students may vary in terms of their personal orientations to learning and how the teacher facilitates it. Judgments of learning may also be influenced by the relationship between a teacher and student. Students may inflate what they learn from a teacher they like and may deflate what they learn from a teacher they dislike.

Hess and Smythe contended that previous studies attempting to delineate the relationship between immediacy and cognitive learning have been misdirected. They argued that immediacy's primary function is to promote a positive relationship with the student. To test their contentions, the authors designed a study to assess the impact of teacher immediacy on student affect and cognitive learning. The results indicated that immediacy was positively related with perceived learning and liking for the instructor. A positive relationship between teacher affect and reported learning was also found. However, immediacy did not impact test performance. Finally, the results indicated that students were motivated by self-interest rather than teacher behavior. Grades were the primary motivating factor for the students.

The results of this investigation support the theory advanced by Hess and Smythe (2001). Immediacy played a substantial role in student perceptions about the teacher, the course and their perceived learning. It had little to do with how they performed on tests.

What can we say then about immediacy and its role in classroom learning? We agree that the primary impact of immediacy is to cultivate a positive relationship with the student. In terms of motivation, immediacy probably has its most pronounced impact on situational interest. This interpretation is closest to the arousal model explicated by Comstock, Rowell, and Bowers (1995). Test scores and other standardized assessments have more to do with student skill and academic engagement time (amount of time studying for a test) than with teacher communication behavior.

We are hesitant to completely abandon the role that immediacy plays in cognitive learning. Let's return to Mehrabian's initial contention that people move toward those they like and away from those they dislike and consider its role in cognition. The research clearly indicates that immediacy teachers are perceived to be approachable. Immediacy helps shape an environment where students feel comfortable to seek clarification and help on academic tasks. Students probably do not think much about their teacher at night when they are studying for a quiz or deliberating on the assignments they should complete. Previous research has not found a link between academic engagement time and immediacy (Powell & Aston 1994; Sine 1995), self-interest, levels of motivation, parents, and the significance of the assignment will influence how much time students spend on academic tasks.

Reflection

♦ **What role does teacher immediacy play in learning?**
♦ **What are some negative aspects of teacher immediacy?**

Communication Apprehension

The previous section examined the communication behaviors and processes that are positively associated with learning. We will conclude this chapter by discussing communication apprehension (CA), a construct that has been found to constrain leaning in the classroom. Communication apprehension is one of the most researched constructs in the discipline of communication but has not been discussed much in education. Literally hundreds of studies have been done and the results have been rather consistent. In terms of the instructional context, the research indicates that students who experience communication apprehension have more difficulty in school than students who are low in communication apprehension.

McCroskey and McCroskey (2002) identified four major effects of communication apprehension: internal discomfort, communication avoidance, communication withdrawal, and overcommunication. The one universal finding is that individuals with high CA experience internal discomfort and negative arousal when they face an event that requires communication. Frequently these feelings are connected with fear. These states may range from a warm flush to terror. Because individuals have such negative responses to the communication events related to the negative states, they frequently attempt to avoid them. Because an oral report may be terrifying, the apprehensive student will do everything to avoid giving it. If it is impossible to completely avoid the situation, a communication apprehensive student may try to physically or psychologically withdraw from it. The student who is scheduled to do a report may say, "I didn't do it," or may respond to a teacher's question by saying, "I don't know." Both strategies allow the student to step back from communication involvement. According to McCroskey and McCroskey (2002), on rare occasions, a student with communication apprehension may attempt to deal with the negative arousal by overparticipating in communication. These students may attempt to "talk" through their anxiety. In these circumstances, the individual may be more concerned with the quantity rather than the quality of the interaction.

There are significant academic consequences for students with high communication apprehension. They obtain lower grade point averages and have poorer attitudes about school (McCroskey & Andersen, 1976). Because of their feelings about communication, apprehensive students are less likely to seek help from teachers and are less likely to articulate their instructional needs. These students also have fewer peer friendships. In a study designed to assess college student retention and academic success, McCroskey, Booth-Butterfield, and Payne (1989) found that high communication apprehensives were more likely to drop out of school than low apprehensives. The effects of communication apprehension had its greatest effect in the first two years of college.

Similar findings have been observed in elementary and middle school. Comadena and Prusank (1988) assessed the relationship between communication apprehension and academic achievement among elementary and middle school students. The findings indicated that students who had high communication apprehension received the lowest scores on all measures of academic achievement. The authors also found that communication apprehension increased with grade level. Communication apprehension increased 17% from the second grade to the eighth grade. The data do not indicate if these shifts are related to academic success or other factors. Whatever the reason, communication apprehension seems to increase with grade levels and is associated with academic success.

Chesebro et al. (1992) conducted an extensive study on the potential role of communication apprehension for "at risk" students. "At risk" students were those failing to achieve in school or dropping out of school. The authors collected data at 14 urban, large predominantly minority middle and junior high school. A total of 2,793 students participated in the study. The results indicated that "at risk" students are substantially more apprehensive about speaking in groups and speaking in dyads. The authors noted that these data are troubling because so much of instruction occurs in these contexts.

The results also indicated that "at risk" students perceived themselves to be less competent in communication. The data indicated that nearly all of the differences were related to communication with acquaintances and strangers. The "at risk" students did not feel competent in these settings. Once more, these data are distressing because students frequently work in groups or teams. Their feelings about communication in these contexts may have deleterious effects on their academic performance.

Rosenfeld, Grant, and McCroskey (1995) reasoned that if communication apprehension negatively affects "at risk" students, it should have the opposite effect for academically talented students. The authors studied (7–10th grade) who were accepted into a gifted program at Duke University and found that gifted students had lower apprehension than the "at risk" students assessed by Chesebro et al. (1992). Further, the findings indicated that gifted students had less apprehension in the small group setting than "at risk" students.

Causes of Communication Apprehension

The data showing the negative effects of communication apprehension are rather consistent. There is controversy about its causes. Daly and Friedrich (1981) stated that communication apprehension might be caused by genetics, skill acquisition, modeling, and reinforcement.

The genetic explanation proposes that communication apprehension is related to factors such as sociability, physical appearance, body shape, and competence in motor skills. Each of these predispositions are enhanced or constrained by environmental factors.

Another way that communication apprehension may emerge, according to Daly and Friedrich (1981), involves the way in which social skills are acquired. Skills such as language use, sensitivity to nonverbal communication interaction management skills may be lacking in the communication apprehensive student. The protypical "geek" or "nerd" may be the student who lacks social skill and cannot "fit into the flow" of social interaction. As a result, communication is not very rewarding and new skills are not developed.

The third explanation that Daly and Friedrich (1981) discussed is modeling. If the child is around communicatively apprehensive individuals, then these are the behaviors modeled. When the individual is asked to engage in communication behaviors which have no frame of reference, the result will be anxiety and apprehension.

According to Daly and Friedrich, the most frequently advanced explanation of communication is explained through reinforcement theory. An individual who receives positive reinforcement for communication will not develop communication apprehension. The child who is told to be quiet, and not encouraged to communicate may develop negative attitudes about communication. McCroskey and Richmond (1978) found that students from rural areas and small towns reported higher communication apprehension levels than students from medium-sized and urban communities. The authors argued that this finding "is the first theoretically projected relationship between an environmental factor and communication apprehension that has been empirically verified" (p. 247). When comparing the environmental factors influencing attitudes about communication, urban children face more communication demands than rural children. For example, the rural students studied by McCroskey and Richmond attended small homogenous schools with little ethnic diversity. A common and narrow set of skills led to communication competence in these communities. In contrast, urban students face a much wider set of communication constraints. As a result, they must develop a broader range of competencies in order to be successful.

A new perspective, one that challenges the reinforcement explanation is emerging. Some researchers (Beatty, McCroskey, & Heisel, 1998; Beatty, McCroskey, & Valencic, 2001) challenge the reinforcement explanation and contend that neurobiological processes primarily determine communication apprehension. Beatty, McCroskey, and Heisel (1998) state that "communication apprehension is primarily a function of two interrelated neurobiological systems, the thresholds of which are the products of genetic inheritance" (p. 224).

Opt and Loffredo (2000) assessed the relationship between communication apprehension and the Meyers-Briggs personality type preferences. The Meyers-Briggs assessment draws from Jungian psychology, a perspective that anchors personality in inborn traits. The authors argued that communication apprehension is not something to overcome but is a preference not to communicate. The participants were assessed on extraversion–introversion, intuition–sensing, thinking–feeling, and judging–perceiving and on their level of communication apprehension. The results indicated that introverts and sensors scored significantly higher on communication apprehension. The authors concluded that communication apprehension is perceived as a problem when it is viewed through the perspective of extroverts. For the introvert, it is normal to not openly communicate or seek out communication exchanges. The introvert prefers quiet places and solitary activities. The authors conclude by suggesting that one way to deal with apprehension is help them become more complete in their personalities by confronting and expanding less preferred competencies.

The nature–nurture debate of communication apprehension has not been resolved and the reader is encouraged to read additional literature on this topic (Beatty, McCroskey, & Valencic, 2001; Condit, 2000. Whether communication apprehension is rooted in learning or theory or in biology, the teacher must have some strategy for dealing with it. The student who exhibits communication apprehension experiences numerous educational disadvantages. McCroskey and McCroskey (2002) discussed several ways that a teacher can prevent and reduce student apprehension. Specifically, they suggested that teachers:

- Reduce oral communication demands

    1   Avoid testing through talk.
    2   Avoid grading on participation.
    3   Avoid alphabetical seating.
    4   Avoid randomly calling on students.

- Make communication a rewarding experience

    1   Praise students when they participate.
    2   Try to avoid indicating that any answer is completely "wrong."
    3   Try not to punish any student for talking.

- Be consistent about communication

    1   Try to be consistent in how you handle student talk.
    2   Be very clear about any rules you must have regarding talking.

- Reduce ambiguity, novelty and evaluation

    1   Make all assignments as clear and unambiguous as you can.
    2   Be clear about your grading system.
    3   Avoid surprises.

- Increase student control over success.

    1   Give the student options.
    2   Be certain that the student can avoid communication and still do well in the course.

Reflection

♦ **How would you deal with communication apprehension in your class?**

Summary

This chapter has attempted to explicate the relationship between communication and learning. We have proposed that students bring a rich set of experiences, language skills, and interests that play an important role in the learning process. We believe that the relationship between classroom communication and learning is a function of three primary factors: student ability, motivation, and communication processes. The research we have reviewed suggests that instructional strategies building on student strengths positively influence academic performance. We also examined different perspectives on motivation and suggested ways to promote self-efficacy and internality. Finally, we examined the communication processes that shape learning experiences. Teacher questions, clarity and immediacy play important roles in the way instructional material is presented, processed, and understood.

Learning Activities

- Complete an assessment of your multiple intelligences. How do these preferences influence the way you approach learning tasks?
- Several of your students do not seem interested in reading. Which perspective on motivation can you use to devise a way to increase their interest in reading?
- Many teachers use external rewards (prizes, stickers, money) to engage students in learning tasks. What can teachers do to increase students, learning goals and internal motivation?

Resources

- Motivating students to engage in class activities
  www.nwrel.org/request/oct00/engage.html
- What do students want and what really motivates them?
  www.middleweb.com/StdntMotv.html
- Encouraging student academic motivation
  www.interventioncentral.org/htmdocs/interventions/motivation/motivation.php

Unit II

Understanding Diversity

This unit focuses on three features of diversity: culture, gender, and exceptionalities. As we noted previously, we consider diversity to be fluid and multidimensional. Culture, gender, and exceptionalities converge and emerge in different contexts. For purposes of clarity, we will deal with each of these areas separately. We will begin with cultural diversity. We will explain the dimensions of culture, the impact of cultural identity, culture and learning style, and ways to engage in culturally responsive teaching. Chapter 4 examines sex and gender. We begin the chapter by differentiating biological sex from gender. This is followed by a review of brain research on males and females. In Chapter 5 we explore students with exceptionalities. The legislation that provides the criteria for students with exceptionalities is reviewed. We describe low and high incidence disability, students with special needs, such as attention deficit/hyperactivity disorder. We conclude the chapter by discussing practices that promote positive interactions with all students in inclusive classrooms.

Chapter 3

Culture and Classroom Communication

On the first day of class, LeAnne Young, a first-year teacher, waits enthusiastically for the students in her first-period English class to arrive. They trickle in, some quietly, others engage in heated conversation. The veritable rainbow of student colors impacts Ms. Young considerably. Finally, the students take their seats and look at Ms. Young as she takes out her roll sheet and begins to call out their names: Eduardo Martinez, Shanisha Knight, Teng Her, Sandi Chalensouk, Gabriela Gamino, Markus Tyson, Michael Smith, Azor Singh, Ignacio Vidales, Danny Castanon, Tamika Yosida, and Brian Moore.

Ms. Young faces a daunting task. She recognizes the vast diversity in her class but is unsure how to address this opportunity. The one cultural studies course she took in college focused on the history of African-Americans. Although interesting, the course did not provide Ms. Young with the skills needed to teach in a culturally diverse classroom.

American classrooms are experiencing profound demographic shifts. In 2006, minorities made up 43% of the U.S. population with Hispanics representing the fastest growing group (United States Department of Education 2008). Asians, a group consisting of Hmong, Laotian, Cambodian, Chinese, Korean, and Japanese, have also shown substantial increases. At the same time, more than 80% of the teaching profession is white.

The demographic changes can be challenging and exciting at the same time. Responsible schools and educators must struggle with ways to meet the needs of students with a wide range of experiences, skills, and interests. Understanding the ways in which culture influences educational contexts can empower teachers to reach all of their students. This is no easy task. Teachers must understand not only how culture influences the behavior of students, but also the way that it influences their own perceptions and behaviors. Like students, teachers come into the classroom with biases, perceptions, skills, and expectations that shape their communication. Teachers, especially white teachers, frequently problematize culture by seeing it as a limitation that the student possesses. Students who "overcome" their culture succeed. Students unwilling to make this adjustment will fail. Teachers seldom reflect on their own biases or the limitations of their pedagogical practices. Rather than placing all the responsibility on the students, we propose that teachers, regardless of their cultural heritage, increase their cultural competence so that they can be better prepared to facilitate student learning.

Reflection

♦ **How do you define culture?**
♦ **To what cultural groups do you belong?**

Culture

Culture is a difficult concept to understand. An examination of some representative definitions might be helpful. Lustig and Koester (1999) defined culture as "a learned set of shared interpretations about beliefs, values, and norms which affect the behaviors of a relatively large group of people" (p. 30). Orbe and Harris (2001) characterized culture as "learned and shared values, beliefs, and behaviors common to a particular group of people; culture forges a group's identity and assists in its survival" (p. 6). Individuals are taught, sometimes implicitly, sometimes explicitly, to view the world in a certain way and to behave in a way that supports this viewpoint. Samovar, Porter, and Stefani (2000) offered the following conceptualization of culture:

> the deposit of knowledge, experiences, social hierarchies, religion, notions of time, roles, spatial relationships, concepts of the universe, and material objects and possessions acquired by a group of people in the course of generations through individual or group striving.
>
> (p. 7)

Culture, then, influences what people know, how they came by that knowledge, what roles they play and how they should play them, what they value, and how they put their values into action. Clearly, culture plays a significant role in the education process.

Dimensions of Culture

A number of scholars have investigated the role culture plays in communication exchanges. The research of Hall (1976) and Hofstede (1980) is particularly relevant to our examination of culture in the classroom. Hall believed that individuals are faced with so many stimuli that they develop mechanisms for filtering and making sense out of them. According to Hall, the context for communication plays a significant role in the way the information is sifted and acted upon. A communication context has physical, social, and psychological features. The physical feature is the actual setting for the interaction (classroom, principal's office, home). The social feature is the relationship among the participants (teacher/student, teacher/parent, teacher/teacher). Psychological features include the attitudes, sentiments, and motivations of the participants. Culture influences the degree to which communicators focus on these features.

Hall postulated a continuum with high-context messages on one end and low-context messages on the other. A high-context message has most of the relevant information in the physical setting or is internalized in the person. Much of the meaning in the message is implied. Japanese, Hmong, Koreans, Chinese, and Latinos are examples of high-context communities. Members of high-context groups have developed similar expectations about how to perceive and respond to a particular communication event. Consequently, explicit verbal messages are not necessary for understanding. Low-context groups, on the other hand require that the message include a great deal of explicit information. Uncertainty is reduced and understandings are obtained through expressed verbal codes.

Most American classrooms are predicated on low-context exchanges. Teachers are expected to be clear, direct, explicit, and linear with their instructions and expectations. Students are expected to be clear, direct, and explicit with their answers. The farther students depart from these communication conventions, the more at risk they become.

Hofstede (1980), another expert on intercultural communication, explained that individuals possess cognitive processes that are shaped by culture and are expressed through the culture's dominant values. He identified four dominant patterns and each has application to classroom exchanges.

The first dimension is *power distance*. This dimension is concerned with the way in which status differences are ascribed and negotiated. Some cultures believe that power should be distributed while others hold that only a few people should possess power and authority. European-American students tend to believe that power should be distributed and that everyone has an equal opportunity to possess it. Students from Latin and Southeast Asian cultures tend to believe that power should be held by a select few. As we noted, clan elders possess a great deal of power in the Hmong community and young women possess very little. Some teachers wield a great deal of power in classrooms. They make all classroom decisions and impose their will on the students. Other teachers share power with students and give them an opportunity to make decisions about instructional issues and class activities.

A second dimension is *uncertainty avoidance*. This dimension is concerned with the ways in which a culture deals with change and unpredictability. Some cultures have very little tolerance for circumstances that may threaten the culture's structure and hierarchy. Severe consequences follow for the individual who does not adhere to the culture's expectations. Individuals from cultures high on uncertainty avoidance have very strict rules governing appropriate behavior and there are severe consequences for violating these rules. Schools and classes also establish rules and policies for appropriate classroom behavior. Some teachers may be very strict and intolerant of student "misbehavior." One teacher stated that the problem with Native American students is that they lack structure at home so he was going to be sure they learned discipline in his classroom. His primary instructional goal was to control student behavior; learning was a secondary goal. Other teachers allow students to make choices, multi-task, and socialize with other students.

A third dimension is *individualism-collectivism*. This dimension is concerned with the degree to which individuals commit to self or community. Competition, autonomy, privacy, personal opinion, and independence are core elements in individualistic societies. The United States is extremely high on this dimension. The school system, with its growing emphasis on grades and test scores, competition, and performance outcomes, strongly promotes individualistic values. Cultures subordinating the needs of the individual to the group are reflective of collectivist societies. Humility and sharing are core values in collectivistic cultures. Thus, focusing attention on the achievements of one individual can bring much stress. For example, it is inappropriate to single out the success of a Native-American individual. Obligation is another core element in collectivist cultures. Some teachers have become frustrated with students who miss class because of family "business." The teachers do not understand that, in some cultures, especially for new immigrants from collectivist societies, family obligation transcends school and education.

The fourth dimension discussed by Hofstede is *masculinity-femininity*. This dimension concerns the degree to which the culture values assertiveness and achievement versus nurturance and social support. Some cultures judge others by their achievements and the manifestations of appropriate masculine behavior. In Mexico, for example, the male is the head of the household, is primarily responsible for the financial security of the family and ultimately makes all important decisions. Women are expected to tend to home duties such as child rearing and cooking. Attitudes about masculinity and femininity are also revealed in America's classrooms. Boys are often encouraged to be assertive, active, and competitive while females are encouraged to be passive, and cooperative. The issue of masculinity and femininity is complex and we discuss this topic in Chapter 4.

After publishing the first four dimensions, Hofstede (2001) added a fifth dimension which he labeled long-term and short-term orientation. According to Hofstede, this orientation is rooted in Confucianism which values thrift, and persistence and a predictable social order. Values of a short-term orientation are a concern for "here and now," a low concern for status and a motivation to protect one's identity. Students from long-term orientation are likely to show great respect for teachers and are concerned with task accomplishment. Students from short-term orientations are more likely to play before work and be more likely to exhibit disrespectful behavior to the teacher.

The perspectives offered by Hall and Hofstede have great application for today's diverse classroom. Recall that culture shapes perceptions, values, and behaviors. The dominant perspective of America's classroom is low-context and individualistic. In most classes, the preferred way of communicating is to be explicit and linear. Yet more and more students are from high-context, collectivistic cultural experiences. For these students, the teacher is considered the expert; knowledge is passed from the teacher to the student. The student's task is to absorb the information. These students are less likely to perceive that knowledge is negotiated. The teacher who is unaware of the way culture informs students of preferences for appropriate behavior may perceive that high-context, collectivist students are disconnected while low-context individualistic students are engaged. Seldom are these issues made clear to the students as they navigate the instructional system.

Cultural Identity

The connection to a culture's values is accomplished through the performance of cultural identity. Cultural identity denotes the ways individuals view themselves and the ways they wish to be viewed by others. Lustig and Koester (2000) noted that cultural identity involves learning about and accepting the traditions, heritage, language, religion, ancestry, aesthetics, thinking patterns, and social structures of a culture (p. 3).

According to Collier (1994), identities are co-created and negotiated through communication exchanges. A person may have different identities, depending on the context. Students may have "home," "playground," and "classroom" identities. A student can be quiet and inattentive in the classroom and loud, boisterous, and aggressive in the school yard. Student identity plays a fundamental role in the groups they move toward and away from. Think about the ways students cluster and the way in which they navigate through the groups in which they participate. "Skaters," "emmos," "preps," "schoolboys," "bandos" dress and talk in ways that support their identities.

Goffman's (1959, 1963) dramaturgical perspective is an excellent framework for viewing the cultural identities of students. He claimed that whenever people participate in social interaction, they are engaged in a type of performance. Like actors in a play, they construct an image they want the audience to accept. Goffman (1959) stated that each person constructs a face and uses a line (way of talking) to support it. A successful performance, according to Goffman, requires the individual to look the part they are trying to play and talk in a way that supports the projected image. These performances are not always positive. For example, some students do not perceive that being a good student is "cool" so they slump in their desks, appear bored, and seldom participate in class discussion. Recall our discussion of self-worth theory and motivation. Students construct a social performance that removes them from academic engagement.

In multicultural classrooms, a student may enact a performance that the teacher misunderstands or does not accept. Cupach and Imahori (1993) examined the way individuals from different cultural backgrounds manage the predicaments (a situation that is embarrassing or unpleasant) created by someone else. Even though their research did not focus on instructional contexts, their research has direct application to the topic we are discussing.

The authors claimed that all individuals want to have their identities supported during social interaction. Receiving undue recognition, being criticized or corrected, having their privacy violated, and being caused to look foolish are the types of situations causing individuals to lose face (Cupach & Metts, 1990, 1992). When individuals are confronted with these predicaments they are compelled to invoke a strategy to save face. Examples of the strategies individuals use to restore their identity are: apology (accepting blame and seeking forgiveness), excuse (minimizing responsibility), justification (downplaying harmful consequences), humor (joking or laughing), remediation (actively attempting to repair damage), avoiding (ignoring the transgression), escape (leaving the scene), and aggression (verbally or physically attacking).

Cupach and Imahori (1993) predicted that American and Japanese students would use different strategies to deal with face-threatening situations. The authors predicted that Americans would use humor, accounts (reasons that justify a behavior), and aggression, while Japanese would use apology and remediation. The results supported the hypotheses. The authors concluded from the findings that Americans use strategies which support their own face and Japanese use strategies to support others.

These findings have direct implications for classrooms. Teachers criticize students for the way they dress, for their taste in music, and on their academic performance. Without meaning to, teachers may also threaten the cultural identities of students. Shortly after the bombing of the World Trade Center, Muslim students and students who looked Middle Eastern were criticized, mocked, and challenged by teachers and students. Students create predicaments for teachers when they question grades, tell a teacher assignments are unclear, or challenge the authority of teachers. The way in which these predicaments are managed can dramatically influence the climate of the classroom.

Reflection

♦ **What are some of the cultural labels you use?**
♦ **How do you feel about the students who perform these identities?**
♦ **How do you respond to face-threatening situations?**

Collier (1994) observed that cultural identities are expressed through core symbols, labels, and norms. Core symbols reference beliefs about the universe and people's positions in it. These symbols direct members of a cultural group to perceive the world in a particular way and behave in a way that is consistent with that definition. Core symbols for African-Americans are authenticity, powerlessness, and expressiveness (Hecht, Collier, & Ribeau, 1993). Latino core symbols are obligation to family, respect, and faith.

Labels are important components of cultural identity. Students with ancestors from Mexico may at different times describe themselves as Mexican, Mexican-American, Hispanic, Chicano, or Latino. Some students say they are African-American, and others call themselves Black. White Hmong are different from Green Hmong, and an Afghan is different from an Iraqi.

Tanno (1997) discussed the different labels characterizing her cultural identity. She spent her formative years in New Mexico, where she used the label Spanish to describe herself. She spoke Spanish and practiced some of the traditions that were introduced into New Mexico by the early Spanish settlers. When she moved from New Mexico she was confronted with a different label. Outside of New Mexico the preferred label for her heritage was *Mexican-American*. This label captured the duality of her heritage: the traditions of Mexico and dominant patterns of America. To be too Mexican was to reject the American in her. To reject the Mexican and become too American was to abandon her historical roots.

A third label found its way into her vocabulary. Whereas, the label *Mexican-American* captured a dual identity, the new label *Latina* captured her connectedness. The Spanish had captured vast territories and merged with indigenous peoples from Cuba, Mexico, and South America. Language, religion, and numerous daily practices were common among a vast group of people. For Tanno, to be *Latina* was to belong to a broad cultural community.

The final label that Tanno discussed is Chicana. This label is unique because it was created by an ethnic group to describe an ethnic group. With this label came a political consciousness. The label *Chicana* recognizes the marginalization that Americans of Latin descent have experienced and the desire to reconstruct these structures through political action.

Tanno concluded her essay by arguing that each label represents a part of her identity. She noted that all individuals take on multiple roles and believed we should be respectful of this complexity. Teachers might also be mothers, fathers, husbands, wives, uncles, little league coaches, and big sisters. Students may be sons, daughters, soccer players, and goddaughters. Further, these labels are not static, but fluid. Individuals may use different labels to define themselves at different times.

Sometimes teachers inappropriately label students or use a label that students do not prefer, like, or perceive to be insulting or embarrassing. Students from Cambodia are often confused with students from China. It is important for teachers to recognize that the way in which they respond to these labels may indicate acceptance or rejection of the student. While labels may seem helpful, they can be problematic. Every African-American student does not have the same attitudes, possess the same skills, or have the same interests.

Group norms also play an important role in cultural identity (Collier, 1994). Norms are the standards for competent participation in a community. There are norms for turning in assignments, participating in class, working individually or in groups. Language performance is a central feature of cultural identity. To competently perform a cultural identity is to use language and behave in a way that sustains and projects that identity. Murrell (2002) draws from the work of Holland, Lachicotte, Skinner, and Cain (1998) and argued that identities are "improvised." That is, identities are tested, negotiated, and reconstructed in each communication context. According to Murrell (2002), identity management is the most significant developmental task facing African-American students.

As we previously discussed, Standard English is the preferred discourse style of the classroom. Some research indicates that students of color assume that in order to be academically successful they must abandon their ethnic identity and assume a white one (Fordham & Ogbu, 1986; Ogbu, 1999). Ogbu (1999) referred to this as a Dialectical Dilemma. In his research in Oakland, California, he found that African-Americans endorsed learning Standard English for education and employment but this mastery also threatened membership in the community. That is, parents and others stated that they did not want students to use Standard English at home or to criticize the use of language styles used in the community. In other words, it appeared to be acceptable to "talk White" at school but not at home. Ogbu's position is that a number of community factors negatively influence the academic performance of minorities. Murrell (2002), a scholar of African-American pedagogy, has a different approach for interpreting the academic performance of African-Americans. He contended that all students experience concern about possible academic failure. Rather than believing that African-Americans must act white to be successful, Murrell (2002) argued they fear that they will confirm negative stereotypes that African-American students and other students of color do not have academic potential. He goes on to contend that schools need to help reshape a construction of African-Americans and we include other groups that require deconstructing a "triple threat." This threat involves teachers, the media, and peers. Many students have teachers who do not expect students of color to be successful (Threat 1). These students face national and local media that reify an achievement gap between white students and students of color (Threat 2). Finally, students of color may see academic achievement as "selling out" (Threat 3). Clearly this is a complicated issue. But we want teachers to think carefully and deeply about their beliefs about students of color, the ways in which they enact their identities, and what this means for their curriculum, evaluative procedures, and relationships.

The research by Rex (2003) illustrates how teachers, even those with good intentions, dismiss and devalue students who do not use mainstream speech. She further contends that high-stakes testing has exacerbated the problem. In one study she observed an exchange between a teacher and an inner city student on the use of topic sentences. In the instructional episode the students were writing sentences about drug use in the community. The student from the inner city wanted to debate the assertion made by the teacher that drug use was a problem. He was from the community and did not use drugs. Rather than engaging the student in the discussion and probing his experience, the teacher moved the focus to the grammatical and syntactical structure of the sentence he was supposed to write. This instructional move was motivated by the desire to help the student improve his writing so that he would score higher on the state test but the effect may have been to disconfirm the student's identity and experiences. Rex (2003) raises several important questions for teachers to consider. For example, she asks, "What if they don't believe they need to talk, read or write in the ways the high stakes tests imply they should" (p. 39). "What classroom conversations are lost and what opportunities for inclusion disappear when much of the talk is about reading and writing as they appear on the test" (p. 39).

The questions posed above are difficult to answer. Yet the students most vulnerable to failure and criticism come from non-dominant communication communities. So how can teachers meet the demands of testing and help students develop more proficiency in language?

Godley, Sweetland, Wheeler, Minnici, and Carpenter (2006) offer recommendations for teachers facing dialectically diverse classrooms. The authors argue that teachers need to change their ideology about teaching English. They state "When teachers engage in teaching of Standard English it is important they frame Standard English as an addition to students' linguistic repertoires, rather than as a more prestigious more 'correct' substitution for the varieties that students already speak".

The authors discuss three ways in which teachers can be more responsive to dialectically diverse classrooms:

1   *Dialect diversity is a resource not a deficit.* Godley et al. (2006) contend that teachers, especially when teaching language arts, should build on and use the dialects that students bring to the classroom. They go on to recommend that teachers should not label non-standard dialects as ungrammatical, illogical, or as slang (p. 35).

2   *Students benefit from learning about dialect diversity.* The authors note that language naturally varies from situation to situation. Helping students analyze and utilize these different forms enriches their understanding of language use. Godley et al. state that programs implemented in middle and high schools have helped students develop a better understanding of regional and social language variation. Teaching about dialectal diversity encourages students to recognize the multiple language forms they use.

3   *Dialect patterns should be distinguished from errors in writing and addressed through a contrastive approach.* This strategy requires teachers to try and understand the underlying patterns of language rather than focusing on correcting errors in language grammar, logic or syntax. Consider the following example of student writing. A student writes, "I seen your buds at the Rodeo Café last night." This sentence has a grammatical structure; there is an object and verb. Godley et al. recommend using a contrasting approach that builds on the student's competence. They suggest that a sentence is "data" that can be analyzed and used to facilitate the use of Standard English. Rather than labeling the error, the teacher might ask the student to reflect on the grammatical pattern that was used. The student can be asked to identify circumstances when it is appropriate to write, "I seen" and when it is appropriate to write "I saw."

The recommendations suggested by Godley et al. (2006) are difficult to implement and take time. However, research indicates that the overall writing performance on standardized assessments has improved when these strategies have been implemented (e.g. Fogel & Ehri, 2000; Schierloh, 1991; Taylor, 1989).

In the previous section we have attempted to describe the role that cultural identity plays in the classroom. Students manage multiple identities through their styles of dress, ways of talking, and norms of behavior. Some of these identities are positively received and others are rejected. All, however, impact the way that interaction unfolds in the classroom.

Culture and Learning

The relationship between student culture and preferences for learning has been discussed frequently, but teachers have not been particularly effective in incorporating culture into classroom practice. Kuykendall (1992) suggested that students who find their culture and learning styles reflected in instruction are more likely to be motivated and less likely to be disruptive. The research by Dunn and Griggs (2000) indicates that student academic achievement increases when instructional practices adapt to the learning styles of students. It is important therefore to understand how culture influences learning and how to integrate this knowledge into instructional practice. The following discussion is introductory so we encourage future teachers to continue to investigate this topic.

Learning style is concerned with the characteristic ways of dealing with instructional information and culture influences this process. For example, observational research suggests that Mexican-American students are more comfortable with broad concepts than with isolated facts (Cox & Ramirez, 1981; Vasquez, 1991). African-American students prefer tactile "hands on" learning (Shade, 1989). Native Americans relate well to instructional tasks requiring skills in visual discrimination, and the use of imagery (ibid.). Mainstream white students value independence, analytical thinking and objectivity.

Cultural differences have been found on self-report measures. Cultural researchers assessing learning styles have found differences in field-independent and field-dependent learning (Gollnick & Chinn, 1994). Field-dependent learners process information holistically and are more concerned with the social context, and are more intuitive. Field-independent learners process information sequentially, do not consider the social situation important, and are rational. Mainstream white students tend to be field-independent and students from minority groups tend to be field-dependent.

It is important to note, however, that there is not a straightforward relationship between culture and learning style. As Guild (1994) noted, there are as many variations within a group as there are commonalities. Moreover, many conceptualizations on learning style are bi-polar. One end is represented by analytic processes while the other end is represented by holistic ones.

Gay (2000), a central figure in multicultural education, argues that learning styles are not "monolithic" or "static traits," but are the "central tendencies" students from different ethnic groups draw upon to engage in learning. According to Gay teachers can utilize these dimensions to develop culturally compatible instruction for ethnically diverse students.

- *Procedural*—the preferred ways of approaching and working through learning tasks. These include pacing rates; distribution of time; variety versus similarity; novelty or predictability; passivity or activity; task directed or sociality; structured order or freedom; and preference for direct teaching or inquiry and discovery learning.
- *Communicative*—how thoughts are organized, sequenced, and conveyed in spoken and written forms, whether as elaborated narrative storytelling or precise responses to explicit questions; as topic-specific or topic-chaining discourse techniques; as passionate advocacy of ideas or dispassionate recorders and reporters; whether the purpose is to achieve descriptive and factual accuracy or to capture persuasive power and convey literary aestheticism.
- *Substantive*—preferred content, such as descriptive details or general patterns, concepts and principles or factual information, statistics or personal and social scenarios; preferred subjects, such as math, science, social studies, fine or language arts; technical interpretive, and evaluative tasks; preferred intellectualizing tasks, such as memorizing, describing, analyzing, classifying, or criticizing.
- *Environmental*—preferred physical, social, and interpersonal settings for learning, including sound or silence; room lighting and temperature; presence or absence of others; ambiance of struggle or playfulness, of fun and joy, or pain and somberness
- *Organizational*—preferred structural arrangements for work and study space, including the amount of personal space; the fullness or emptiness of learning space; rigidity or flexibility in use of claims made to space; carefully organized or cluttered learning resources and space locations; individually claimed or group-shared space; rigidity or flexibility of habitation of space.
- *Perceptual*—preferred sensory stimulation for receiving, processing, and transmitting information, including visual, tactile, auditory, kinetic, oral, or multiple sensory modalities.
- *Relational*—preferred interpersonal and social interaction modes in learning situations, including formality or informality, individual competition or group cooperation, independence or interdependence, peer–peer or child–adult, authoritarian or egalitarian, internal or external locus of control, conquest or community.

- *Motivational*—preferred incentives or stimulations that evoke learning including individual accomplishment or group well-being, competition or cooperation, conquest or harmony, expediency or propriety, image or integrity (pp. 151–152).

According to Gay (2000) some ethnic group members display "purer" learning style characteristics than others. The degree of purity is determined by group identification, gender, social class, and level of education. African-American students with a high degree of ethnic identification may relate best to instruction that is based on group activities in procedural, motivational, relational, and substantive dimensions of learning. Traditional Japanese or Chinese students might be bi-stylistic, because of their collectivistic cultural values they may respond well to activities requiring group problem solving. At the same time these students may perform well on mechanistic, technical, and atomistic learning tasks. Teachers need to understand that one set of strategies will not work with all students.

Reflection

♦ Consider the dimensions discussed by Gay. Identify your preferences for each category. Share your perspective with a classmate. What are the commonalities and differences?
♦ How could you use this information to develop a math lesson?

For many years educators have acknowledged the relationship between culture and orientations to learning, but few have offered concrete recommendations on how a teacher can integrate culture into classroom practice. Claxton (1990) provided a framework that serves the interests of both minority and non-minority students. He argued that "Recognizing the need to teach minority students well . . . must also involve teaching white students more effectively" (p. 35). Claxton's framework is built on two approaches to learning; the first he called *separate knowing* and this entails the separation of the object of inquiry and the knower. Ideas, facts, and information are isolated from the larger contexts in which they are found. The second approach is *connected knowing*. This implies a relationship with the thing being studied. The closer the relationship, the deeper the understanding.

Claxton advocated developing teaching strategies which integrate the two ways of knowing. The model he develops is called the connected teaching model and consists of five central features. The central metaphor of the connected learning model is the teacher as midwife rather than the teacher as banker. Bankers, according to Claxton, deposit knowledge, whereas midwives help students draw it out. The role of the teacher is to help students build on what they know and connect to what they do not know.

The second feature of connected teaching is a focus on problem posing. Traditional teaching focuses on imparting information through lecture or print. Connecting teaching requires students to solve problems that are significant and relevant. When learning is relevant, students become engaged. Delpit's (1995) work on writing resonates with Claxton's position. She stated, "Actual writing for real audiences and real purposes is a vital element in helping students to understand that they have an important voice in their own learning processes" (p. 33).

The third feature of connected teaching is the insistence that dialogue is not one-way communication. This idea reinforces the points made by Sprague in Chapter 1. Knowledge is not located in the teacher and transmitted to the student; it comes through the interaction between and among learners. In this view, learning is emergent and negotiated between and among participants.

The fourth feature of connected teaching is disciplined subjectivity. In traditional teaching, students are held accountable for the knowledge presented by the teacher. The instructor is the center and students are expected to report what the teacher wants. In connected teaching, the emphasis is on the student. Teachers attempt to view content from where the students stand. Reflect on the study conducted by Rex (2003) discussed earlier in the chapter. The teacher missed an opportunity to view the instructional task from the student's perspective. He wanted to discuss drug use and she wanted him to write a topic sentence. These are not mutually exclusive goals.

The final feature of connected teaching is fostering collaboration and community rather than competition and individualism. Students do not compete for grades but create a community where knowledge is discovered. Cleary and Peacock (1998) reported that such cooperative environments are particularly useful for Native-American students. Similar findings have been identified with other cultural groups.

Culturally Responsive Teaching

We believe that the key to managing cultural diversity is to develop intercultural competence. Wlodkowski and Ginsberg (1995) offered the following definition of culturally responsive teaching:

> Teaching that is culturally responsive occurs when there is equal respect for the backgrounds and contemporary circumstances of all learners, regardless of individual status and power, and when there

is a design of learning processes that embraces the range of needs, interests, and orientations to be found among them.

(p. 17)

Gay (2000) outlined the core characteristics of culturally responsive teaching: First, culturally responsive teaching is *validating*. It draws upon the cultural knowledge, traditions, and styles, of diverse students, extending and affirming their strengths of competencies. Among its other features, culturally responsive teaching incorporates multicultural information into the instruction of all subjects and uses a variety of instructional strategies.

Second, culturally response teaching is *comprehensive*. Teachers use cultural referents to impart knowledge. This requires teachers to be willing to learn about the cultural backgrounds, traditions, and histories of the students represented in the classroom. In addition, teachers must make efforts to enhance connections to the community, maintain cultural identity, and to instill attitudes of success and commitment. Responsibility and commitment to self and others are encouraged. They are expected to internalize the value that learning is a communal, reciprocal, interdependent affair, and manifest it habitually in their expressive behaviors (Gay, 2000, p. 430)

Third, culturally responsive teaching is *multidimensional*. Any topic or issue can be approached from multiple perspectives. Gay describes ways that teachers could collaborate to teach the concept of protest. Students could be encouraged to discover the ways different groups symbolize their issues and concerns. By examining, literature, poetry, music, art, interviews, and historical records, students could learn both about what gives rise to protest and how it is exhibited. Assessments should also be multidimensional. In this framework, the teacher does not use one standardized assessment but uses multiple assessments. Howard Gardner and his seminal work on multiple intelligence is applicable to culturally responsive teaching.

Fourth, culturally responsive teaching is *empowering*. Teachers who successfully implement culturally responsive teaching expect all students to succeed and develop structures that increase the probability of student success. Success is accomplished by "boostering students' morale, providing resources and personal assistance, developing an ethos of achievement, and celebrating individual and collective accomplishments" (p. 32). Culturally responsive teaching shifts the emphasis from external to internal forces, thus engaging students in the learning process.

Fifth, culturally responsive teaching is *transformative*. Instructional practices build upon the students' strengths and extend them further in the learning processes. According to Gay, success is perceived to be a "non-negotiable mandate" for all students. Students are encouraged to give back to their respective communities and participate fully in the national society. Education is transformative when students come to understand the structures and processes that are related to discrimination and prejudice and when they develop skills to combat them.

Finally, culturally responsive teaching is *emancipatory*. Students are given the freedom to move beyond the traditional canons of knowledge and explore alternative perspectives and ways of knowing. Within this perspective, students challenge and question and come to understand that no truth is total and permanent. According to Gay (2000), "These learning engagements encourage and enable students to find their own voices, to contextualize issues in multiple cultural perspectives, to engage in more ways of knowing and thinking, and to become more active participants in shaping their own learning" (p. 35). Consider, for example, the various ways that a lesson on the "discovery" of America could be taught. Loewen (1995) thoughtfully outlined what is omitted from most textbooks about the circumstances, and events and tragedies involving the voyages of Columbus. Allowing students to explore and examine alternative stories may help them find connections that are not possible with dominant interpretations.

Reyes, Scribner, and Scribner (1999) show that culturally sensitive teaching has tremendous payoffs. These authors studied eight high performing Hispanic schools. These schools were located in lower socioeconomic communities along the border of Texas and Mexico. One of the most significant findings was that the eight schools studied had a strong commitment to culturally responsive teaching. The authors reported:

> Perhaps the most powerful finding pertaining to the classroom learning was the incorporation of the students' interests and experiences, the "funds of knowledge" they bring with them into the learning situation, whether it be reading, writing, mathematics, or other subjects.
> (p. 14)

Teachers built upon the cultural values of the students and made the classroom a culturally inviting place.

Gay (2002) made specific recommendations on ways to accomplish culturally responsive teaching. She contended that culturally responsive teaching has four primary features. First, the teacher develops a cultural knowledge base. Developing this base requires teachers to understand the cultural characteristics and contributions of different cultural groups. Cultivating a cultural data base on the specific contributions of specific cultural groups helps the teacher establish a context for learning. She stated that culturally sensitive teaching deals as much with multicultural strategies as it does with adding specific content into lessons. Weaving this knowledge into instructional practice helps the teacher make the connections necessary for learning.

The second feature involves converting cultural knowledge into relevant curricula. According to Gay, three types of curricula are present in the classroom. The formal curriculum entails the standards approved by state policy boards. Gay recommends that teachers carefully assess the strengths and weaknesses of this curriculum and make the necessary changes to improve overall quality. The second type of curriculum Gay identifies is the symbolic curriculum. This involves the images, symbols, and awards that are used to promote learning and values. Images displayed on bulletin boards, pictures of heroes, and statements about social etiquette are examples of this type of curriculum. Teachers need to ensure that these displays are representative and accurate extensions of what is taught in the formal curriculum. The final type of curriculum is the societal curriculum. This curriculum involves the images about cultural groups that are reflected in the mass media. Culturally responsive teachers ask students to question and challenge the representations that appear on television and in news.

The third feature of culturally responsive teaching is demonstrating cultural caring. To accomplish this, teachers need to build on the experiences of the students and broaden their intellectual horizons. Understanding the communication styles and knowing how to connect them to learning goals is a crucial feature of culturally responsive teaching. Teachers, thus must have "knowledge about the linguistic structures of various ethnic communication styles as well as contextual factors, cultural nuances, discourse features, logic, rhythm, delivery, vocabulary usage, role relationships of speakers and listeners, intonation, gestures, and body movements" (p. 111). Culturally responsive teachers must also understand different "protocols of participation in discourse" and different ways that groups engage in task. The IRE pattern we discussed in Chapter 2 is dominant in mainstream classes. Students from groups of color, however, are more active, participative and circular in their interaction patters. Serious classroom management problems can unfold when teachers do not understand these communication differences. Wlodkowski and Ginsberg (1995) observed: "Probably the area where the dominant perspective in education is in greatest conflict with other behavioral styles is that of language and dialect" (pp. 146–147). It is therefore crucial that teachers increase their communication competency in intercultural exchanges.

The fourth feature of culturally responsive teaching concerns the actual delivery of instruction. Gay argues that teachers need to *multiculturalize* instructional practice. This final feature involves the strategies teachers use to bring the material to life. Cooperative learning strategies follow from a knowledge that some ethnic groups prefer tasks that allow them to work with others. Knowing that some groups do not communicate in a linear analytic fashion allows the teacher to use narrative as a way to present material. Finding ways to integrate diversity into the high status academic areas (i.e. math, reading, and science) is an excellent way to show a commitment to the world views of students).

The recommendations advanced by Gay (2000, 2002) can help teachers understand the role of student culture and preferences for learning and what teachers can do. However, this goal is difficult to achieve. Teachers, administrators, school boards and some parents may not support this type of approach. One school board in a rural California would not allow students to do projects on Cesar Chavez, event though 90% of the students were Mexican-American. Some teachers fight against the goals of these perspectives and school boards may criticize these types of strategies. Even with this information, however, some teachers will favor students whose behavioral and learning styles match their own. When there are language distinctions between teachers and students, teachers may use their own language as an evaluative lens for judging the abilities of the student. The student who uses nonstandard speech may be perceived as less intelligent and less competent. The notion that students with nonstandard English patterns are considered less competent has been documented in research (e.g. Powell & Avila, 1986).

In addition to speech pattern and accent, a teacher may respond negatively to other stylistic features of a student's communication. Latin students may use metaphor and other ornamental forms of speech. These forms depart from linear, reductionistic features of individualistic cultures. Teachers may consider the comments unclear or inappropriate.

Reflection

◆ **How can a teacher develop a cultural knowledge base?**
◆ **How do teachers signal their lack of understanding of culture?**

Cultural Alignment

We take the position that everyone is cultural, yet teachers, especially teachers whose ancestors are from Europe have difficulty understanding their cultural presuppositions. As a consequence, they may not reflect on the ways in which culture influences their attitudes, behaviors, and beliefs. Orbe and Harris (2001) suggested that whiteness signals dominance, normalcy, and privilege. Yet many whites do not accept these descriptions as portraying their lived experience. McAllister and Irvine (2000) argued that in order to be effective, teachers must critically examine their world-views and confront their personal biases. Kumashiro

(2000) contended that educators can easily oppress students of color or students from other marginalized groups when those students are seen as the "other." Teachers take important steps toward inclusion when they examine their own world-views. Because the overwhelming majority of teachers are white, we wish to conclude this chapter by exploring "whiteness" as a cultural construct.

Paley, in her book *White Teacher* (1989), examined the challenges societal values reflected in today's classrooms through an examination of her own prejudices as a white teacher. In her work with African-American children, she stated:

> The black child is Every Child. There is no activity useful only for the black child. There is no manner of speaking or unique approach or special environment required only for black children. There are only certain words and actions that cause all of us to cover up and there are other words and actions that help us reveal ourselves to one another. The challenge in teaching is to find a way of communicating to each child the idea that his or her special quality is understood, is valued, and can be talked about. It is not easy, because we are influenced by the fears and prejudices, apprehensions, and expectations, which have become a carefully hidden part of every one of us.
>
> (p. xv)

Before beginning the discussion, answer the questions posed by Manning and Baruth (2000).

Ask yourself these questions:

1 Are my opinions of parents and families based on myths and stereotypes or on accurate and objective perceptions?
2 Have my experiences included positive firsthand contact with people from culturally different backgrounds?
3 What means have I employed to learn about the customs, traditions, values, and beliefs of all people?
4 Do I understand the extended-family concept or do I only think "too many people live in the same house because of poverty conditions"?
5 Am I prejudiced, or do I have genuine feelings of acceptance for all people regardless of culture, ethnicity, race, and socioeconomic background?
6 Do I hold the perceptions that Native Americans are alcoholics, that African-American families are headed by single females, that Asian-Americans are the model minority and have achieved what

represents the American Dream, or that Hispanic-Americans have large families and live on welfare?

7 Can I perceive that aunts, uncles, and grandparents are as important as more immediate family members (i.e. the mother and father)?

8 Do I understand the rich cultural backgrounds of families, and am I willing to base educational experiences on this diversity?

9 Do I know appropriate sources of information to learn more about parents and families from culturally diverse backgrounds?

10 Do I have the motivation, skills, and attitudes to develop close interrelationships with parents and families from culturally different backgrounds? (p. 284)

Some of these questions are very difficult to answer. Few of the white individuals we know openly state that they have privilege and opportunity because of their ethnicity. Yet as Howard (2000), a white multi-educational scholar, noted:

> White Americans are caught in a classic state of cognitive dissonance. Our collective security and position of economic and political dominance have been fueled in large measure by the exploitation of other people. The physical and cultural genocide perpetrated against American Indians, the enslavement of African peoples, the exploitation of Mexicans and Asians as sources of cheap labor—on such acts of inhumanity rests the success of the European enterprise in America.
>
> (p. 326)

Howard (2000) further contended that daily survival for people of color is related to their knowledge of white America. On the other hand, the survival of white Americans has not depended on an understanding of the structures, institutions, and language of minority groups. One area where this disparity is most obvious is in the area of education. We believe that all teachers should examine their cultural assumptions and consider ways these assumptions may influence their teaching.

McAllister and Irvine (2000) reviewed three process models that have been used to explain the transitions from culturally ethnocentric to culturally sensitive orientations: Helms' (1990) Racial Identity model, Banks' (1994) typology of ethnic identity, and Bennett's (1986) Developmental Model of Intercultural Sensitivity. Each model focuses on a different feature of cultural identity and awareness but each suggests that individuals progress through different stages of awareness and differentiation. In the early stages, individuals have limited and naïve orientations about culture.

White teachers, for example, are not inclined to view themselves as cultural or to see how their "whiteness" influences their orientation to the world in general or the classroom in particular. In later stages, there is an understanding of cultural norms, expectations, and actions. In these stages, individuals are able to take the perspective of individuals from different cultural orientations and make context appropriate adaptations.

After reviewing the studies conducted on these models, McCallister and Irvine (2000) concluded that the results offer important challenges for those involved in teacher education programs. The first challenge is realizing that individuals are at different places in their level of cultural awareness and understanding. For some, cultural sensitivity is simply an unnecessary waste of time, for others, it is vital to effective pedagogy. The process models reviewed provide a framework for understanding where teachers stand on intercultural issues including resistance and denial.

Second, teacher training programs should be sensitive to the stages individuals experience as they struggle with cultural issues. Teacher training programs cannot assume that after one class or one workshop teachers are going to leap into cultural sensitivity. Teachers entrenched in the early stages will need to move incrementally. In addition, individuals must come to understand their own culture before they can begin to understand someone else's. In one professor's class, students are required to give micro lessons on cultural artifacts. White students typically have the most difficulty with this assignment because they do not see themselves as cultural. After a discussion of core symbols and cultural orientation, they "discover" that their world is full of cultural artifacts and symbols. After the lesson, they learn of great connections between themselves and those presumed to be culturally different.

Finally, and perhaps the most difficult challenge, is that teacher education programs need to invite honest conversations about race, racism, privilege, marginalization, and oppression. Frequently these topics invoke hostility, anger, guilt, and confusion. Although difficult, these conversations are necessary if we are going to help teachers face the complexity of today's diverse classroom. A teacher's sentiment about race, culture, and ethnicity will be revealed in both subtle and explicit ways. Teachers' affective posture, the way they teach the "facts" of history, how they ask questions, how they discipline, who they call on and who they talk to outside of class say much about how they view culture and cultural issues. Once teachers acknowledge the role of culture in the instructional process, they are in a better position to meet the needs of all the students in their classrooms.

The goal, then, for all teachers is to strive for culturally responsive teaching. Our teacher, Ms. Young, should start her journey by increasing her knowledge and understanding of the cultural backgrounds of the students enrolled in her classes. But it is not enough to understand the cultures but to exhibit a genuine respect and interest in them. According to the research, students who feel respected and understood are more likely to connect with the teacher and classroom experiences. Ms. Young also needs to examine her own cultural presuppositions and attitudes. In understanding the way in which culture shapes her orientations, she will be in a better position to understand her students. Additionally, we believe that schools, and school districts should commit to culturally responsive teaching and provide support for all teachers. The end result will be a better learning situation for everyone.

Learning Activities

- Who am I?
  On a piece of paper write the numbers 1–20. For each item provide a description of yourself. These descriptions may be a social role (i.e. father, student) and psychological (i.e. emotional, humorous). After completing this task, form a group and share your lists with the other students.
- Dialectical diversity
  Maintain a journal of different dialects and language styles you observed in a 24-hour period. In your journal explain your impressions of these different language forms. Did you respond positively to some and negatively to others?
- How will you use a "cultural data base" to accomplish culturally response teaching?

Resources

- Teaching diverse learners
  www.alliance.brown.edu
- Culturally response teaching
  www.intime.uni.edu/multiculture/curriculum/culture/teaching.htm
- Geert Hofstede cultural dimensions
  www.geert-hofstede.com
- Multicultural activities
  www.edchange.org/multicultural/activityarch.html
- Teaching multicultural literature
  www.learner.org/workshops/tml/workshop1/commentary3.html

Chapter 4

Gender and Classroom Communication

Leticia and Danny, two sixth graders, have just returned from school and are greeted at the kitchen door by their dad, Antonio who asks, "How was school today?" "Good," says Danny as he opens the refrigerator door and forages through each shelf for something to eat. Leticia silently goes to her bedroom and takes out her calendar to check her homework. Antonio notices that Leticia seems bothered by something and follows her to the bedroom and asks her if everything is OK. She sits on her bed and says that everything is fine. Danny bounces down the hallway and asks his dad when soccer practice is. "Don't interrupt, I'm talking to your sister, " Antonio barks. Once more Antonio asks his daughter "Are you sure everything is OK, mi hija?" Danny hangs back in the hallway when Leticia opens up and says, "I don't get it, Mr. Hayes never calls on me in class. I work hard and know the answers, but every time I hold up my hand he ignores me and calls on Danny or one of the other guys in the class. Today he told me I was showing up the boys for doing so well in math. I don't think he likes me."

A substantial body of research has investigated male and female differences on a variety of instructional processes and outcomes (Condravy, Skirboll, & Taylor, 1998; Gurian & Stevens, 2005; Hall & Sandler, 1982; Murphy & Gipps, 1996; Nadler & Nadler, 1990; Pollack, 1998; Sadker & Sadker 1994; Wood, 2001). Some of this research suggests that educational practices have privileged males (e.g. American Association of University Women, 1991). Others argue that current approaches place males at risk for failure (Gurian & Stevens, 2005). The situation is complex and exacerbated by the fact that teachers are not adequately prepared to deal with gender issues and therefore use their personal theories to guide instructional practices. Schools of education typically dedicate only two hours of instruction per semester to gender issues (American Association of University Women, 1995). We agree with Wood (2001) who argued that teachers need to do all they can to understand the way in which gender dynamics influence student and teacher behavior. In this chapter, we will examine the ways that gender impacts the instructional process. Specifically we will examine the developmental and socio-cultural factors that impact attitudes and behavior, intellectual differences between males and females, and the ways that males and females are treated by teachers. We will conclude the chapter by exploring ways to create and sustain a more gender responsive classroom climate.

Sex and Gender

Teachers often use the terms sex and gender interchangeably. Sex, however is a biological designation and gender is a social psychological one. Boys are not made of frogs and snails and puppy dog tails but a XY chromosome pair and girls are not made of sugar and spice and everything nice but by a XX chromosome pair. Although there is a prevailing sentiment that "boys will be boys" and "girls will be girls," biology alone does not determine behavior. However, it is instructive to examine some of the biological factors that may influence the ways that females and males respond to academic tasks.

Gurian and Henley (2001) focused on recent developments in brain-based learning. They discussed five differences between male and female brains that influence learning. The first is structural. Females have a much larger corpus callosum, the bundle of nerves that connects the two lobes of the brain. This allows females to access both sides of the brain during certain tasks. For example, brain scans indicate that when females are listening, both sides of the brain are activated. This is not the case for males. Does this mean that females attend to academic instructions better than males? Or does it mean that they add information that may not be directly related to the task? Males, on the other hand, may only listen for the bottom line and not attend to nuances in the instructions. We do not believe that females listen better but it appears they listen differently from males.

The second area is chemical. Females secrete more serotonin vasopressin and oxytocin. These chemicals are related to impulsivity and the ability to experience empathy. The greater production in these chemicals may explain why females are less fidgety and more able to connect emotionally with others.

The third area is hormonal. Estrogen and progesterone are the dominant hormones in females and testosterone is the dominant hormone in males. The authors contend that hormonal differences play a significant role in the behavior of males and females. Males with high levels of testosterone tend to be aggressive while those with low levels tend to be sensitive and nurturing. Female hormones influence mood and responses to certain academic tasks.

The fourth area is functional. Gurian and Henley (2001) claimed that males are more inclined to use the right hemisphere while females use both. Males tend to access the left hemisphere which directs analysis and critical thinking. Females are more right hemisphere dominant. This part of the brain controls artistic activity, and intuitive thinking.

Emotional stimuli for males is channeled from limbic system to the brain stem whereas emotional stimuli for females is processed in the upper brain where higher order processing occurs. Thus females view relationships and interpersonal situations from a more complex perspective. Gurian and Henley (2001) also stated that the female brain has a greater capacity for memory and sensory intake and the male brain is predisposed to special tasks and abstract thinking.

The final area is emotional. According to Gurian and Henley (2001), the female brain processes more data through more senses. The authors speculated that because males may be more emotionally fragile because their brain is less able to process a wide variety of emotional stimuli. Consequently they may be more affected by problems at home or with other students.

What do these differences mean in terms of education and academic performance. Jensen (2000) provided a summary of some of the differences. For example, females generally outperform males in:

fine motor skills
computation tests
multi-tasking
recalling the position of objects
spelling
fluency of word generation
those that require being sensitive to external stimuli
remembering landmarks
use of verbal memory
appreciation of depth and perceptual speed
reading body language/facial expressions.

While males generally outperform females in:

targeting skills
working vocabulary
extended focus and concentration
mathematical reasoning and problem solving
navigation with geometric properties of space
verbal intelligence
habit formation and maintenance
most spatial tasks.

How might these predispositions play out in classroom activities? Females may have better penmanship, may be more proficient in art, such as coloring between lines, math worksheets, and reading comprehension, and remembering instructions, and perceiving if someone is frustrated or upset. Males, on the other hand, may be better at word problems, drill and rehearsal tasks, gross motor tasks such as throwing and running, and spatial tasks.

While biology is important, it is not the primary factor that explains the way males and females perform in academic settings. According to Wood (2001), it is the way we deal with differences that is most important to understand. The sentiments, expectations, attitudes, behaviors are connected to but not directed by biological sex or the way in which the brain is hardwired. However, there are deeply rooted cultural expectations about male and female behavior and schools are a place where these attitudes are reinforced. As a consequence, the interaction that occurs in schools can perpetuate and reinforce gender stereotypes to the detriment of the intellectual and emotional development of students. In the next section we will explore the way in which communication influences attitudes about males and females and the way they should act and perform in educational contexts.

Gender

Gender is a social and symbolic construction. Individuals are born male or female but are taught how to be masculine and feminine (Wood, 2001). Ivy and Backlund (2000) argued that the family is the most significant agent of gender socialization. Parents, siblings and relatives send explicit and implicit messages about what it means to be male and female in the larger culture. In the United States, for example, masculinity is frequently connected with strength, ambition, rationality and assertiveness. Femininity, on the other hand, is usually associated with physical attraction, emotionality, and cooperation. Little boys are encouraged to roughhouse, to be aggressive, and to explore their surroundings. Little girls are encouraged to be cheerful, gentle and cooperative. Research suggests that these expectations begin the day of birth and continue as they mature (e.g. Block, 1984; Stern & Karraker, 1989; Rubin, Provensano, & Luria, 1974).

The attitudes and expectations established in the family carry on into the school setting. Messages about gender are communicated in a number of ways. A "tomboy" will be criticized for acting too masculine and a boy who likes to play with dolls is teased and called a sissy. A teacher's attitude about gender will influence the way s/he manages a classroom and will affect his or her expectations about student ability. Finally, the curriculum, the texts students read, and the assignments they do may contain implicit and explicit themes about gender.

In the attempt to maximize the talents, ambitions, and interests of all students it is helpful to understand the way in which the "gendering process" unfolds in the schools. In the next section we will examine the forces that influence attitudes about appropriate male and female behavior.

Reflection

♦ **What does it mean to be male in our culture?**
♦ **What does it mean to be female in our culture?**

Females

Females struggle with a number of factors that influence classroom attitudes and performance. Females are bombarded with a multitude of contradictory messages about what it means to be female. These messages come from the media, family members, peers and the schools. Research from the American Association of University Women indicates that females aged 8–9 are comfortable and confident with their identities but their attitudes decline until they leave high school. The largest drop occurs between elementary and middle school (American Association of University Women, 1991). In middle school, many females begin to lose their interest in intellectual ideas and increase their interest in relationships and romance (Bate, 1992). At this stage one of the biggest factors influencing girls' self-esteem is how they look. According to Wood (2001), females who feel that they do not meet the cultural standard of attractiveness also believe they are less competent and capable in other areas.

Pipher (1994), the author of *Reviving Ophelia: Saving the Selves of Adolescent Girls,* wrote that young girls feel an enormous pressure to be beautiful and are keenly aware of the evaluations about their appearance. Young women perceive that their popularity is connected to physical beauty. The media is powerful in communicating the social significance of attraction. As a consequence, young girls spend a tremendous amount of time focusing on their looks. Pipher (1994) observed:

> Beauty is the defining characteristic for American women. It's the necessary and often sufficient condition for social success. It is important for women of all ages, but the pressure to be beautiful is most intense in early adolescence. Girls worry about their clothes, makeup, skin, and hair. But most of all they worry about their weight.
>
> (p. 18)

Because of the pressure to be thin and attractive, many females, especially European Americans, start to develop eating disorders in middle school.

Females predisposed to eating disorders embody popular culture's definition of femininity—they are thin, passive, attractive, and eager to please. While these students may be bright, their identities seem to be tied more in their looks than in their intellect. Schools, teachers, and peers may reinforce this cultural value. Teachers too often comment on how pretty a young girl is and not enough on the quality of her thinking (Sadker & Sadker, 1994).

The preoccupation with looks and the larger culture's ideal about women manifest themselves in peer group relations as well. Girls who wear the "wrong" clothes, who do too well in school, who are too large, who are too athletic, may be severely criticized by other girls. Because aggressive behavior is considered unacceptable for females, they learn to develop verbal competencies that serve to chastise, evaluate, and dissect others. Think about the conflicts that have occurred among adolescent girls. What were the topics and who were the targets of the conflict? Over time, these verbal abilities become more refined and sophisticated.

Martin (1989) observed that peer groups are more accepting of individuals who adhere to gender stereotypes. However, peers seem to be more accepting of females who engage in masculine behaviors than males who engage in feminine ones. Girls who play sports and roughhouse are perceived more positively than boys who want to play with dolls.

Peer groups also play an important role in the way values are tested. Young females use communication to test the boundaries of appropriate behavior. "Girl talk," for example plays a role in the construction of normative behavior. Discussions that focus on the behavior, dress, or activities of other girls help shape boundaries and expectations. Consider the following example of the way values are tested in peer communication exchanges. Three middle school females, Elizabeth, Natalie, and Julie are discussing Natalie's interest in Tony. The focus of Tony's affection is Monica, a girl outside of the clique described above. During their discussion, Elizabeth calls Monica a "skank," a label used to describe someone who is overly sexual and violates the normative expectation for dress and behavior. The girls conclude the session by noting that if Natalie must "stoop" to Monica's level, Tony isn't worth having as a boyfriend. This discussion reveals the group's values and expectations of behavior. Through this interaction the girls establish how far one should go to pursue a boy. Eder and Sanford (1986) stated that gossip, teasing, and humor are other ways to communicate unacceptable behavior without direct confrontation.

The larger society places substantial pressure on females to embrace certain values. They should be physically attractive, feminine, and passive, especially in public contexts. In addition, females are discouraged from maximizing their intellectual abilities.

Males

The school setting also influences the gender identity of males. Research indicates that boys account for the majority of behavior problems in schools and represent a large proportion of students in special education classes. Educational difficulties with boys start in elementary school and continue through high school. Expectations about appropriate male behavior are also shaped by the media, families, peers, and schools.

William Pollack (1998) author of *Real Boys: Rescuing Our Sons from the Myths of Boyhood*, addressed many of the factors that place boys at risk. At the core of boys' development is the "boy code," a masculine ethic directing feelings and emotions inward. Boys are encouraged to wear a "mask" that hides or obscures any difficulty or problem. Pollack concludes that boys are quick to state that everything is fine when it is not.

Young boys may be very expressive at birth, but by the time they reach elementary school begin to hide their feelings as their gender identity starts to take shape. Pollack (1998) identified two important processes that influence the gender identity of boys. The first is the use of shame. Little boys are made to feel ashamed of feelings, weakness, vulnerability, anxiety, or fear. The second is the separation processes. Boys are encouraged to separate from their primary caretakers before they are emotionally ready.

The use of shame to control boys is significant according to Pollack (1998). The pressure to "act" like a man comes from many directions. The media idealizes men who are strong, aloof, and detached. Peers refer to each other as "woman," "sissy," "faggot," "mama's boy," when emotions are not held in check. Parents communicate concern if a young boy does not act "masculine" enough. Teachers are not tolerant of boys who play "too much" with girls or have a communication style or interests that seem "feminine."

The second contributor discussed by Pollack (1998) is the premature separation from their primary caregiver. In most cases, this is the mother but it can be father, grandmother, aunt, or some other significant person. The 5-year-old who wails after being dropped off at kindergarten is often told to be "a big boy, stop crying." The boy who falls off a swing is not held and comforted but told to "be tough."

Some research suggests that the different emotional struggles that young boys face influence their orientations to learning situations. Hudson and Jacot (1991) suggested that boys must learn to compensate in some way if they are taken from a primary caretaker before they are emotionally ready. Because of their limited social skills, boys are often drawn to material objects not requiring the management of relationships. Interest in science, computers, and math may be related to these social processes.

Pollack (1998) argued that in elementary school teachers see little boys as the feeling vulnerable beings they are. As they grow older, the emotional core of the boy is lost in a body that appears masculine. Their vulnerability is hidden in faces with growing facial hair, voices that grow deeper, and bodies that sometimes tower over their teachers. In addition, teachers may not understand the "Boy Code," or be sensitive to the range of messages that inform a boy to be tough, aggressive, and strong. Teachers may in fact reinforce the very behaviors they are critical of in other contexts.

Sex and Learning Style

A number of studies have investigated the way in which males and females approach learning tasks. Head (1996) argued that males and females could be differentiated on four categories of cognitive style. The first, he discussed, is field independence and dependence. Field-independent learners approach the environment in an analytic fashion. Responses to assessments, such as the Group Embeddedness test, shows that males more than females are inclined to extract figures from the backgrounds in which they are embedded. Field-dependent learners consider the larger context and approach learning tasks from a more connected standpoint.

A second category discussed by Head (1996) is impulsiveness and reflection. Males have been found to be more impulsive while females exhibit care and deliberation. It is not uncommon, for example, for boys to race through multiple choice items or blurt out answers without carefully evaluating the questions. Head argued that the consequences for an incorrect response are not as high for boys. Think about student responses to questions in the classroom. The research indicates that males are called on in the class more than females. This pattern may unfold because males may leap into the interaction and capture the attention of the teacher. Females may think more about the question because they want to answer it correctly. This pattern of male dominance may create an implicit assumption that the voices of males should be heard and voices of females should be quiet. Wood (2001) argued that classrooms are masculine speech communities which reward students who compete and speak in absolute terms.

The third category discussed by Head (1996) is locus of control. Males tend to attribute academic success to their own efforts and failures to external factors. Females exhibit a different response. Success is attributed to luck and failures to internal factors.

When individuals feel that they have the skills necessary to complete a task, they will put in the effort to accomplish it. However, if an individual does not feel they can achieve a task, they do not expend the necessary effort. This pattern can lead to what Dweck (1986) labeled learned help-lessness. Teachers, then, need to develop teaching strategies that require females to take personal responsibility for success and thus build internal locus of control.

The final category discussed by Head (1996) is cooperation versus competition. Much educational philosophy is driven by a competitive sys-tem of external rewards. Competition is believed to motivate students to achieve. However, this system may work better for boys who are social-ized through athletics and other activities to be aggressive, assertive, and dominant. Females, on the other hand, may work better on tasks that require cooperation and the management of relationships. A competitive classroom may at the same time motivate and intimidate students. We will explore the benefits of cooperative learning in Chapter 9. The point we want to stress here is that several factors may influence the way a student moves toward or away from a learning goal.

Other researchers have examined differences between males and females. Belinky Clinchy, Goldberger, & Tarule (1986), for example, investigated the ways females come to know. The authors contended that traditional educational curriculum is predicated on a masculine way of knowing, where rationality and objectivity are valued over intuitive and personal knowledge. After interviewing 135 women, the authors identi-fied four ways of knowing: silence, received knowledge, subjective knowledge, and constructed knowledge. These orientations or styles depart from the rational orientation that appears to dominate educa-tional practice. From this research a coding system called Educational Dialectics was developed. The assessment consists of 12 bi-polar scales; one choice is masculine, the other is feminine.

Kolb (1976) provided a typology of learning that is based on two dimensions: active experimentation versus reflective observation and concrete experience versus abstract conceptualization. Four styles can be identified with the system. An accommodator is best at a hands on expe-rience. Divergers are best at learning requiring imagination, and brain-storming. Convergers are best when seeking practical solutions, and assimilators are most adept at logic and organization.

Philbin, Meier, Huffman, and Boverie (1995) examined sex differences on educational dialectics and learning style. The authors asked 45 females and 25 males to complete the Learning Style Inventory (Kolb, 1985) and the Educational Dialectics Instrument (Belinky et al., 1986). The results indicated that the preponderance of males used an assimila-tor learning style. In terms of educational dialectics, the majority of males were more concerned with self than others when it came to edu-cational decisions. The authors contend that the traditional learning environment, one that celebrates rationalism may not fit the learning style of females. Even though this study is exploratory, the findings and recommendations do resonate with authors like Gilligan (1982) who contended that education does not do enough to find a best fit between educational practice and learning style. The manner in which content is presented and the methods used to assess learning may favor the learning preferences of males.

While the studies examining the effects of sex on learning style have yielded some noteworthy findings, there is not overwhelming evidence that these results warrant the conclusion that often males are superior in some intellectual endeavors and females are superior in others. Much of the dialogue about the differences between males and females may be exaggerated and driven more by gender expectations than by fact. In the next section we will review research that has systematically analyzed the effect of sex on several important areas. We will begin by examining the findings on math, science, and verbal performance.

Sex and Intellectual Ability

There is a prevailing belief that males are good at math and females are good in language arts. Theorists such as Gurian and Stevens (2005) would argue that these differences are a function of brain structure. Scores on standardized tests tend to reflect this commonly held belief. The standardized tests used nationally are the ACT (the American College Testing Program), the PSAT (Preliminary Scholastic Assessment Test), and the SAT (Scholastic Assessment Test). Between 1990 and 1997, males outscored females on the verbal and math sections of the SAT. Females outscored males on the verbal section of the ACT but males scored higher than females on the mathematics and scientific reasoning sections of the ACT (American Association of University Women, 1999). With the inclusion of the writing portion of the PSAT, differences in gender showed a "dramatic" shift. The differences between boys and girls were narrowed considerably.

Recent data from the National Center for Education Statistics (U.S. Department of Education, 2008) indicated that the largest difference between males and females is in the areas of reading and writing. Females have closed the gap in mathematics performance. Tables 4.1, 4.2, and 4.3 report the test scores in these areas.

These data indicate that the greatest difference between males and females was in the area of verbal linguistic competence (reading and writing). Females consistently scored higher in these areas. The largest difference occurs in writing in the twelfth grade where females outscored males by 24 points. There were virtually no differences between males and females on mathematical competence. These results appear to support the assertion that females are more proficient in verbal abilities but they do not support the claim that males are superior in math.

Table 4.1 Average Mathematics Scores for Students in Grades 4, 8, and 12, 2005, 2007

Sex	Grade 4		Grade 8		Grade 12
	2005	2007	2005	2007	2005
Male	239	249	280	282	151
Female	237	239	278	280	149

Source: U.S. Department of Education (2008).

Table 4.2 Average Reading Scores for Students in Grades 4, 8, and 12, 2005, 2007

Sex	Grade 4		Grade 8		Grade 12
	2005	2007	2005	2007	2005
Male	216	218	257	258	279
Female	222	224	267	268	292

Source: U.S. Department of Education (2008).

Table 4.3 Average Writing Scores for Students in Grades 8 and 12, 2002, 2007

Sex	Grade 8		Grade 12	
	2002	2007	2002	2007
Male	143	146	136	144
Female	164	166	160	162

Source: U.S. Department of Education (2008).

We believe it is important to be cautious about drawing hard and fast conclusions about sex differences and academic ability. Hyde and McKinley (1997) reviewed meta-analytic studies conducted on gender differences on a variety of achievement tests. Meta-analysis is a procedure for aggregating results across a series of studies thus reducing the possibility of error that may result from a traditional review of literature. The aim of their investigation was to determine if some of the findings on gender abilities reported in the literature were supported by the meta-analytic procedures. Four areas were analyzed: verbal ability, mathematics performance, spatial ability, and science achievement.

In terms of verbal ability, the results of two meta-analysis studies (Hedges & Nowell 1995; Hyde & Linn, 1988) were examined. The results indicated that any general difference between males and females is extremely small. The authors argued, however, that there are different types of verbal ability that may be lost in traditional testing. Females, for example, may be superior in speech production and males may have more difficulties with verbal performance.

The results of the meta-analyses conducted on mathematical ability did not indicate male superiority. Males obtained higher scores but the amount of this difference was minimal. Similar to verbal ability, there are different types of mathematical competency that are not frequently discussed in the literature. Mathematical ability entails computation, concepts, or problem solving. Each of these subsets may be lost when scores are summarized. A meta-analysis conducted by Hyde et al. (1990) found that females scored higher than males on computation tasks by a small amount in elementary school and junior high but not in high school. There were no differences at any age in understanding mathematical concepts. And there were no differences in problem solving in elementary or junior high. Males did obtain higher scores in problem solving in high school and in college.

The third area reviewed by Hyde and McKinley (1997) was spatial ability. They reviewed a meta-analysis conducted by Linn and Petersen (1985). Three types of spatial ability were analyzed: spatial perception, (the person's sense of horizontality or verticality), mental rotation, (how well one can mentally rotate a three-dimensional object that is depicted in two dimensions and match it to other illustrations), and spatial visualization (visually locating a simple figure within a complex one). The results of the analysis conducted in spatial ability yielded no clear-cut gender differences.

Finally, Hyde and McKinley (1997) analyzed science achievement. Three meta-analytic studies were reviewed (Becker, 1989; Fleming & Malone, 1983; Hedges & Nowell, 1995). Fleming and Malone (1983) analyzed the science performance of kindergarten to twelfth grade students. Boys scored higher than girls but the differences were small. The largest gender difference was found in the middle-school age group. An analysis conducted by Becker (1989) found that the largest gender difference was related to the subject matter tested. Boys received significantly higher scores in physics. Hedges and Nowell (1995) investigated high school achievement and found that males outscored females in science. Hedges and Nowell (1995) noted that fewer females elect to take science in high school and therefore the findings are subject to bias.

The results of the science performance meta-analyses indicated that males outscored females by a relatively small amount. Further, the findings seem to relate to the particular subject matter examined. Males did best in physics and physical science.

The research reported above does not provide compelling evidence for sex differences in intellectual capacity. This is not to say that there are no cognitive differences between males and females but it is difficult to ascertain what these differences are and what they mean in actual practice. Numerous methodological problems cloud the research on sex and gender. One problem is that the research tends to focus on biological sex and not on the social-psychological features of gender. This approach makes it difficult to ascertain if any difference found is related to sex, gender, or some other intervening variable. One study that tried to account for the effects of gender was conducted by Kirtley and Weaver (1999). These authors argued that gender conceptions serve as filters that modify cognitions and behaviors. They identified two cognitive schemes. The agentic role construct includes characteristics such as goal-orientation, assertiveness, and self-activation. In contrast, a communal orientation involves characteristics such as selflessness, openness, caring, and kindness. In the classroom an individual with an agentic role identity may positively respond to tasks requiring analytical thinking while an individual with a communal identity may prefer verbal learning tasks.

Reflection

◆ **What role does gender play in learning?**
◆ **Do you believe that males are naturally inclined to be better than females in math and science?**

Interaction Patterns

A rather substantial body of literature indicates that males and females are not treated the same in the classroom (Diller, Houston, Morgan, & Ayim, 1996; Sadker & Sadker, 1994). Diller et al. (1991) summarized the findings by stating:

> Studies on teacher–student interactions indicate that within the coeducational classrooms, teachers, regardless of sex, interact more with boys, give boys more attention (both positive and negative) and that this pattern intensifies at the secondary and college levels. Girls get less attention and wait longer for it. When they do get attention, it is more likely that the teacher will respond to them neutrally or negatively (although this depends some on the girls' race and class). The reinforcement girls do get is likely to be for passivity and neatness, not for getting the right answer.
>
> (p. 52)

Sadker and Sadker (1994) have conducted a great deal of research on gender differences and emphasize the following points:

- Teachers typically initiate more communication with boys than with girls in the classroom, strengthening boy's sense of importance.
- Teachers tend to ask boys more complex, abstract, and open-ended questions, providing better opportunities for active learning.
- In class projects and assignments, teachers are more likely to give detailed instructions to boys, and more likely to take over and finish the task for girls depriving them of active learning.
- Teachers tend to praise boys more often than girls for intellectual content and quality of their work. They praise girls more often for neatness, and form.
- When boys perform poorly, teachers often blame failure on lack of effort. When girls perform poorly, it is for reasons other than effort.
- All too often teachers discourage girls from courses of study that lead to high-skilled, high-paying careers.

Sadker and Sadker (1994) further noted that when student culture is included in the analysis of interaction patterns, another trend emerges. White males received the most attention, followed by minority males, white females and minority females. The group of students most impacted by the lack of teacher attention may be minority females. The American Association of University Women reported that African-American girls, while entering school with high self-esteem, grow increasingly negative about school and their teachers. Hispanic girls show the most negative shifts. Between elementary school and high school the self-esteem of Hispanic girls drops more than any other ethnic group studied (American Association of University Women, 1991).

Sadker and Sadker (1994) identified four types of responses from teachers: praise, ("good job"), remedies ("check your addition"), criticism ("this is not correct"), and accepts ("okay"). Teachers praise only 10% of the time and criticize 5% of the time. The most frequent form of feedback provided by teachers is a verbal or nonverbal "Okay." Boys receive the most praise. Praise is an important educational resource and one that seems to benefit boys the most because it is typically tied to intellectual endeavors.

When females receive praise, it is frequently for the way they look. Teachers complement hair styles, dresses, smiles. These comments do not come during lectures but in small group discussions and between class exchanges. Sometimes, students pull the teacher into this "gendering exchange." Think about how you would respond to the following: "Teacher what do you think of the dress my dad brought me from his trip to Albuquerque?" The culturally reflective teacher would consider ways to offer a complement but also to make an intellectual comment as well.

Research also indicates that teachers give males more time to answer questions. Most teachers wait about one second for a student to answer but teachers wait less time for females. Further, boys are more likely to display non-verbal cues that they want to answer a question. Hands leap in the air and some boys may blurt out an answer before being called on. Sadker and Sadker (1994) call these "green arm" students. Their arms are in the air so long the blood seems to drop from their arms. Females may be more passive and hesitant in the way they signal an answer. Also, knowing the correct answer may be more important to the females so they may be more tentative in their responses.

Houston (1996) summarized the problem:

> If teachers fail to notice the gender of the student who is talking, if they pay no attention to who is interrupting whom, whose points are acknowledged and taken up, who is determining the topic of discussion, then they will by default perpetuate patterns that discourage women's participation in the educational process.
>
> (p. 54)

Nonverbal Behavior

The nonverbal orientations of the student and the teacher play an important role in the way in which communication is managed in the classroom. Research suggests that males and females developed different orientations to nonverbal behavior. Wood (2001) noted that nonverbal codes are significant in managing identities and interpersonal relationships. She drew from the work of Mehrabian (1981) and identified three features of nonverbal communication that are used differently by females and males. These features are: responsiveness, liking, and power. Understanding these features of communication helps teachers manage the communication exchanges in the classroom.

Responsiveness is concerned with how expressive individuals are in interaction. Both females and males are responsive but communicate it in different ways. Generally, males are more expansive in their gestures. Wood contended that males are socialized to command attention. Think about the number of times young boys are told to look at someone in the eye and speak up when asked a question. Females, on the other hand, learn to use nonverbal behavior to manage interpersonal connection. Females learn to read subtle cues such as eye contact, and males learn strategies for getting and holding the attention.

A second important dimension of nonverbal behavior is liking. Some theorists suggest that females are encouraged to put more stock into this feature of their communication and as a consequence develop more skills in communicating liking than males (LaFrance & Mayo, 1979; Wood, 2001). Females tend to sit closer than males and engage in more eye contact and use affiliative touch more than males. It is not uncommon for middle school females to hug and walk with interlocked arms. Some research suggests that females are much more concerned with how the teacher feels about them.

The final dimension discussed by Wood is power or control. Control is concerned with who decides topics, who interrupts whom, who has the most space, who initiates touch. Males tend to engage in more nonverbal behaviors of control than females. Young males wrestle slap, poke and push to gain control and authority. Males tend to interrupt females more, command more space in interaction. Look around the classroom and compare how males and females sit.

Minimizing Differences

What can teachers do to create environments that are safe and provide opportunities for males and females to be academically successful? We will close this chapter by discussing some ways that teachers can create learning environments that affirm all students. We will begin by examining language processes. In Chapter 1, we contended that individuals act upon the meanings they construct. Language has a substantial effect on classroom exchanges. Some of the effects are subtle but others are most substantial and significant.

Sexist language can be defined as "words, phrases, and expressions that unnecessarily differentiate between females and males or exclude, trivialize, or diminish either gender" (Parks & Roberton, 1998, p. 455). Many teachers unfortunately see little need or value to be aware of the way in which language creates images and shapes expectations.

It has been consistently documented, for example, that male generic language excludes women (Wood, 2001). Words like chairmen, mailmen are not inclusive. What are teachers implying when they say that a young female student is a "hottie." or a young male is a "stud." It is not enough for teachers to change the pronouns they use to recognize that language shapes deeper expectations about gender. Wood (2001) observed that language could be used to devalue and trivialize females. Richmond and Dyba (1982) identified four effects of sexist language: (1) the use of sexist language promotes sexual stereotyping and the adoption of sex-typed attitudes and behaviors; (2) teachers serve as important models for language learning of children; (3) when teachers employ sexist language, their behavior is likely to promote sexism and sexist behavior in their students; and (4) when the use of sexist language on the part of the teachers can be reduced, an attendant reduction in sexism and sexist behavior in their students can be expected.

Richmond and Dyba (1982) tested the effects of modeling on a group of elementary and secondary teachers. They found that teachers frequently engaged in sexist language by using the generic "he" or masculine pronouns. However, after intervention, teachers learned to reduce the use of these language forms. Similar positive effects on teacher modeling were obtained by Cronin and Jreisat (1995). The authors studied the effects of modeling nonsexist written language and found that students could learn to incorporate nonsexist language into written messages. The research does suggest that teachers can have a positive effect on students' use of sexist language

In addition to modeling non-sexist language, teachers need to select curriculum that stresses accomplishments of women and men and notes their achievements in other ways. In Chapter 3 we discussed the way the social curriculum influences expectations based on ethnicity. In terms of gender, teachers need to utilize curriculum that provides a balanced viewpoint on the contributions of males and females. Further, teachers need to shed the cultural expectation that males are mathematically and logically inclined and that females are verbal and emotional. A safe environment would provide opportunities based more on gender identity than on biological sex. Teachers need to be aware of larger culture's expectations about intelligence, academic success, physical attraction, beauty, health, masculinity, and femininity. In other words, females who are logical and interested in science should receive as much encouragement as males interested in these areas. Similarly, males who are interested in literature should receive the same support as females interested in these areas.

Teachers need to be sensitive to learning style and try to create activities and assessments that are matched with students' abilities. It may be unreasonable to expect a teacher to abandon multiple choice tests, which seem to favor males, but they can limit how much weight such assessments have in the allocations of grades. Research suggests that there are a number of other instructional strategies that can benefit boys and girls. Cooperative learning and active learning strategies, for example, have been found to be helpful for a wide range of learning styles. Our discussion on multiple intelligences will provide more guidance on these issues.

The powerful effect of peer groups should also be recognized. Research by Ryan (2001) indicated that peer groups have a dramatic affect on male attitudes toward school. Peers who enjoy school create social groups with peers who enjoy school. Similarly, peers who dislike school tend to select friends who also dislike school. Ryan (2001) also found that the students who "hung out" with friends who disliked school grew more negative about school over time. This research suggests that peer groups influence attitudes about school and academic achievement. Some peer groups create norms and expectations for success while others create expectations for failure. Additional research suggests that peer groups influence attitudes about gender identity and norms for appropriate behavior (Eder & Sanford, 1986). While it may be difficult for teachers to influence peer group selection, they can influence the way that students group in the classroom. Encouraging connections among a wide range of students with a wide range of abilities may prove helpful. Through these connections, students, especially those who do not like school, may discover new areas of interest. Facilitating new relationships may garner positive academic rewards.

Teachers should help young women filter the multitude of confusing messages they receive about physical beauty, popularity, health, femininity, and intelligence. Helping females understand and embrace the significance of intellect and good health will empower them in important ways. Females need to understand that the world of math and science is not the sole territory of males. Teachers play an important role in the way in which gender messages are processed.

Teachers ought to address the needs of boys as well. Pollack (1998) suggested that schools fail boys in four ways: (1) they do not recognize the problems boys face in certain academic areas such as reading, and writing; (2) schools and teachers tend to be poorly versed in the special social and emotional needs of boys and mishandle their difficulties; (3) a good number of schools are not environmentally friendly or warm for boys; and (4) schools do not have curricula and teaching methods designed to meet boys' needs and interests.

One important step that teachers can take is to recognize the forces that contribute to the "boy code." In early elementary school, teachers may have difficulty recognizing little boys as vulnerable and feeling. But as Pollack (1998) noted, when they grow older and become adolescents, we start to see them in a different way. Yet underneath their façade of strength is swirling pool of emotions and feelings. One moment boys may be aloof and the next fighting back tears from a poignant movie. Teachers do much to reinforce the gender stereotypes and view boys as the "bad guys," who should be controlled in order to accomplish learning goals.

Summary

This chapter has examined the various ways that sex and gender intersect in classroom communication. Even though gender expectations run very deep, classrooms can be a place where new insights and expectations are shaped and formed. Teachers who understand gender issues can do much to manage curriculum and communicate in ways that build on or extend the talents of all students. We encourage future teachers to incorporate our recommendations for minimizing differences into their instructional repertoires.

Learning Activities

- Identify the various ways gender is communicated through popular culture, such as film, music videos, clothing, and television.
- Divide the class into two groups, males and females. As females to answer the following question: What do males need to know to communicate effectively with females? Ask males the following question: What will females say that males need to understand to communicate effectively with females? Identify the similarity and difference among the responses.
- What types of strategies can teachers use to increase male interest in reading and writing?
- How can teachers ensure that their class is safe for gay and transgendered students?
- How do beliefs about femininity and masculinity vary by culture?

Resources

- Male and female brains
  http://faculty.washington.edu/chudler/heshe.html
- Neuroscience for kids
  http://faculty.washington.edu/chudler/experi.html
- Brain activities
  http://www.funbrain.com/

Chapter 5

Students with Special Needs

The following story, "Welcome to Holland," appeared in *The Fresno Bee* newspaper in October, 2002.

I am often asked to describe the experience of raising a child with a disability—to try to help people who have not shared that unique experience to understand it, to imagine how it would feel. It's like this ...

"When you're going to have a baby, it's like planning a fabulous vacation trip—to Italy. You buy a bunch of guidebooks and make wonderful plans. The Coliseum, The Michaelangelo David. The gondolas in Venice. You may learn some handy phrases in Italian. It's all very exciting."

"After months of eager anticipation, the day finally arrives. You pack your bags and off you go. Several hours later, the plane lands. The stewardess comes in and says, 'Welcome to Holland.'"

"Holland?" you say, "What do you mean, Holland? I signed up for Italy! I'm supposed to be in Italy. All my life I've dreamed of going to Italy!"

"But there's been a change in the flight plan. They've landed in Holland and there you must stay.

"The important thing is that they haven't taken you to a horrible, disgusting, filthy place, full of pestilence, famine and disease. It's just a different place.

"So you must go out and buy new guidebooks. And you must learn a whole new language. And you will meet a whole new group of people you would never have met.

"It's just a different place. It's slower paced than Italy, less flashy than Italy, But after you've been there for a while and you catch your breath, you look around, and you begin to notice that Holland has windmills; Holland has tulips; Holland even has Rembrandts.

"But everyone you know is busy coming and going from Italy, and they're all bragging about what a wonderful time they had there. And for the rest of your life, you will say, 'Yes, that's where I was supposed to go. That's what I had planned.'

"And the pain of that will never, ever, ever go away, because the loss of that dream is a very significant loss.

"But if you spend your life mourning the fact that you didn't get to Italy, you may never be free to enjoy the very special, the very lovely things about Holland."

(EMILY PERL KINGSLEY)

This story from a parent of a child with a disability reminds us of the experience of new teachers as they plan for the perfect group of students: school-ready, enthusiastic, motivated. But no situation is perfect. Early on many teachers become disenchanted as they learn that they will be responsible for teaching students from differing cultural backgrounds, representing different spoken languages and, with varied learning abilities.

Students with disabilities often present physical, social, and academic challenges to classroom teachers. The inclusion of students with special needs into general education classrooms has increased in recent years. According to the 22nd Annual Report to Congress on the Implementation of the Individuals with Disabilities Education Act (IDEA), 75% of the more than 5.5 million 6- through 21-year-olds with disabilities served under IDEA were educated in regular classrooms, with their nondisabled peers. General education teachers can expect to have several students with mild disabilities included in each of their classes. Students with moderate to severe disabilities are included less frequently.

In the first chapters of the book we discussed different types of diversity: ethnic, cultural, linguistic, sexual, and gender, as they relate to classroom communication. Students with disabilities present another type of diversity challenge for classroom teachers. The term disability, exceptionality, handicap, and special needs are often used interchangeably to refer to the categories of disabilities specified by the federal law. Students with special needs have skill diversity significant enough to require a specialized program of instruction in order to achieve educational equity. Most students with special needs are educated in the general education classroom. We will discuss the benefits of inclusion. Pertinent legislation and eligibility criteria that qualify students for special services will be discussed. We will define the low-incidence disability categories, those less commonly served in public and private school settings. Next, high-incidence disabilities, those most often served in public and private school settings, will be defined and practices that promote positive social interactions in inclusive education settings will be highlighted. The importance of collaboration in the delivery of services to students with disabilities will be discussed and finally, strategies for working effectively with parents and families will be recommended.

The Spirit of Inclusion

Today, most students with special needs receive the majority of their education in general education classes, with special services provided as needed either in the classroom or in a learning lab. This has not always been the case. In the early days of education in the United States, students with special needs were placed in general education classes but without the assistance of trained specialists. Students with severe disabilities were often excluded from school. As special education grew, students with severe disabilities were sent to special schools and students with milder disabilities, who presented a difficult challenge to general education teachers, were removed and placed in separate special classes. Concerns regarding issues such as segregation, labeling, and high incidence of minority students identified as disabled, led parents and educators to question current practices. The pendulum swung from segregation of special students in separate schools and separate classes toward inclusion into the mainstream of education. Inclusion is the term most often used today to refer to the placement of students with special needs in general education. Today, students with disabilities are served in general education classrooms with the assistance of specialists including special education teachers, speech and language pathologists, and other service providers deemed necessary for students to succeed in school.

One of the most important goals of inclusion is to help students with special needs succeed academically and socially. Most students who are eligible for services have identified academic goals they are working toward. Socially, a goal for these students is to learn to perform competently in interactions with others, to invoke social support, and to develop long-lasting friendships with others.

Gresham (1981b) identified peer acceptance, positive judgments by significant others, improved classroom behavior, high self-esteem, play skill acquisition, and academic achievement as positive effects of social competence. Social skills are the specific abilities required to work and socialize with other people. Students with special needs often exhibit deficits in social skills (Hallahan & Kauffman, 1994; Kavale & Forness, 1996; Walker & Leister, 1994). They experience lower self-perceptions, and are often less accepted and more often rejected by their non-disabled peers.

The good news is that studies have shown that students with disabilities can benefit both academically (Helmstetter, Curry, Brennan, & Sampson-Saul, 1998; Malian & Love, 1998; Shinn & Powell-Smith, 1997) and socially (Kennedy & Itkonen, 1994; Kennedy, Shukla, & Fryxell, 1997) from being educated alongside their nondisabled peers. Benefits include more opportunities for social interaction; improved communication and social skills; friendships; appropriate models of behavior; and perceived higher standards of performance from teachers. Researchers have found that students without disabilities can also benefit from association with their peers with special needs. They benefit as role models for students with disabilities, thereby improving their social competence and decreasing feelings of loneliness and rejection in inclusive classrooms (Pavri & Monda-Amaya, 2000). Students without disabilities also benefit by learning about tolerance, individual difference, and human exceptionality. They learn that students with disabilities have many positive characteristics and abilities.

Academic achievement and improved social competence are most likely to be achieved when instruction is individualized and when support is provided to teachers as well (Madden & Slavin, 1983; Schulte, Osborne, & McKinney, 1990). Teachers play a critical role in developing a climate of acceptance through curriculum design, instructional strategies, and activities that encourage positive social interactions among students with special needs and their non-disabled peers.

Reflection

♦ **What experience have you had working with students with disabilities?**
♦ **Do you think students with disabilities should be included into general education classrooms? Explain your answer.**

Pertinent Legislation for Students with Disabilities

Teachers working with students who have disabilities should understand three major laws—the Individuals with Disabilities Education Act (IDEA), Section 504 of the Rehabilitation Act of 1973, and the Americans with Disabilities Act (ADA). IDEA is a federal law that governs all special education services in the United States. Funding is provided to state and local education agencies to guarantee special education and related services to students who meet the eligibility criteria within the categories of disabilities. Each category has specific criteria defining the disabling condition. In each category, the disabling condition must adversely affect the student's educational performance. IDEA ensures that all children, from 3 through 21 years of age, regardless of type or severity of disability, are entitled to a free, appropriate, public education. An individualized education plan (IEP) is developed for every child served under IDEA.

In contrast, Section 504 of the Rehabilitation Act of 1973 is a civil rights law. It prohibits discrimination against a person with disabilities. The statute states, in part, that:

> No otherwise qualified handicapped individual in the United States ... shall, solely by reason of his [her] handicap, be excluded from the participation in, be denied benefits of, or be subjected to discrimination in any program or activity receiving federal financial assistance.

This means that individuals eligible for accommodations under this law must demonstrate the existence of an identified physical or mental condition (e.g. asthma, attention deficit disorder) that substantially limits a major life activity (e.g. walking, seeing, hearing breathing, caring for oneself). Section 504 does not require that the student needs special education to qualify. The school district determines eligibility. Both IDEA and Section 504 require that school district personnel develop a plan for eligible students, which includes specialized instruction, related services, and accommodations within the general education classroom.

The Americans with Disabilities Act was signed into law in 1990 and provided that individuals with disabilities not be discriminated against and that such individuals be provided with "reasonable accommodations" in the workplace. This law is an important extension of IDEA in that it provided protections for individuals with disabilities enrolled in colleges and universities, meaning that they are also entitled to appropriate accommodations in the classroom. ADA extends services beyond the high school years. High school teachers are often involved in transition planning for youth with disabilities.

Eligibility for Services

Under IDEA, students who exhibit academic and/or social and behavior problems that negatively affect their education performance may qualify for services under one of the following disability categories: learning disabilities, mental retardation, emotional disturbance, speech or language impairments, autism, hearing impairments, visual impairments, traumatic brain injury, orthopedic impairments, other health impairments, or multiple disabilities. Infants and toddlers with disabilities birth through age 2 and their families receive early intervention services. These children may need early intervention services because they are delayed in one or more of the following areas: cognitive development; physical development; vision and hearing; communication development; social or emotional development; adaptive development; or have a diagnosed physical or mental condition that has a high probability of resulting in developmental delay. School-aged children and youth, aged 3 through 21, receive services through the school system. These children may experience delays in one or more of the following areas: physical development, cognitive development, social or emotional development, or adaptive development. Each child seeking services under IDEA must receive a full evaluation including academic and psychological testing.

Children with attention deficit/hyperactivity disorder can be served under the federal law if they meet eligibility criteria for a learning disability, emotional disturbance, or other health impairments. Students who are gifted and talented are not served under the federal special education law for students with disabilities unless they qualify as learning disabled, emotionally disturbed, or communication disordered. Most states provide for initial screening and adapted instructional programs for gifted students. Special education eligibility provides students with disabilities opportunities for specialized instruction designed to more appropriately meet their needs in general education and/or special education classrooms.

Low-Incidence Disabilities

Low-incidence disabilities include autism, visual impairments, hearing impairments, physical and other health impairments, traumatic brain injury, and severe and multiple disabilities. Lower-incidence disabilities are often present at birth or can be acquired later in life.

IDEA defines *autism* as a developmental disability significantly affecting verbal and nonverbal communication and social interaction, generally evident before age 3, that "adversely affects educational performance." Characteristics associated with autism are engaging in repetitive activities and stereotyped movements, resistance to changes in daily routines or the environment, and unusual responses to sensory experiences. The term autism does not apply if the child's educational performance is adversely affected primarily because the child has emotional disturbance (U.S. Department of Education, 2000).

Related to autism is autism spectrum disorder, which may be diagnosed after the age of 3, and implies a qualitative impairment of social interaction and communication (Hallahan & Kauffman, 2003). Included are several disorders: Asperger Syndrome, Rett's disorder, childhood disintegrative disorder, and pervasive developmental disorder. Children who have Rett's disorder, for example, develop normally for five months to four years followed by regression and mental retardation.

Peterson and Hittie (2003) have identified two programs that have been successfully implemented with students who have autism. Each program is built on a very different philosophy. One program is referred to as TEACCH: Treatment and Education of Autistic and Related Communication-Handicapped Children. Teachers organize the school environment by visual materials to create schedules that students can follow to learn new skills. Initially, the teacher prompts students but the goal is that students will learn to move through their daily tasks independently. The visual schedule is based on student's skills, interests, and needs. A program called PECS, Picture Exchange System, provides students with a concrete way to communicate their needs. Two computer programs, Boardmaker and Writing with Symbols 2000, can be used to share information.

Visual impairment means impairment in vision that, even with correction, adversely affects a child's education performance. The term includes both partial sight and blindness. An educational definition of *blindness* suggests that a student must use Braille or aural methods in order to receive instruction (Heward, 2000). Visual impairment accounts for less that 0.5% of the total special education population (U.S. Department of Education, 2000).

Deaf-Blindness means concomitant [simultaneous] hearing and visual impairments, the combination of which causes such severe communication and other developmental and educational needs that they cannot be accommodated in special education programs solely for children with deafness or children with blindness (U.S. Department of Education, 2000).

Under IDEA, *hearing impairment* is defined as a loss, whether permanent or fluctuating, that adversely affects a child's educational performance but is not included under the definition of "deafness." *Deafness* refers to a hearing impairment so severe that a child has difficulty processing linguistic information through hearing, with or without amplification that adversely affects a child's educational performance. Hard of hearing describes individuals who have hearing loss, but are able to use the auditory channel as their primary mode for perceiving and monitoring speech or acquiring language (Diefendorf, 1996).

Turnbull, Turnbull, Shank, Smith, and Leal (2002) recommended the following strategies for inclusion of students with disabilities in general education classrooms:

1   Utilize activities that allow students to experience concepts such as role play, experiments, and field trips.
2   Make use of collaborative learning and peer tutoring to provide students who are deaf or hard of hearing with opportunities to be equal participants with peers during learning activities.

3   Present information visually or in sign language. Use illustrations, semantic maps, graphic organizers, flowcharts, and computer technology.

4   If the students use an assistive listening device, use the microphone at all times. Pass the microphone to other students who are talking.

5   Always speak with the light on your face, not behind you.

6   Speak slowly and distinctly; but do not exaggerate your mouth movements or speak more loudly. Keep your hands away from your face while talking.

7   If the child uses a sign language interpreter, provide enough time between asking a question and calling on a student so that the interpreter has enough time to interpret the question. Most students who are deaf in general education classrooms will have sign language interpreters and note takers.

IDEA refers to *physical disabilities as orthopedic impairments*:

The term includes impairments caused by congenital anomaly (e.g., clubfoot, absence of some member, etc.), impairments caused by disease (e.g., poliomyelitis, bone tuberculosis, etc.), and impairments from other causes (e.g., cerebral palsy, amputations, and fractures or burns that cause contractures).

(C.F.R. Sec. 300.7 (b)(7)

Curricular goals for students with physical disabilities vary depending on the specific disability. Teachers will need to work with other service providers (e.g. nurses, occupational and physical therapists) and families to help students improve mobility, increase communication, learn daily living skills, and learn self-determination skills. Special education teachers and students' parents are an important resource for general education teachers. They are familiar with adaptive equipment to improve mobilization, technology to improve communication, medical technology assistance (e.g. tracheotomy, colostomy) utilized to replace or augment vital body functions.

Other health impairments, often referred to by educators as physical disabilities, is another category of disabilities covered by IDEA. Individuals with *other health impairments* have limited strength, vitality, or alertness, including a heightened alertness with respect to the educational environment, that are due to chronic or acute health problems such as asthma, attention deficit disorder or attention deficit hyperactivity disorder, diabetes, epilepsy, a heart condition, hemophilia, lead poisoning, leukemia, nephritis, rheumatic fever, and sickle cell anemia; and adversely affects a child's educational performance.

Students with human immunodeficiency virus (HIV) and students with acquired immune deficiency syndrome (AIDS) are served under this disability category. Students who have cancer, diabetes, or epilepsy are also served under the *other health impairment* category.

The educational needs of students with health impairments are similar for those students without disabilities. However, the teacher should be willing to make allowances for absences. Keeping in close contact with family members and medical personnel is necessary when working with students with health impairments. Other students in the class may need to be educated as to specific health issues. Peers may be helpful in assisting with a student's care or with classroom and homework assignments.

Under IDEA, *Traumatic Brain Injury* means

> an acquired injury to the brain caused by an external physical force, resulting in total or partial functional disability or psychosocial impairment, or both, that adversely affects a child's educational performance. The term applies to open or closed head injuries resulting in impairments in one or more areas, such as cognition; language; memory; attention; reasoning; abstract thinking; judgment; problem solving; sensory, perceptual, and motor abilities; psychosocial behavior; physical functions; information processing; and speech. The term does not include brain injuries that are congenital or degenerative, or brain injuries induced by birth trauma.
>
> (34 C.F.R., Sec. 300.7[6] [12])

Children with mild to severe traumatic brain injury often have poor coping and social skills. Traumatic brain injury thrusts them into a situation dramatically different from the one they previously knew. Relationships are often strained as these individuals respond with anger, anxiety, fatigue, and depression (Tyler & Mira, 1999). Tyler and Mira suggested that teachers should obtain as much knowledge as they can about the injury and long-term outcomes. Behavior and instructional expectations should be clearly stated. Do not assume that the student knows what is expected. Learning to foresee what triggers problem behavior will help both teacher and student to respond appropriately.

IDEA defines *Multiple Disabilities* as follows:

> *Multiple Disabilities* means concomitant impairments (such as mental retardation—blindness, mental retardation—orthopedic impairment, etc.), the combination of which causes such severe educational problems that they cannot be accommodated in special education programs solely for one of the impairments. The term does not include deaf-blindness.
>
> (34 C.F.R., Sec 300: (b) (6))

Severe Disabilities is defined as follows:

> The term "children with severe disabilities" refers to children with disabilities who, because of the intensity of their physical, mental, or emotional problems, need highly specialized education, social, psychological, and medical services in order to maximize their full potential for useful and meaningful participation in society and for self-fulfillment ... Children with severe disabilities may experience severe speech, language, and/or perceptual-cognitive deprivations, and evidence abnormal behaviors, such as failure to respond to pronounced social stimuli, self-multilation, self-stimulation, manifestation of intense and prolonged temper tantrums, and the absence of rudimentary forms of verbal control, and may also have intensely fragile physiological conditions.
>
> (34 C.F. R. Sec. 315.4(d))

Students who have multiple or severe disabilities are likely to receive service in a variety of settings including a special education classroom within a regular school, separate schools, residential facility or at home or in the hospital. Curricular goals for these students include teaching skills that will help them to be successful at school, home, and in the community.

Reflection

♦ **Emily is a seventh-grade student, with a mild hearing impairment, in your physical education class. Today you will be requiring students to work in teams for basketball practice. What accommodations might be needed to include Emily in this activity?**

♦ **What types of information would a general education teacher need to obtain to adequately serve students with other health impairments such as diabetes or epilepsy in the classroom?**

High-Incidence Disabilities

The disabilities most commonly seen in schools are high-incidence disabilities. High incidence disabilities include learning disabilities, emotional or behavioral disorders, mild or moderate mental retardation, and speech and language disorders. Under the Individual with Disabilities Education Act, these disability areas make up about 90% of the total population of students' ages 6–21 served. General education teachers will likely serve students with high-incidence disabilities in their classrooms.

Learning Disabilities

The National Joint Committee on Learning Disabilities (NJCLD) defines learning disabilities:

> Learning disabilities is a general term that refers to a heterogeneous group of disorders manifested by significant difficulties in the acquisition and use of listening, speaking, reading, writing, reasoning, or mathematical abilities. These disorders are intrinsic to the individual, presumed to be due to central nervous system dysfunction, and may occur across the lifespan. Problems in self-regulatory behaviors, social perception, and social interaction may exist with learning disabilities but do not by themselves constitute a learning disability. Although learning disabilities may occur concomitantly with other handicapped conditions (for example, sensory impairment, mental retardation, and serious emotional disturbance) or with extrinsic influences (such as cultural differences, insufficient or inappropriate instruction), they are not the result of those conditions or influences.
>
> (NJCLD, 1994)

Students with learning disabilities constitute the largest percentage of students, about 50%, served in special education. Clearly, the predominant problem for students with learning disabilities is academic. These students achieve at a level far below what is expected given their intellectual abilities. Learning problems may occur in the area(s) of reading, written language, mathematics, memory, and metacognition. They often avoid asking questions and participating in class activities. Teachers can best serve these students by varying instruction (e.g. lecture, small group, discussion, video); academic activities (e.g. journaling, storytelling, activity centers, cooperative groups, role-play), and evaluation (e.g. presentation, project, portfolio). Refer to Thomas Armstrong's book, *Multiple Intelligences in the Classroom* (2000) for other suggestions. Explicit instruction is often needed for students to learn main concepts. The student's special education teacher should be consulted for specific educational goals and for recommendations regarding instructional strategies and accommodations. This is of course needed when working with any student identified as having a disability and who has an individualized education plan. Harwell (2002) offered some of the following accommodations that are beneficial for students with learning disabilities:

1 Seat student near teacher.
2 Assess prior knowledge.

3 Use high-interest materials of the student's choosing when possible.
4 Teach students to use mnemonics, story mapping, advanced organizer, and webs to organize and remember information.
5 Prioritize tasks to be done.
6 Break down assignments into shorter tasks.
7 Give extra time to complete assignments and tests.
8 Provide a buddy or peer-tutor to help with clarifying and completing assignments.
9 Use a calculator, computer, spell check, tape recorder.
10 Provide immediate, specific feedback.
11 Use rewards to encourage effort and completion of work.
12 Involve parents with homework, field trips, and in-class activities.

Students with learning disabilities also lack social and communicative competence. Kavale and Forness (1996) analyzed over 100 independent studies and found that 80% of students with learning disabilities are perceived to have deficits in social competence. These children tend to be less accepted and are less socially skilled than their nondisabled peers (Coleman, McHam, & Minnett, 1992; Toro, Weissberg, Guare, & Liebenstein, 1990; Vaughn & Hogan, 1994). Students with learning disabilities exhibit deficits in verbal and nonverbal communication skills and are less able to adjust to changing social situations than are their nondisabled peers (Weiner & Harris, 1997). Other social-emotional problems presented by students with learning disabilities include low self-esteem, anxiety, depression, and delinquency (Scruggs & Mastropieri, 1996; Bryan, Pearl, & Herzog, 1989). Students with learning disabilities often report feelings of isolation and alienation toward peers and teachers as reasons for dropping out of school (Bryan, Pearl, & Herzog, 1989; Seidel & Vaughn, 1991). Researchers offer varied explanations for these problems from neurological deficits (Little, 1993) and cognitive processing problems (Mathinos, 1991) to difficulty perceiving the feelings and emotions of others (Stone & LaGreca, 1983).

Peer tutoring is a strategy that has been successfully used to improve socialization and academic performance of students with learning disabilities (Fuchs & Fuchs, 1998). Guidelines for developing class-wide peer tutoring, an approach to benefit all students, have been developed by Fulk and King (2001). Students are trained in the roles of tutor and tutee and further taught feedback for correct and incorrect responses and error correction procedures. Peer-Assisted Learning Strategies (PALS) in reading has been quite successful with students with learning disabilities (Fuchs, Fuchs, & Burish, 2000). Cooperative learning activities provide students with learning disabilities opportunities to practice social skills while working on academic tasks. In one study, middle school students with learning disabilities were taught to recruit peer assistance during cooperative learning activities (Wolford, Heward, & Alber, 2001). This skill is especially important in small group instruction arrangements in general education settings where most students with learning disabilities are educated.

Emotional and Behavioral Disorders

Children with emotional or behavioral disorders have IQs that range from low average to gifted (Duncan, Forness, & Hartsough, 1995). The Individuals with Disabilities Education Act (IDEA) definition of serious emotional disturbance specifically recognizes the difficulties these children have in establishing and maintaining positive relationships.

The term serious emotional disturbance means a condition exhibiting one or more of the following characteristics over a long period of time and to a marked degree, which adversely affects educational performance:

1   An inability to learn that cannot be explained by intellectual, sensory, or health factors.
2   An inability to build or maintain satisfactory relationships with peers and teachers.
3   Inappropriate types of behavior or feelings under normal circumstances.
4   A general pervasive mood of unhappiness or depression, or
5   A tendency to develop symptoms or fears associated with personal or school problems.
    The term includes children who are schizophrenic. The term does not include children who are socially maladjusted unless it is determined that they are seriously emotionally disturbed (U.S. Department of Education, 1998).

These children may exhibit internalizing or externalizing behaviors. Internalizing behaviors may include social withdrawal, anxiety, or depression. Externalizing behaviors include aggressive, acting-out, and noncompliance behaviors. Students with externalizing behaviors often have difficulty adjusting to the behavioral expectations of their teachers, are often rejected by peers and have difficulty developing and maintaining friendships (Schonert-Reichl, 1993; Walker & Leister, 1994). It is usually the social skill deficits, not academic difficulties that cause these children to be removed from general education settings. Smith (2001) noted that young children without disabilities responded negatively to children exhibiting externalizing types of behavior whereas children with internalizing behaviors were less likely to be noticed. Adolescents rejected their disabled peers who exhibited externalizing and antisocial behaviors. Children with psychological problems were viewed less favorably by their nondisabled peers than were those with medical problems.

Gresham and Elliot (1989) reference social learning theory to explain social skill deficits in students with disabilities:

> A social skill deficit results from failure to acquire a social skill due to lack of opportunity to learn the skill and/or lack of exposure to models of appropriate social behavior. A social performance deficit results from a lack of opportunity to perform social skills and/or lack of reinforcement for socially skilled behaviors.
>
> (p. 122)

There is a plethora of evidence showing that students with emotional and behavioral disorders can benefit from specific social skills instruction (Mathur, Kavale, Quinn, Forness, & Rutherford, 1998; Forness & Kavale, 1999). Numerous commercial programs are available for teaching social skills to students with mild disabilities. These include: the ACCEPTS Program (a Curriculum for Children's Effective Peer and Teacher Skills) (Walker, McConnell, Holmes, Todis, Walker, & Golden, 1983; the ACCESS Program (An Adolescent Curriculum for Communication and Effective Social Skills) (Walker, Todis, Holmes, & Horton, 1988); and Skillstreaming the Adolescent (Goldstein & McGinnis, 1997). These programs all focus on teaching specific skills (e.g. listening, asking for assistance, resolving conflicts peacefully) rather than global skills (e.g. self-esteem building). All three programs have pre- and post-assessment measures to determine whether teaching certain skills is necessary and whether students have learned skills taught.

The following effective instructional strategies are recommended by Wehby, Symons, Canale, and Go (1998):

- providing appropriate structure and predictable routines;
- establishing a structured and consistent classroom environment;
- implementing a consistent schedule with clear expectations, and set rules and consequences;
- fostering positive teacher–student interaction with adequate praise and systematic responses to problem behaviors;
- promoting high rates of academic engagement;
- encouraging positive social interaction and limited seatwork (p. 52);
- Medication can be helpful in increasing attention and reducing aggressive behaviors (Forness & Kavale, 1988). It is important for teachers to collaborate with parents and physicians to monitor behavior and side effects.

Mild or Moderate Mental Retardation

The American Association of Mental Retardation (AAMR) definition reads:

> Mental retardation refers to substantial limitations in present func-
> tioning. It is characterized by significantly sub-average intellectual
> functioning, existing concurrently with related limitations in two or
> more of the following applicable adaptive skill areas: communica-
> tion, self-care, home living, social skills, community use, self-direc-
> tion, health and safety, functional academics, leisure, and work.
> Mental retardation manifests before age 18.
>
> (Luckasson et al., 1992, p. 5)

Greenspan and Granfield (1992) argued that determining an individual's ability "to perform certain crucial social roles (e.g. worker, friend, neighbor) more than ability to master academic tasks" (p. 443) should be the determining factor when diagnosing mental retardation. Children with mental retardation exhibit a variety of social problems. They often have difficulty making friends and have low self-esteem (Luftig, 1988; Hallahan & Kauffman, 1994). These deficits may be the result of low cognitive ability making it difficult for them to process social cues and other information or may be the result of a display of disruptive behavior, due to frustration when they experience difficulty, that is interpreted as inappropriate by their nondisabled classmates (Hallahan & Kauffman, 1994).

Teaching life skills and self-determination skills is a main goal for teachers working with students who have mental retardation (Wehmeyer & Schwartz, 1997). Training is focused on helping students adjust to environments where they will live, work, and play after they leave school. Instructional strategies are varied from large group instruction and individual conferences to one-on-one behavioral interventions. Students are taught to set goals, solve problems, and to advocate for themselves. Wehmeyer, Argan, and Hughes (1998) proposed that students learn to be "causal agents" or actors in their own lives instead of being acted upon. A synthesis of research in the area of self-determi-nation for individuals with disabilities can be found in (Algozzine, Browder, Karvonen, Test, & Wood, 2001). Many of the strategies rec-ommended for students with learning disabilities, emotional and behav-ioral disorders, and ADHD, such as cooperative learning, peer tutoring, praise and reinforcement, are also successful for students with mental retardation.

For students with special needs to be successful in inclusive settings, they must learn and exhibit socially competent behaviors. It's not enough to assume that exposure to their nondisabled peers alone will help students with special needs learn appropriate social skills (Gresham, 1981b; Sale & Carey, 1995).

Communication Disorders

The American Speech-Language-Hearing Association (1993) differentiates language and speech disorders. A speech disorder is characterized by an inability to deliver messages orally such as an individual's production of sounds, rhythm of speech, or voice quality. A language disorder is characterized by difficulty in receiving, understanding and formulating ideas and information. Approximately 22% of all students receiving special education services are provided speech and language services.

Smith, Polloway, Patton, and Dowdy (2001) recommend some of the following classroom accommodations for students with speech and language disorders:

- Work closely with the speech-language pathologist, following suggestions and trying to reinforce specific skills. Also consult with the special education teacher to determine IEP goals and objectives specific to speech and language development.
- Provide opportunities for students to participate in oral group activities.
- Give students lots of opportunities to model and practice appropriate speech.
- Maintain eye contact when the student speaks.
- Increase receptive language in the classroom.
- Teach listening skills for class discussions.
- Encourage students' conversations through story reading.
- Use music and play games to improve language.
- Be a good listener and don't interrupt or finish the student's sentence for him or her.
- When appropriate, educate other students in the class about speech disorders and about acceptance and understanding.

As we discussed in Chapter 3, culture influences communication in small ways. Children's speech and use of language reflects their culture. Teachers must be careful not to assume a difference in dialect means disorder. Walker et al. (1983) stressed the importance of teachers making home visits, trying to understand the world from the student's perspective, and allowing flexible hours for conferences. He encouraged teachers to consider student behavior in the context of the student's cultural values, motivation, and worldview.

Advances in technology such as communication boards and mechanical or electronic communication devices will allow students with severe communication disorders to communicate with teachers, peers, and family members. For example, a voice synthesizer is used to produce speech output. Communication boards can be made of paper or a sturdier material, and allow students to point to words or pictures to communicate. Computers can be used to make communication boards with programs such as Boardmaker from Mayer-Johnson Company. This program contains more that 3,000 picture symbols in black and white or color. The print labels accompanying each symbol are available in more than 10 languages. These devices are easy for teachers to program and allow students with communication disorders to participate in classroom activities.

Other Students with Special Needs

Most discussions of inclusion concentrate on children and adolescents with disabilities. In this book, we have expanded the concept of special students to include those who are gifted and talented. Gifted, as defined in the Gifted and Talented Children's Act of 1978 (PL 95–561, Section 902), is a term meaning:

> [C]hildren, and whenever applicable, youth who are identified at the preschool, elementary, or secondary level as possessing demonstrated or potential abilities that give evidence of high performance capabilities in areas such as intellectual, creative, specific academic, or leadership ability, or in the performing and visual arts, and who by reason thereof, require services or activities not ordinarily provided by the school.

Gifted students, while they do not qualify for special education services, often provide challenges, both academically and socially, for classroom teachers. Gifted students are often rejected by their peers and feel isolated in school. Classroom teachers must consider the unique needs of these students. Teachers should be aware that many gifted students, including underachievers, girls, students from culturally and linguistically diverse backgrounds, and students with learning or physical disabilities remain unidentified and therefore may not receive appropriate educational services.

Kennedy (1995) offered several inclusion tips for teachers working with gifted learners:

- Resist policies requiring more work of those who finish assignments quickly and easily. Instead, explore ways to assign different work, which may be more complex and more abstract. Find curriculum compacting strategies that work, and use them regularly.

- Seek out curriculum and supplementary materials, which require analysis, synthesis, and critical thinking, and push beyond superficial responses.
- De-emphasize grades and other extrinsic rewards. Encourage students to learn for learning's sake, and help perfectionists establish realistic goals and priorities.
- Encourage intellectual and academic risk-taking. The flawless completion of a simple worksheet by an academically talented student calls for little or no reward, but struggling with a complex, open-ended issue should earn praise.
- Help all children develop social skills to relate well to one another. Help them see things from other's viewpoints. Training in how to "read" others and how to send accurate verbal and nonverbal messages may also be helpful. Tolerate neither elitist attitudes nor anti-gifted discrimination.
- Take time to listen to responses that may at first appear to be off-target. Gifted students are often divergent thinkers who get more out of a story or remark and have creative approaches to problems. Hear them out, and help them elaborate on their ideas.
- Provide opportunities for independent investigations in areas of interest.
- Be aware of the special needs of gifted girls. Encourage them to establish realistically high-level educational and career goals, and give them additional encouragement to succeed in math and science.
(pp. 223–234)

Attention Deficit/Hyperactivity Disorder

Attention deficit/hyperactivity disorder (ADD/ADHD) is not a specific category under IDEA. However, students with ADD or ADHD may be served under IDEA if they meet the criteria under the category of learning disabilities or emotional disturbance, or under "other health impairment." The American Psychiatric Association (1994) defines attention deficit disorder as a "pervasive pattern of inattention, impulsivity, and/or hyperactivity-impulsivity that is more frequent and severe than is typically observed in individuals at a comparable level of development" (p. 78). Children can experience an attention deficit disorder with or without hyperactivity or both. Students with ADHD have poor attention, impulsive behavior, and overactivity. They often have difficulty staying in their seats and rarely complete assignments, as they tend to shift from one activity to another. Students with ADHD are estimated to be rejected 50–60% more often than their nondisabled peers (Guevremont, 1990). Students who present with hyperactivity (ADHD) are most challenging to classroom teachers. Teacher intolerance of movement in the classroom is often blamed for the over identification of ADHD.

Parker (1996) has offered numerous strategies for accommodating students with ADHD in the classroom. For example, to improve socialization, Parker recommended that teachers utilize the following strategies:

1   Praise appropriate behavior.
2   Monitor social interactions.
3   Set up social behavior goals with student, and implement a reward program.
4   Prompt appropriate social behavior either verbally or with private signal.
5   Encourage cooperative learning tasks with other students.
6   Provide small group social skills training.
7   Praise student frequently.
8   Assign special responsibilities to student in presence of peer group so others observe student in a positive light.

To reduce motor activity, Parker suggested the following:

1   Allow student to stand at times while working.
2   Provide opportunity for "seat breaks," i.e. run errands, etc.
3   Provide short break between assignments.
4   Supervise closely during transition times.
5   Remind student to check over work product if performance is rushed or careless.
6   Give extra time to complete tasks.

Medical management is also an important component in managing students with ADHD. Teachers need to work closely with parents and physicians to monitor side effects and behavior changes.

Practices that Promote Positive Interactions among Students with and without Disabilities in Inclusive Classrooms

Salend in his text, *Creating Inclusive Classrooms: Effective and Reflective Practices* (2001), recommends strategies for teaching about individual differences. Some of those strategies include utilizing:

1   Disability simulations (contact the American Red Cross for sample simulations and questions).
2   Successful individuals with disabilities as guest speakers (contact community agencies, parent organizations, special education teachers).
3   Films (e.g. *My Left Foot, Dead Poet's Society, Children of a Lesser God, What's Eating Gilbert Grape? Shine*).

4   HBO specials (e.g. *Educating Peter*).
5   Books (local bookstores will have numerous suggestions as well as on-line information specific to children's literature and disability: www.kidsource.com/NICHCY/literature.htm).
6   Information about adaptive devices (contact special education teachers or speech and language pathologists).
7   Collaborative problem solving (e.g. cooperative groups, project-based learning, service learning, class meetings).
8   Multicultural materials.

Salend further suggested that teachers teach about language diversity and different dialects, family differences, gender equity, homelessness, stereotyping, and discrimination.

As stated earlier, most students with disabilities receive instruction in general education or inclusive classrooms. The philosophy of inclusive education requires the building of community support and a strong sense of belonging in all students. Villa and Thousand (1995) have identified a number of promising practices that support the philosophy of inclusive education: outcome-based education; multicultural education; multiple intelligence theory; constructivist learning; interdisciplinary curriculum; community-referenced instruction; authentic assessment of student performance; multi-age grouping; use of technology in the classroom; peer-mediated learning; teaching responsibility and peacemaking; and collaborative teaming among adults and students. Many of these strategies are discussed in detail in preceding chapters.

Collaborating to Meet Student Needs

Students with disabilities are entitled to receive a variety of services that enable them to be successful in school. Many individuals play an important role in providing these services to students with special needs. Special education teachers have the primary responsibility for managing and coordinating the services a student receives. Students with disabilities have individualized education plans (IEPs) that indicate educational goals and objectives and services needed to enable each student to maximize their potential. Special education teachers must learn to collaborate with other teachers, parents, administrators, and other service providers (e.g. psychologists, social workers, speech/language therapists, interpreters, and paraprofessionals) to provide the best service to students. General education teachers must take responsibility and ownership for the students with disabilities included in their classrooms. They are responsible for identifying students who exhibit suspected disabilities. They attend IEP team meetings and participate in development, review, and revision of students' programs. Implementation of a student's program may include classroom accommodations, modifications, and other supports.

Collaboration can be defined as working with other people to meet shared goals. For example, a team of individuals, sometimes referred to as a multidisciplinary team meets to determine where, when, and how a student with special needs will be educated. Collaboration also takes place when a teacher meets individually with parents, siblings, guardians, or other service providers to discuss issues related to students with disabilities. Collaboration is voluntary, requires parity among participants, is based on mutual goals, depends on shared responsibility for participation and decision-making, and requires shared accountability for outcomes (Friend & Cook, 1996). Collaboration is the process for ensuring that students with special needs receive a free, appropriate education mandated by IDEA. The goal is for all of those involved to work together to meet the needs of students with disabilities.

Working Effectively with Parents and Families

Establishing a good relationship with parents and/or family members is important to the success of students with special needs. Parents come from varied ethnic/racial, and socioeconomic backgrounds. They bring a day-to-day understanding of their children that, as teachers, we may not have. Their perspective on the goals of education for their children is important for teachers to understand. It is important for teachers to encourage parents/families to be partners in the education of their children.

Research links parent involvement to both academic and social success of children in school (Liontos, 1992). Some of the results of parent involvement include:

1   Improved academic achievement.
2   Improved student behavior.
3   Greater student motivation.
4   More regular attendance.
5   Lower student dropout rates.
6   A more positive attitude toward homework.
7   Improved attitudes, and better parent ratings for teachers.
8   More positive interaction with children for parents.
9   More parental cooperation with school personnel in solving children's academic and behavior problems (p. 14).

Some of the obstacles to parent involvement involve emotional barriers felt by the parents themselves. Parents may have negative attitudes based on their own bad experiences with school. A level of distrust and anger results when parents pick up the phone only to hear, "Your son is causing problems in math class again." Many low-income parents and parents from other cultures see teachers as authority figures and believe it is best left to the schools to educate their children. Cultural and language barriers often lead parents to maintain a respectful distance from the schools. Educators often misinterpret this choice as a lack of concern for their child's education. Other barriers evolve out of time constraints and logistical problems such as transportation or child care.

Mostert (1998) noted that facilitating parent involvement could be both rewarding and frustrating. He reminds us that the assumptions that we make can enhance or destroy relationships with parents and families. Mostert recommended that teachers begin by assuming that parents want the best for their children.

Effective communication is essential for collaboration to be successful. Gordon (1987) identified the following common elements in effective interpersonal interactions: active listening, depersonalizing situations, identifying common goals and solutions, and monitoring progress to achieve goals. Families should be included whenever possible in the decision-making process involving their child's education. Home visits, newsletters informing parents of class activities, asking for parents to volunteer in the classroom or to share their wisdom with students are all examples of ways to show respect to families and to encourage their involvement.

Response to Intervention and Universal Design

Sugai (2009) suggested that:

> Schools are complex environments where the collective skills, knowledge, and practices of a culture are taught, shaped, encouraged, and transmitted. Teachers are challenged to provide effective and explicit instruction that maximizes students' acquisition of concepts, skills, and information, and students are challenged to remain attentive, responsive, and engaged to benefit from these instructional opportunities.

Sugai (2007) highlighted the challenges schools face in reaching these goals:

> In recent years, achieving these goals has required that schools a) increase instructional accountability and justification, b) improve the alignment between assessment information and intervention development, c) enhance use of limited resources and time, d) make decisions with accurate and relevant information, e) initiate important instructional decisions earlier and in a more timely manner, f) engage in regular and comprehensive screening for successful and at-risk learners, g) provide effective and relevant support for students who do not respond to core curricula, and h) enhance fidelity of instructional implementation.

Two recent initiatives, Response-to-Instruction (RTI) and Universal Design for Learning (UDL) represent problem-solving frameworks to address the needs of students at risk and students with disabilities. According to Fox, Carta, Strain, Dunlap, and Hemmeter (2009), RTI is a systematic, data-driven process that attempts to resolve students' academic and/or behavioral challenges using scientific, research-based interventions in the educational environment. Response to intervention integrates assessment and intervention within a multi-level prevention system to maximize student achievement and to reduce behavioral problems. RTI seeks to prevent academic failure through early intervention, frequent progress monitoring, and increasingly intensive research-based instructional interventions for children who continue to have difficulty. This model is intended to reduce referrals to special education while allowing children in the general education setting to have access to a high quality of curriculum and instruction matched to his/her level of need.

Fox et al. (2009; pp. 2–3) identified several features of RTI that allow school programs to identify students who are at risk or who have delays in learning and behavior and to provide them with the supports they need to be successful. Those features include the following:

1   *Universal screening*: In RTI approaches, the performance of all students is evaluated systematically to identify those who are (a) making adequate progress; (b) at some risk of failure if not provided extra assistance; or (c) at high risk of failure if not provided specialized supports.

2   *Continuous progress monitoring*: In RTI approaches, student progress is assessed on a regular and frequent basis in order to identify when inadequate growth trends might indicate a need for increasing the level of instructional support to the student.

3   *Continuum of evidence-based interventions*: RTI approaches assume multiple levels, or a "cascade," of interventions that vary in intensity or level of support derived from scientifically validated research. An individualized intensive curriculum is implemented for students who do not show adequate growth in response to the modified curriculum.

4   *Data-based decision making and problem solving*: At the heart of the RTI approach is instructional decision-making based on student performance or growth on curricular outcomes and modifications when insufficient growth is noted.

5   *Implementation fidelity*: RTI requires specific procedures for regular documentation of the level of implementation (e.g. were the modifications of the teaching practices implemented consistently and with a high degree of accuracy?) of each of the features of the model.

Academic Systems

☐ Intensive, Individual
   Interventions
   • Individual students
   • Assessment-based
   • High intensity
   • Longer duration

☐ Targeted Group
   Interventions
   • Some students (at-risk)
   • High efficiency
   • Rapid response

☐ Universal Interventions
   • All students
   • Preventive, proactive

Behavioral Systems

☐ Intensive, Individual
   Interventions
   • Individual students
   • Assessment-based
   • Intense, durable
     procedures

☐ Targeted Group
   Interventions
   • Some students (at-risk)
   • High efficiency
   • Rapid response

☐ Universal Interventions
   • All settings, all students
   • Preventive, proactive

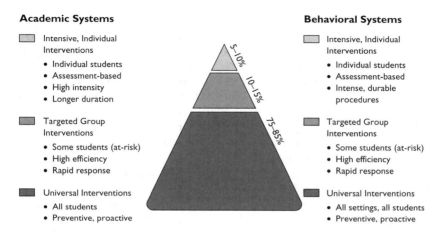

Figure 5.1 RTI, a School-Wide System for Student Success.

Source: North Star Educational Tools: http://www.northstaret.com/rti_01.shtml

RTI is conceptualized as a multi-tiered service delivery model including primary, secondary, and tertiary levels of support. RTI is broken into multiple tiers of instruction with various levels of intervention that increase in intensity as you progress up the pyramid (see Figure 5.1). What distinguishes this approach is that the interventions occur within the classroom and are individualized to the student. The focus on individual instruction is based on the belief that no single intervention will be successful for all students. All tiers include a four-step process: (1) problem identification; (2) problem analysis/selection of intervention; (3) implementation of intervention; and (4) progress monitoring (Fuchs & Fuchs, 2006).

The primary, or first, tier is focused on all students receiving high-quality, scientifically based instruction in the core curriculum. Ongoing progress monitoring allows for identification of students who are struggling learners and need additional support. In this tier approximately 75–85% of the general student body should be able to meet grade level norms without additional assistance.

The 10–15% of students who are not showing progress in the regular classroom are provided with increasingly intensive instruction matched to their needs. Instruction is provided in small group settings in addition to instruction in the general education curriculum. Students who continue to show little progress at this level of intervention are then considered for more intensive interventions at Tier 3.

Tier 3 will provide services to 5–10% of the students who will continue to show resistance to intervention provided at Tier 2. Hence, the intensity of intervention increases as the severity of the problem increases. At this level, students receive individualized instruction that target specific skill deficits. Students who do not achieve at this level are referred for a comprehensive evaluation and considered then for eligibility for special education services under IDEA 2004. The data collected in all three tiers are used to make the eligibility decision.

The key goal in using the RTI model is to improve outcomes for all students. Students with academic and behavioral needs are identified early. Evidence-based interventions are individualized according to student need. Early intervention is likely to reduce the number of students referred to special education for learning disabilities.

Universal Design for Learning (UDL) is a framework for designing curriculum (goals, materials, methods, and assessment) that is grounded in the belief that every learner is unique and brings different strengths and weaknesses to the classroom (Rose & Meyer, 2002). UDL is designed to enable all students to learn by reducing the barriers to the curriculum and by providing additional supports for learning. Rose & Meyer identify three UDL principles to guide the design of a flexible curriculum.

1   To represent information in multiple and flexible formats and media to give students with diverse learning styles ways of acquiring information and knowledge.
2   To provide multiple and flexible pathways for students action and expression.
3   To provide multiple and flexible means of engaging students interest and motivation to learn.

The new age of digital multimedia, adaptive technologies, the World Wide Web, and other advancements make it possible to individualize education for all students, not just students with disabilities. Developers and practitioners of UDL apply the intrinsic flexibility of digital media to individualize educational goals, classroom materials, instructional methods and assessments. Thus, each student has an appropriate point-of-entry into the curriculum—and a pathway toward attainment of educational goals.

New curricular materials and learning technologies should be designed from the beginning to be flexible enough to accommodate the unique learning styles of a wide range of individuals, including children with disabilities. Some examples of UDL include: accessible Web pages; electronic versions of textbooks and other curricular materials; captioned and/or narrated videos; word processors with word prediction; speaking spell checkers; talking dialog boxes; voice recognition; and picture menus. Some students with disabilities will still need assistive technology devices such as communication aids, visual and hearing aids, wheelchairs, etc. However, using UDL will help to ensure that students with disabilities will have access to core curriculum and new technologies available to all children. The Center for Applied Special Technology (CAST) is a great resource for teachers to learn how to customize instruction using the above- mentioned principles of UDL.

A major goal of both RTI and UDL is to improve educational outcomes for students with disabilities. Strangeman, Hitchcock, Hall, Meo, Gersten, and Dimino (2006) identify three common goals of RTI and UDL: First, both RTI and UDL recognize that poor achievement does not necessarily reflect disability, but rather also reflect poor instruction. Both support the notion that curriculum may need to be adapted to meet the individual needs of students. Second, RTI and UDL both reflect the understanding that one size does not fit all. In other words, what works for one student does not necessarily work for another. Third, both RTI and UDL support the use of multiple assessments to guide instruction. Ongoing progress monitoring is used to guide decision-making regarding the appropriate instruction and intervention. The authors suggest that, "by simultaneously implementing RTI and using UDL to build the capacity of the general education curriculum, it may be possible to realize broadly effective general education curricula that anticipate students' difficulties and eliminate the need for intervention" (pp. 7–8).

Summary

An important goal for any classroom teacher is the participation of all students in as many classroom activities as possible. For students with special needs, this means that teachers must be able to identify academic and social disabilities, and further, to choose strategies that help these students succeed in the classroom. In this chapter we have defined the 13 categories of disabilities eligible under IDEA. In each category we have provided some suggestions for teachers to facilitate inclusion of students with special needs. The successful inclusion of students with special needs can only be met when we develop an attitude of acceptance and model that acceptance to students in the classroom. We also discussed two models, RTI and UDL, which may represent innovative approaches to addressing the academic and behavioral needs of students with disabilities.

Learning Activities

- Bobby is a student who does not believe that he is capable of being successful in school (low efficacy). He can be moody and frequently resists his teacher by saying "I can't do this." Draw upon the information you have learned (use material from any chapter) and develop a strategy for changing his sense of efficacy.
- Based on your understanding of attention-deficit/hyperactive disorder (ADHD), what criteria must be met before classifying a student as having this disability? You may want to consult several outside sources.
- Roberto is a third-grade student with attention deficit disorder. He is larger and louder than his classmates. He always wants to be the center of attention, which he accomplishes through clowning around, making jokes, and entertaining his classmates with a variety of sound effect noises. If you knew Roberto was coming into your classroom, how would you help him succeed?
- Tamara's parents are divorced and, for the last few years, she and her mother have moved from one place to another, sometimes living out of their car. Tamara is often absent and when she is in class, she seems withdrawn and disinterested in class assignments. What are the issues involved in working with Tamara?
- Yenny is a fourth-grade student who, just this year, became eligible to receive special education services for emotional and behavioral disorders. Yenny is included, for the first time, in your general education classroom. Her IEP goals are mainly behavioral. She has average intelligence but has difficulty relating to her peers. Yenny has been known to have a quick temper and often hits other students when things don't go her way. How could you find out more about Yenny? What strategies could you implement in your classroom to help Yenny improve her relationships with other students?

Resources

- ADD in School
  http://addinschool.com
- American Association for Mental Retardation
  www.aamr.org
- The American Speech-Language Hearing Association
  www.asha.org

- Center of the Study of Autism
  www.autism.org
- Children and Adults with Attention Deficit Hyperactivity Disorder
  www.chadd.org
- The Council for Exceptional Children: the Division for Diverse Exceptional Learners
  www.cec.sped.org/dv/ddel.html
- The Council for Exceptional Children with Behavior Disorders
  www.ccbd.net
- The Inclusion Network
  www.inclusion.org
- International Society for Augmentative and Alternative Communication (ISAAC)
  www.isaac-online.org
- LD Online
  www.ldonline.org
- The National Information Center for Children and Youth with Disabilities
  www.nichcy.org
- TASH Organization, addressing the needs of individual with significant disabilities
  http://tash.org

Unit III

Building and Managing Positive Teacher–Student Relationships

Unit III focuses on ways to build and maintain positive relationships between teachers and students. Chapter 6 discusses research examining teacher–student interactions. The first part of the chapter discusses why positive relationships between teachers and students are important, especially for students from diverse backgrounds. The second part of the chapter examines the ways that the teacher–student relationship evolves and changes over time. The third section reviews constructs that positively influence student feelings about teachers, academic material, and motivation. Chapter 7 moves away from a microscopic focus on teachers and students and looks at the larger classroom community. Research indicates that when students feel part of a community, they learn more and behave more appropriately. Among the topics discussed are the defining features of a learning community, the importance of teacher support, peer tutoring, cooperative learning, peer mediation, classroom meeting, and service learning. Research on behavioral management is reviewed in Chapter 8. The chapter begins by reviewing different perspectives on behavior. Teachers' beliefs about the causes of behavior will influence their strategies for managing it. The way culture influences behavior and a teacher's response to it are also discussed. We also discuss ways to use positive reinforcement and review strategies for managing minor classroom disruptions.

Chapter 6

Building Relationships

Wen Shu runs up to her teacher, Mr. Puentes, to show him the kocapeli figure that her mother bought her on a recent business trip. Mr. Puentes interrupts Wen Shu's story about the doll and tells her to get back to her seat because the class needs to study for the state examinations that come at the end of the month. Dejected and somewhat embarrassed, Wen shu returns to her seat but is not very interested in completing the practice multiple choice test Mr. Puentes wants her to take.

In the era of high stakes testing and accountability, teachers are pressured to meet or exceed state standards and expectations. However, some of the moves that teachers make to meet these expectations may in fact be counterproductive. Specifically, teachers may be putting less effort into cultivating positive relationships with their students. This is unfortunate because the interpersonal relationship between a student and teacher has a profound effect on instructional outcomes and activities. Research consistently shows that interpersonal processes influence the way that students feel about the content they study and their motivation to study it (e.g. Davis, 2003; Friedriksen & Rhodes, 2004; Frymier, 1994; Perry, Vandekamp, Mercer, & Nordby, 2002). Teachers are also affected by the relationships they have with their students. The desire to prepare for class, to give extra attention to students, and to develop creative teaching strategies, is related to the types of relationships teachers establish and maintain. This chapter, therefore, focuses on the interpersonal processes that play a role in the classroom context. In this chapter we discuss the importance of positive teacher–student relationships, discuss the perspectives that describe the way these relationships develop, and review the communication processes found to promote positive teacher–student relationships.

Teacher–Student Relationships

How students feel about school and their classes is in a large part determined by the quality of the relationships they have with their teachers.

Teachers who are caring, friendly, helpful, understanding, and dependable foster supportive relationships with their students (Goodenow, 1993; Rosenfeld & Richman, 1999; Skinner & Belmont, 1993; Teven & Hanson, 2004). Noddings (1995) argued that "we should want more from our educational efforts than adequate academic achievement and … we will not achieve even that meager success unless our children believe that they themselves are cared for and learn to care for others" (pp. 675–676). Noddings argued that spending time developing relationships with students, talking to them about their problems, and guiding them toward sensitivity and competence are significant teaching activities. These connections are important because they encourage learning that they may not occur otherwise.

Kohn (1996) also stressed the role of positive teacher–student relationships when he stated:

> Caring teachers converse with students in a distinctive way; they think about how what they say sounds from the students' point of view. They respond authentically and respectfully rather than giving patronizing pats on the head (or otherwise slathering them with "positive reinforcement"). They explain what they are up to and give reasons for their requests. They ask students what they think, and then care about their answers.
>
> (p. 112)

Bosworth (1995) interviewed middle school students regarding their ideas of what it means to be a caring teacher. Helping with schoolwork was the frequently mentioned characteristic of a caring teacher. Valuing individuality and recognizing different learning styles were important to seventh- and eighth-graders and among males. Providing guidance and helping with problems outside of school time was the second most frequently mentioned characteristic. Teven and Hanson (2004) found that caring was related to teacher credibility.

Gettinger and Stoiber (1999) reviewed literature on teaching excellence and highlighted the significance of positive teacher–student relationships. Specifically, they stated: "Positive teacher-student social interactions contribute to students' self efficacy and intrinsic interest in learning, and they foster a sense of identity as a member of a learning community" (p. 940).

Croninger and Lee (2001) argued that a quality teacher–student relationship is a form of social capital that has particular benefits for students who are at risk for academic failure. They analyzed data collected over several years by the National Center for Educational Statistics. They found that at risk students who dropped out of high school had a less positive relationship with teachers than at risk students who stayed in school. They also found that students who were academically at risk benefited more from a positive relationship with teachers than students who were not academically at risk.

Brewster and Bowen (2004) found that a positive teacher–student relationship positively influenced academic engagement of Latino middle and high school students who were at risk for school failure. The authors stated that school engagement "includes a student's affective, cognitive, and behavioral responses related to attachment, sense of belonging, or involvement in school" (p. 49). They surveyed 699 Latino middle and high school students from the United States and school personnel who identified the students as at risk for school failure. The results indicated that teacher support (e.g. My teachers really care about me. My teachers are willing to work with me after school) had the greatest impact on the meaningfulness of school. They also found that students who had a positive relationship with a teacher exhibited fewer behavioral problems in school. The authors concluded by observing that teacher support may be more important for students at risk than for other students.

Davis (2003) conducted an extensive review of the literature on the influence of teacher–student relationships on cognitive and social development. She concluded that the quality of the teacher–student relationship influences social cognitive outcomes from preschool to early adolescence.

Perspectives on Teacher–Student Relationships

Three primary perspectives have been used to study the role of the teacher–student relationship on academic and social performance. One approach, attachment theory, contends that student–teacher interaction is driven by students' beliefs about adults, teachers, and adult–child interaction. These beliefs, in turn influence the processes used to guide students toward academic goals. An attachment perspective considers the teacher–student relationship to be an extension of the parent–child relationship. Teachers who are nurturing appear to create positive bonds that positively influence a student's orientation to the learning tasks. Research suggests that students who have a positive relationship with a teacher also have better peer relationships, manage their emotions better and experience fewer behavioral problems (Pianta & Steinberg, 1992).

A second perspective reviewed by Davis (2003) focuses on the way a teacher motivates a student to accomplish academic goals. As we discussed in Chapter 2, a significant amount of attention has been given to this topic. Motivational studies examine the communication skills and instructional strategies that impact student motivation to learn. According to Davis, teachers who promote autonomy and help students become self-directed are particularly effective. In contrast, teachers who engage in power struggles have more problematic relationships. For these teachers, the goal has more to do with control than with student learning.

Motivation is impacted by the socio-emotional connections between teachers and students. Research from education and communication show that teachers who exhibit positive affect, promote positive attitudes about instructional material, increase a sense of belonging, and increase student self-efficacy (Brophy, 1998; Christophel, 1990, Comstock, Rowell, & Bowers, 1995; Moos & Moos, 1978).

Students are also motivated to obtain goals that are not related to academic success. For example, the need for peer acceptance may in some instances be more important than academic performance. Indeed, the teacher–student relationship is influenced by numerous factors. Teachers have values, beliefs, and expectations about students and course content. Students have attitudes about their teachers, their peers, and themselves. In some cases, teachers and student connect in positive ways and sometimes they struggle as they attempt to work through the instructional experience.

The third area discussed by Davis (2003) is the socio-cultural perspective. This perspective views the teacher–student relationship as mutually negotiated. Teachers and students are in a continual process of defining and redefining their relationship. The social-cultural perspective challenges teachers to understand the forces that influence the development and maintenance of interpersonal relationships.

Two approaches are prevalent in the socio-cultural perspective: the ecological and the social constructivist views. The ecological view focuses on the physical setup, class size, and the social pressures the student experiences. The effects of class size have received considerable attention. As the classes become larger, it becomes more difficult for teachers to make connections with their students. Often, teachers and administrators create policies and structures that privilege the test scores at the expense of building positive relationships. As a consequence, students will seek out and develop alternative relationships with classroom aids, student teachers, and peers.

The second approach, the social constructivist, considers knowledge as co-constructed between teachers and students. We discussed the constructivist view in Chapter 1. According to this perspective, learning is considered a social activity. Students must make sense out of both cognitive (learning math) and social (teacher immediacy) material. In order to be effective, teachers need to connect with student sense-making processes Social constructivists attempt to promote autonomy through cooperative learning, sharing classroom rules, and providing students with the resources to navigate the material. This perspective requires teachers to understand the diverse lived experiences of their students. While teachers utilize strategies for accomplishing intellectual goals, students create mechanisms for managing their own goals. For example, students who do not want to study math may "act out" or in some way sabotage the lesson. Teachers may refer to these students as "their problem children," or "troublemakers." This relationship may be more contentious and difficult. If we return to the discussion in Chapter 3, some teachers may hold negative stereotypes about students of color and project these attitudes to them.

One final point that Davis (2003) makes about teacher–student relationship is how they change as students move from elementary school to high school. In elementary school, learning is a community enterprise; students have one teacher for a school year and work in numerous cooperative groups and teams. When students advance to middle school and high school, learning becomes more individual. Students have more than one teacher, move from class to class and have different social relationships. For some, the bonds established in elementary school are broken in middle school. Thus, as the context changes the expectations about teacher–student relationships change.

The previous discussion outlines the value of developing positive teacher–student relationships. However, this discussion provides little guidance on ways to obtain these goals. We believe it is helpful to examine the ways that the student–teacher relationship develops in the classroom context. Once we outline these developmental processes we will turn our attention to the ways that teachers can use friendship as a context for promoting care in the classroom.

Reflection

♦ **Think about your favorite teacher. How did this person communicate?**
♦ **What can a teacher do to facilitate positive relationships with students?**
♦ **How is learning affected by the teacher–student relationship?**

Relationship Development

The student–teacher relationship evolves and changes over the school year. As the school year unfolds, teachers and students share information and experiences and as their understanding of each other increases, the way in which they communicate changes. Two prominent theories that have been used to describe this relationship change are Social Penetration Theory (Altman & Taylor, 1973) and Social Intercourse Theory (Knapp, 1978). Both theories are predicated on a belief that relationships move from superficial to deeper levels. Even though the bulk of research testing these theories has been applied to intimate interpersonal relationships, they offer important insight into how teacher–student relationships evolve over time.

Managing two aspects of communication, breadth and depth, are central to relationship development (Altman & Taylor, 1973; Knapp, 1978). Breadth refers to the number of different topical areas that are available during communication. As teachers get to know students, they learn about their family situations, their extracurricular interests, their academic strengths and weaknesses. Depth refers to how much information a person has about a particular topic. A teacher may learn that a student's mother, who is recently divorced, is starting to date someone that the child does not like. When the child reveals how he or she feels about this circumstance, the dialogue involves more depth. It is not uncommon for teachers to learn a great deal from a student when they discuss the reasons why homework was not turned in on time, why a student seems lethargic, or why a student misbehaves. Over time, the number of topics and opportunity to explore them increase.

Communication changes in other ways over time. Knapp and Vangelisti (2000) stated that communication moves along eight primary dimensions. Communication in developing relationships becomes more:

1   *Broad*—more topics are discussed in more depth.
2   *Unique*—people are viewed as unique individuals rather than in stereotyped roles.
3   *Efficient*—accuracy, speed, and efficiency of communication increase as a relationship develops.
4   *Flexible*—the number of different ways an idea or feeling can be communicated verbally—and nonverbally.
5   *Smooth*—the ability to predict the other's behavior increases so that there is "greater synchrony in interaction.
6   *Personal*—people reveal more about themselves, such as fears, feelings, likes, and dislikes.
7   *Spontaneous*—informality and comfort increase and we feel less hesitant about how to react, what topics to discuss, and how much can be said about a topic.
8   *Overt*—praise and criticism are less inhibited as a relationship grows.

According to Knapp and Vangelisti (2000), as relationships start to unravel or deteriorate, communication becomes narrow, stylized, difficult, rigid, awkward, public, hesitant, and judgments are suspended. Teachers frequently, have difficulty with one or more students. Communication in this stage may be strained, difficult, and awkward. Sometimes, teachers search for ways to reconnect and even start over, but they find that such attempts are difficult if not impossible. Because the relational reservoir is not as deep in teacher–student relationships, damage or hurt can have severe consequences.

Knapp (1978) explicated several stages that mark the development of intimate relationships. In his theory, relationships go through a linear progression of stages. His theory can be extended to the student–teacher relationships as well. The stages we believe are applicable to teacher–student interactions are initiating, experimenting, intensifying, differentiating, and dissolution. It is also important to note that teachers and students go through the stages at different rates. Some relationships develop rapidly while others trudge along and seem locked in one place.

Initiating

The first relationship stage we enter is initiating. As a popular television ad states "we don't get a second chance at a first impression." The moment students walk into the classroom, teachers start to form impressions that in many cases are difficult to change. In turn, students develop expectations based on limited data. They respond to the teacher's nonverbal behavior (does he or she smile and seem approachable and enthusiastic?) and they respond to the way a teacher explains the academic goals for the semester or year (will it be hard or easy?) and they respond to the organization of the classroom (does it feel inviting?).

Friedrich and Cooper (1999) discussed the importance of the first day of class and provide strategies for managing it. They argued that early meetings play an important role in initiating students to the knowledge and skills they need to successfully perform the role of student in a particular context. Students also obtain a great deal of information about the teacher's affective orientation to the class. A smiling and expressive teacher is perceived to be friendly and a frowning neutral teacher is considered mean or grumpy. These first impressions play an important role in the trajectories of teacher student relationships.

Experimenting

A second stage of development is experimenting. During this stage teachers and students try to identify common ground and locate points of difference. In the experimenting stage, teachers start to obtain information about the student that might influence a teaching strategy. For example, teachers may ask students about their favorite hobbies, activities, and family situations. These conversations sometimes occur during class discussion, in a student conference or, during recess. The information obtained in these exchanges provides data that is used to form impressions about students and helps shape subsequent communication behavior.

Similarly, students *experiment* with teachers. Students try to sort out teacher likes and dislikes, their real rather than professed boundaries (if you give a real good excuse, he will let you turn in late work), and their grading biases. In Chapter 3 we discussed ways that teachers can gain and use cultural knowledge. Obtaining this information and testing its use relates to the experimenting stage of development. In many ways, elements of experimenting exist throughout the academic year as students and teachers explore ways to manage their relationships.

Intensifying

As students and teachers obtain more depth and breadth in their inter-actions, their relationship moves to an intensifying stage. This label is most suited for romantic partners, but the communication reflected in this stage is illustrative of teacher–student interactions as well. During this stage participants make communication choices based on psycho-logical rather than socio-logical information. That is, the communicators make choices based on the individual rather than stereotypic roles. It is in this stage that teachers start to communicate authentic care for the students and the circumstances that enhance and constrain learning.

According to Knapp (1978), there are several features of the intensify-ing stage. In romantic relationships, forms of address become more infor-mal, use of first personal plural becomes more common, private jargon may be used, verbal shortcuts built on background information may be used, and more direct expressions of commitment may be employed.

Differentiating

Over time, as participants learn more about each other, they may deter-mine that they really don't care for the other person very much. Even though it is socially inappropriate to admit it, the fact remains that teachers sometimes dislike some of their students and students may come to dislike their teachers. In this stage participants try to distance themselves physically and emotionally. The most obvious indicator of differentiating is conflict. Teachers will sometimes say "it's like pulling teeth to get her to work," or "he argues about every assignment I give." Students may argue that they do not do well in class because they have a personality conflict with the teacher. Every teacher has a story about a difficult student and every student has had a teacher they felt was Cruella Daville. Unfortunately, this stage is particularly prob-lematic for learning. The negative affect accompanying this stage influ-ences motivation and the willingness to learn. Students avoid the teacher and the teacher avoids the student and as a consequence, learn-ing is compromised.

Deterioration and Dissolution

The final stage is dissolution. In this stage the formal teacher–student relationship is severed. There are several ways that this occurs. In some cases, a student–teacher relationship becomes so problematic that the student is removed from the class. Another example is when a student is moved because he or she has special learning needs that the teacher is not prepared to address or accommodate. A third way is through matriculation. Each year a class is ushered to the next grade. Even for students who are not passed, it is unlikely that they will have the same teacher.

Even though the formal teacher–student relationship can be dissolved (the teacher no longer has the student in class), the interpersonal relationship does not evaporate. Rather, the teacher–student relationship is redefined. Teachers and students cannot erase the history they shared and the way they affected each other. Relationships between teachers and students never really stop but are transformed or redefined. As students move to the next level or transfer to another school, they take a part of that teacher with them. Many students return to their teachers many years later to praise their efforts. When these relationships rekindle, they do not start from scratch but are based on the history and events that were shared. We prefer to say, then, that a teacher–student relationship is never really terminated but is redefined.

The developmental perspective advanced by Knapp helps teachers understand some of the ways their relationships with students develop and change over time. Teacher–student relationships may not follow the linear progression explicated by Knapp (1978), however, the communication that characterizes these stages does appear in teacher–student relationships. Teachers worry about the ways to start the school year positively (initiating), try different teaching strategies (experimenting), delight when feel a special connection with a student (intensifying), and obsess when they have conflicts that seem to have no end (differentiating). Knapp's perspective provides one view of the developmental features of the teacher–student relationship, other theorists have looked at this relationship from different perspectives.

Reflection

♦ Think about a teacher you liked. Why did you like this teacher?
♦ How would you describe the different stages in this relationship?

Relational Dialectics

Relational Dialectics, initially advanced by Leslie Baxter and her colleagues (e.g. Baxter, 1987, 1988, 1990, 1992, 1993; Dindia & Baxter,

1987; Rawlins, 1992, 2000), proposed that in every relationship there are contradictory tensions and the way individuals deal with these tensions influences they way in which it evolves. The key features of Dialectical Theory are *Contradiction* and *Process*. Contradiction is conflict between two opposing forces such as the desire for closeness and the desire for distance. People in long-term relationships know about the need to "have space" and the need to be close and connected. The need for space finds its meaning through its opposite, the need for connection.

The second feature of Dialectical Theory is Process. Like our theory of communication, relationships are fluid and always in a state of adjustment. Participants continually struggle and work through tensions through communication and other symbolic activities.

Researchers have identified three relational dialectics: *integration/separation*, *stability/change*, and *expression/privacy*. The *integration/separation* dialectic involves the tension between wanting to integrate with other persons and wanting to be separate from them. The *stability/change* dialectic involves the tensions between wanting predictability and wanting novelty or stimulation. The final dialectic involves the desire to be *open/expressive* on one hand and *private* and reserved on the other.

William Rawlins (2000) applied the Theory of Relational Dialectics to the instructional context. Specifically he used a dialectic perspective to explore teaching as a mode of friendship. According to Rawlins (2000), friendship consists of affection, equality, and mutuality.

Affection means caring about and for others. Rawlins stated: "We can care deeply and significantly about students without desiring an exclusive, intimate connection with them, either as a close friendship that might imply unwarranted favoritism, or as a sexual relationship that involves exploitation and abuse of power differences" (p. 6). Rawlins contended that in the instructional context, affection is concerned with the classical tradition of *philia*, a posture concerned with good will and helping the other prosper. With good will come respect and a concern for the student to do well.

Equality is the second facet of friendship and is more problematic for the teacher–student relationship. Teachers are considered authorities on most issues that touch classroom life. Theoretically they have more knowledge of content and are in positions of power. For Rawlins, however, it is not necessary to exercise these power differences. Rather, teaching as friendship attempts to minimize status differences and create an atmosphere where all can learn. Teachers can learn a great deal when they open themselves to the world of students.

The final feature of friendship is mutuality. This aspect of friendship follows from the previous ones. According to Rawlins, learning is promoted when teachers and students "create an enterprise of co-learning." Mutuality occurs when teachers and students recognize their interdependency in the pursuit of academic goals. For example, when a teacher acknowledges and thanks a student for proposing a new way of solving a math problem, he or she is demonstrating in co-learning.

Rawlins outlined four dialectical tensions that characterize interaction between teachers and students in the context of educational friendship. The first is the dialectics of freedom to be independent and the freedom to be dependent. The degree to which educators direct and the degree to which students are allowed to discover have been historical issues. Individuals typically have freedom to choose friendship but such volition is constrained in the educational context. Teaching as friendship entails cultivating a student's independence in thought and action while being available to provide expertise and guidance when necessary.

Rawlins acknowledged that some students should not be pushed into independence when they are not ready for it. The degree of independence that is appropriate depends on the grade level and the amount of competence the student has to complete the task. However, the sense of independence and accountability also fosters attitudes of accountability and ownership—important features of academic success.

The second dialectic involves affection and instrumentality. Most teachers will admit they want their students to like them but this is not the only goal that teachers should seek. Rawlins cautioned teachers not to be too hard on students they like to guard against the perception of favoritism, and not to be too easy on them because they feel they deserve the benefit of the doubt. Similarly, teachers should not be too hard on students with whom they have not established good will. Teachers ought not give themselves permission to dislike students without giving students permission to dislike teachers. The key here is that the way in which teachers manage this dialectic influences how safe students feel to take risks and develop new competencies.

The third dialectic is concerned with judgment and acceptance. Teachers must balance feedback about how they feel about a student as a person and how the student has completed an instructional task. This is perhaps one of the most difficult dialectic tensions to manage. Students may misread the fun expressive teacher as one who does not have high academic standards and is overly flexible on requirements. Teachers who have the best interests of the student have high expectations but are flexible in how they are obtained.

The fourth dialectic is concerned with expressiveness and protectiveness. On the one hand, being open and expressive in pursuing knowledge is important but so is discretion and respect. One university professor loved to put students on the spot in seminars. He played a game called "shooting fish in a barrel." He required students to give reports on a research article. After the report, the professor would literally "shoot" question after question at the student with the goal of showing the class that the student did not understand the article, thus requiring the sage professor to explain it. The professor was verbally aggressive as he challenged students to respond to his questions. This strategy did little to foster interest in the topic but much in creating anxiety and anger. A thoughtful teacher helps create trust and comfort so that students do not feel overly vulnerable about what they do not know but not too smug in what they do.

Relational dialectics provides a useful perspective for understanding the daily strains of interpersonal relationships. Rawlins' notion of teaching as a mode of friendship is particularly interesting. Effective teachers manage relationships that promote the best interests of the students they teach. These teachers recognize that the student–teacher relationship establishes a context that facilitates learning and motivation. The next section of this chapter reviews five major constructs that positively influence the student–teacher relationship: teacher immediacy, affinity seeking, self-disclosure, humor, and credibility, and impact the development of a positive teacher–student relationship.

Teacher Immediacy

Teacher immediacy was introduced in Chapter 2 and has a profound effect on the teacher–student relationship. Immediacy consists of the verbal and nonverbal behaviors that reduce psychological distance. Smiling, eye contact, touch, a relaxed body orientation, and close physical proximity are examples of nonverbal immediacy behaviors. Addressing students by name, using appropriate humor, using personal examples and referring to the class as "my class" are examples of verbal immediacy behaviors. While the thrust of research on teacher immediacy has attempted to assess its role in motivation and learning, we agree with Hess and Smythe (2001) who argued that its function is primarily relational.

One consistent finding is that teacher immediacy promotes affective learning, the feelings students have about the instructor and course content. Nonverbal immediacy appears to play a significant role in the feelings the student have about the teacher and course. Richmond (2002), a leading scholar on teacher immediacy, argued that:

> The primary function of teachers' nonverbal behavior in the classroom is to improve affect or liking for the subject matter, teacher, and class, and to increase the desire to learn more about the subject matter. One step toward this is the development of a positive affective relationship between the student and the teacher. When the teacher improves affect through effective nonverbal behavior, then the student is likely to listen more, learn more, and have a more positive attitude about the school.
>
> (p. 70)

The research conducted on immediacy shows that it is positively associated with a number of affective factors that unfold in the classroom. Students who view a teacher as approachable may feel more comfortable in the learning situation and may be more inclined to listen to instructional material and may be more comfortable in seeking clarification on information they do not understand. Frymier and Houser (2000) found that immediacy was positively correlated with two important communication skills: referential skill and ego support. Referential skill is concerned with explaining content and ego support is how teachers meet student needs. The way in which a teacher explains instructional material is mediated by immediacy. This finding is consistent with research by Powell and Harville (1990) who found that immediacy was related to teacher clarity, especially for students from Latino and Asian backgrounds. Immediacy may help teachers give form to important instructional contexts. Also, the immediate teacher may also be more psychologically connected to students. During instructional episodes immediate teachers may consistently assess student feedback and adjust instructional messages to meet their needs.

Research by Baringer and McCroskey (2000) investigated the effects of student immediacy on teachers. The authors reasoned that the nonverbal behavior of students is one way that students indicate that they are accurately receiving information and are positively disposed to it. The authors examined the effects of student immediacy and found that teachers are more positively disposed to students who engage in immediacy behaviors and are more motivated to teach them.

It is important to emphasize that immediacy involves implicit codes. Therefore, maximum effects will occur when teachers interpret the immediacy cues in the same way. Difficulty will arise when implicit codes are misinterpreted, not acknowledged or inconsistent. An immediate teacher may be perceived as easy or less rigorous. Students may believe that a teacher they like will accept late work or give them the benefit of the doubt. Other difficulties can arise when the immediate teacher fails a student or is critical on an assignment. In addition, because most of the studies are correlational, it is difficult to sort out the causal direction of the effects. Do the positive effects start with the student, the teacher or some combination of both? Our belief is that teachers who exhibit immediacy behaviors will foster positive relationships and these in turn will promote positive attitudes about learning.

Affinity Seeking

As the above research suggests, liking is an important part of a positive relationship. Researchers have examined the strategies teachers use to get students to like them. Bell and Daly (1984) developed a typology of the strategies individuals use to generate liking that have been extended to the classroom context. Richmond (1990), for example, identified five affinity-seeking strategies that influence motivation and affective and cognitive learning (facilitate enjoyment, assume control, nonverbal immediacy, optimism, and self-concept definition). For the complete list of affinity seeking strategies, see Table 6.1.

Frymier and Thompson (1992) investigated the relationship between affinity seeking and credibility and found that nonverbal immediacy was significantly related to perceptions of teacher character. This dimension of credibility is concerned with how much a person is liked, respected, and admired. Immediacy appears to increase the positive regard for the teacher, which in turn may influence student attitudes about learning.

Frymier (1994) built on the previous research and proposed a causal model of affinity seeking, liking, and learning. A causal model charts the direction and strength of a set of variables. Frymier contended that affinity seeking strategies increases liking, which in turn impacts motivation and learning. Frymier found that the use of affinity seeking had a significant effect on the degree to which students liked their teachers. The strategies most predictive of liking were *assume equality* (teacher does not appear superior), *dynamism* (teacher is active and enthusiastic), and *facilitate enjoyment* (teacher develops a classroom environment that is enjoyable). Six other strategies were associated with liking and motivation: *comfortable self* (the teacher is at ease and relaxed), *concede control* (the teacher allows students to control the relationship), *conversational rule-keeping* (teacher is polite and follows rules for appropriate conversation), *elicit other's disclosure* (teacher inquires about student's interests), *nonverbal immediacy* (teacher signals liking and interest), and *optimism* (teacher presents a positive outlook). Frymier argued that teachers' improved interpersonal relationships help motivate students to work on instructional tasks.

Wanzer (1998) explored the strategies students use to engender liking from an instructor. She also examined how instructors respond to the strategies students use. Students were asked to identify five examples of the ways they get a teacher to like them. Some 66% of the responses fell into five categories: conversational rule keeping (19%), nonverbal immediacy (13%), elicit disclosure (13%) requirements (11%) and self-inclusion (10%).

Teacher perceptions of student strategies fell into five categories, accounting for 53% of the total responses. Teachers viewed students using self-inclusion (16%), conversational rule keeping (14%), achievement (8%), elicits other's self-disclosures (8%), and self-concept confirmation (7.5%).

While the data on teacher immediacy and affinity seeking is overwhelmingly positive, there are some additional issues to consider. The bulk of the research has been conducted on young adults in university or

Table 6.1 Affinity-Seeking Strategies

1	Altruism: The affinity-seeker strives to be of assistance to the target in whatever she or he is currently doing.
2	Assume Control: The affinity-seeker presents himself or herself as a person who has control over what ever is going on.
3	Assume Equality. The affinity seeker strikes a posture of social equality with the target.
4	Comfortable Self. The affinity seeker ignores annoying environmental distractions, seeking to convey a "nothing bothers me" impression.
5	Concede Control. The affinity seeker allows the target to assume control over relational activities.
6	Conversational Rule-Keeping. The affinity seeker adheres closely to cultural rules for polite, cooperative interaction with the target.
7	Dynamism. The affinity-seeker presents herself or himself as an active, enthusiastic person.
8	Elicit Other's Disclosures. The affinity-seeker encourages the target to talk by reinforcing the target's conversational contributions.
9	Facilitate Enjoyment. The affinity-seeker tries to maximize the positiveness of relational encounters with the target.
10	Inclusion of Other. The affinity-seeker enthusiastically participates in an activity the target is known to enjoy.
11	Influence Perceptions of Closeness. The affinity-seeker engages in behaviors which cause the target to perceive the relationship as closer than it actually has been.
12	Listening. The affinity-seeker listens actively and attentively to the target.
13	Nonverbal immediacy. The affinity-seeker signals interest in the target through various nonverbal cues.
14	Openness. The affinity-seeker discloses personal information to the target.
15	Optimism. The affinity-seeker presents himself or herself to the target as a positive person.
16	Personal Autonomy. The affinity-seeker presents herself or himself to the target as an independent free thinking person.
17	Physical Attractiveness. The affinity-seeker tries to look and dress as attractively as possible in the presence of the target.
18	Present Interesting Self. The affinity-seeker presents herself or himself to the target as someone who would be interesting to know.
19	Reward Association. The affinity-seeker presents himself or herself in such a way that the target perceives the affinity-seeker can reward the target for associating with him or her.
20	Self-Concept Confirmation. The affinity-seeker demonstrates respect for the target and helps the target to "feel good" about himself or herself.
21	Self-Inclusion. The affinity-seeker arranges the environment so as to come into frequent contact with the target.
22	Sensitivity. The affinity-seeker acts in a warm, empathic manner toward the target.
23	Similarity. The affinity-seeker seeks to convince the target that the two of them share many similar tastes and attitudes.
24	Supportiveness. The affinity-seeker supports the target in the latter's social encounters.
25	Trustworthiness. The affinity-seeker consistently fulfills commitments made to the target.

college settings. The studies have been based on self-report data. Few observational or experimental studies have been conducted. Status differences and relationship expectations are not the same at this level as they are in elementary, middle, and high school. While we have reason to believe that immediacy and affinity seeking are also important to younger students, their role in learning and attitudes about instruction may be different from those in older audiences.

Also, the research has not explicated all the consequences of being perceived as approachable. In some cases, a student may perceive that an approachable teacher will accept an excuse for not turning in work on time. An approachable teacher might be expected to give students the benefit of the doubt or not grade as rigorously. Uncertainty is created when the interpersonal behavior does not seem to match the instructional behavior.

Self-Disclosure

One of the processes that is central to management of interpersonal relationships is self-disclosure. Cooper and Simmonds (1999) argued that self-disclosure is necessary for effective teacher–student interactions. Self-disclosure occurs when someone reveals something of themselves the other person would not know unless otherwise disclosed. Through direct comments, stories, and illustrations, teachers reveal themselves to students. These revelations, in turn, influence relationships with students, which influence how students feel about the content. Several investigators have explored the effects of self-disclosure in the instructional context. Nussbaum and Scott (1979) were among the first to investigate the role of self-disclosure in instructional relationships and found that the perception of honesty in disclosure had the most positive effect. Downs, Javidi, and Nussbaum (1988) found that award-winning teachers tended to use moderate amounts of self-disclosure. Further, the disclosures of these teachers were relevant to course content or utilized for the purpose of clarifying course material. When teachers overdisclose or share information that is unrelated to the course, then self-disclosure may have more negative consequences. At one university, students frequently complained about one of the professors who spent an inordinate amount of time discussing the difficulties in her personal life. While the students did not dislike the professor, they did feel that that the class was becoming a waste of time.

Sorensen (1989) investigated how the management of self-disclosure differentiated good and poor teachers. She found that good teachers were more likely to engage in disclosive statements reflecting a concern for students. Evaluative disclosures or ones reflecting a negative outlook were reflective of poor teachers. These types of messages were also related to affective learning. Positive disclosures positively impacted affective learning while negative ones did not. Culture plays a significant role in self-disclosure. Individuals from individualistic cultures are the most likely candidates for self-disclosure because explicitness and revelation are part of their cultural experience. Students from Euro-American backgrounds will probably disclose the most in a class. Students from high-context cultures are less likely to engage in self-disclosure. Native Americans, Asians, and Latinos are less likely to engage in self-disclosure or feel that it is appropriate. Effective use of self-disclosure requires that teachers be attentive to students. When teachers use self-disclosive statements to help illustrate a concept or reveal a struggle or difficulty learning a concept, then the disclosure is likely to have positive effects. Disclosures about personal life issues are more problematic and risky.

During class discussions and in individual meetings or conferences, teachers need to be attentive to the role of culture. Students from high-context cultures may be less willing to volunteer information or reciprocate when the teacher discloses. One of the least effective strategies that a teacher can use is to demand that students reveal something they are uncomfortable sharing.

Humor

In our judgment, a sense of humor is a powerful way to promote positive relationships in the classroom. Whether students are in kindergarten or college, they respond positively to teachers who can make them laugh as well as laugh at themselves. Humor also appears to be a cross-cultural phenomenon. Kluver (1990) found that a sense of humor was the most frequently ranked characteristic of effective teachers in China. Through humor, important connections both affectively and cognitively are made.

Meyer (2000) contended that humor has four major functions. The first two serve to create connections and the second serve to differentiate and create distance. The first connecting function is identification. Humor can be used to link speakers with their audiences which helps create group cohesiveness. For example, when teachers make fun at themselves, they lower their personal status while raising the status of the students. Humor that reduces tension and reveals that the teacher is also human increases the connection between teacher and student.

A second connecting function is clarification. Humor that is used to encapsulate a view or idea may result in more clarity. Meyer notes that ideas referenced in memorable stories or phrases may lead to greater recall. Humorous stories, because they are frequently presented incongruously or unexpectedly, make the receiver do a bit more cognitive work which influences recall of information.

A third function of humor, according to Mayer, is enforcement. Humor can be used to level criticisms while maintaining some degree of identification with the audience. Teachers frequently use this type of humor to reinforce class rules and expectations for normative behaviors. Students may ask a teacher to repeat instructions to a task because they were talking to a neighbor and not paying attention. A teacher may use any number of humorous statements to comment on the students' lack of attention.

The final function that Meyer discussed is differentiation. People use humor to contrast themselves with the views of others. Humor of this kind is frequently revealed in political humor. In the classroom, humor of this type may come in the form of sarcasm, or teasing. One professor with a class full of athletes once claimed the phrase "scholar athlete" was an oxymoron. She asked one member of the class if he was a student or an athlete because he did not have the skills to be both. Needless to say, her "humor" did little to connect the student with the teacher or the class. When humor is used effectively, positive outcomes can be achieved.

Pollack and Freda (1997) outline six positive effects of teacher humor in the middle school context. Their recommendations apply to a broad range of instructional settings. The first is *building rapport*. Teachers who can laugh at themselves and with students shape a climate where students are more willing to work together on instructional tasks. Students like teachers who can laugh. The second is *empowering* learners. Humor helps level status differences and create a culture of learners. Teachers frequently make mistakes and the degree to which these "errors' are accepted with humor models appropriate behavior for students. Teachers who want to passionately hold on to the mantle of authority do not do much to create positive learning environments. The third is *thinking creatively*. Creative thinking requires individuals to see things from different perspectives. Humor is a way to sort through the incongruous or incompatible which in turn promotes problem solving. The fourth is *creating interest*. Humor serves to increase arousal and attention. Students tend to remember content and lessons that are presented in an exciting and humorous way. The fifth is *enhancing self-esteem*. Teachers can help students laugh at themselves, discover realistic expectations, and promote a willingness to work through difficult situations. Teachers with no sense of humor are perceived to be rigid and students perceive they have little room to make mistakes. The final feature is *emphasizing socialization*. A good sense of humor can help teachers turn a tense situation into a challenging intriguing one. Humor helps students discover appropriate models of behavior and helps establish a sense of "intellectual humility." Humor can do much to engender the joy of learning.

Several attempts have been made to categorize teacher humor. (Bryant, Comisky, & Zillmannn, 1979; Gorham & Christophel, 1990; Nussbaum, Comadena, & Holladay, 1985). Neuliep (1991), for example, developed a taxonomy of high school teachers, humor. He asked high school teachers to assess their humor using the taxonomy developed by Gorham and Christophel (1990). The teachers were also asked to indicate how frequently they used humor and their reasons for using humor. Finally, teachers were asked to describe their last attempt at humor.

Based on the responses, Neulip developed a 20-item taxonomy of humor consisting of five major sections: (1) teacher-targeted humor; (2) student-targeted humor; (3) untargeted humor; (4) external source humor; and (5) nonverbal humor.

1   *Teacher-targeted humor.* The teacher is the object of humor. Three types of teacher-targeted humor emerged. One type involves the teacher self-disclosing personal information that may be related to the course content, not related to the course content, or something of an embarrassing nature. The second form of teacher-targeted humor involves role-playing by the teacher. A teacher imitating a public figure is an example of this type of humor. The final type of teacher target humor involves the use of self-deprecating humor where the teacher pokes fun at himself or herself.

2   *Student-targeted humor.* The student is the target of this type of humor. Four types of student-targeted humor emerged. The first involves a teacher making fun of a student mistake. A second involves teasing in non-hostile or friendly fashion. The third type of student-targeted humor involves the teacher insulting the student in a non-hostile manner. The final type of humor involves student role-playing.

3   *Untargeted humor.* The third type of humor is untargeted. The focus of the humor is not on a teacher or student but an issue or topic. Three types of untargeted humor were identified. One involves an awkward comparison or incongruity. For example, one teacher likened the sword fight between Tybalt and Romeo to a WWF wrestling match. The teacher blended Shakespearean language with wrestling jargon to make his point. The second type of untargeted humor is when a teacher tells a joke. The joke may or may not be related to the topic being studied. A third type of untargeted humor entails a play on words or puns. The final type of untargeted humor was labeled tongue in cheek or facetious humor. This type of humor involves witty remarks by the teacher that are not directed at the student or the teacher.

4   *External source humor.* External source humor requires the teacher to draw upon a source other than the teacher. One type of external humor is to relate some historical event to something the students find humorous. For example, numerous comedians made fun of the ballot counting process during the 2000 Presidential Campaign. A second type of external source humor is when the teacher utilizes

cartoons, photos, or editorials that have humorous intent. Calvin and Hobbs is a popular comic strip that reveals many of life's difficulties and dilemmas. In the final type of external source humor, the teacher demonstrates some natural phenomena in a way that the class finds amusing. Neulip uses the example of a teacher releasing a balloon to demonstrate high versus low pressure.

5   *Nonverbal humor.* Nonverbal humor entails affect displays and kinesic humor. Using funny face or other type of gesture to accentuate a point or using your body to mock or illustrate something are illustrative of this type of humor.

Civikly (1992b) provided five guidelines for the use and assessment of teacher humor (p. 137):

1   *Review and assess how humor has been used in the class.* Placement of a tape recorder in an unobtrusive location while teaching is simple and review of the tape can provide excellent feedback.
2   *Analyze and assess the classroom atmosphere.* Each class develops norms and relational bases distinctive to itself.
3   *Identify humor styles comfortable for you.* There is a wide range of choices from which to select: stories and anecdotes, puns, riddles, limericks, cartoons and visuals, understatement and exaggeration, impersonation, mime, teasing, satire, witticisms, jokes on oneself, and political humor.
4   *Work on "planned spontaneity" of instructional humor.* This involves doing some preparation of examples and incidents that the students see as relevant and humorous and then presenting these in a "spontaneous" manner.
5   *Evaluate the humor developed and used.* Watch for student reactions and ask for feedback regarding their interest, attentions, liking, and comprehension of the material presented. Use this feedback to direct use of humor in class and refine any rough edges that may be identified.

The research indicates that there are numerous advantages to using humor in the classroom. While we do not advocate that teachers attempt to be stand-up comedians, we do believe that humor should be integrated into teaching. Appropriate humor is the key however. Humor for humor's sake, tasteless and off-color jokes, hostile teasing, and mocking have no place in the classroom. Teachers also need to be aware of the cultural factors influencing humor. Humor is inextricably defined by context ("I guess you had to be there phenomena") and students from some cultures may not have the background information necessary to understand the joke. To test this notion, ask a student from a culture different from yours to tell a story or joke from his or her native orientation. Then ask the student to explain why the example is humorous. This exercise should illustrate how context influences humor.

Teacher Credibility

The last concept we believe is important to the teacher–student relationship is credibility. We typically apply the concept of credibility to political or legal contexts, yet the principles have a great deal of application to instructional settings. Two primary dimensions are related to teacher credibility: competence and character. Competence refers to content knowledge that the teacher possesses. Character refers to the trustworthiness of the person.

The interplay of competence and character appears to be important in the classroom as well. At lower grades, many students are most concerned about the social characteristics of the teacher. One second grader indicated that she wanted to be placed in Ms. West's class because she is nice. Even in college, students seek instructors who have positive personal characteristics. Content competence is seldom the only factor influencing the choice to enroll in a particular class. At the same time, students form judgments about how well teachers present instructional information, clarify instructional goals, and criticize student work. These judgments also influence the perception of teacher credibility.

Frymier and Thompson (1992) investigated the relationship between affinity-seeking strategies and credibility and found that affinity seeking was positively related to the character dimension of credibility and moderately related to the competence dimension. The authors acknowledged that it is possible to view someone as competent but not likeable. Teaching effectiveness is enhanced when a teacher is judged highly on both dimensions. Frymier and Thompson identified 12 strategies that relate to both character and competence. The strategies were:

1 *Listening*—paying close attention to what the student says and querying to ascertain if the student's intended meaning is the interpreted meaning.
2 *Facilitate enjoyment*—developing a classroom environment that is enjoyable, an environment in which learning is both interesting and entertaining.
3 *Dynamism*—physically indicating to students that one is dynamic, active, and enthusiastic via physical and vocal animation.
4 *Elicit other's disclosure*—inquiring about student's interests and opinions and providing positive reinforcement for responses.
5 *Optimism*—presenting a positive outlook and one's self as someone who is pleasant to be around, someone who will not be self-critical or critical of others.

6 *Sensitivity*—communicating empathy, sympathy, and a "I care about you as a person and what you think about" attitude.
7 *Conversational rule-keeping*—following the cultural norms for socializing, being polite.
8 *Demonstrating interest in what the student says.*
9 *Comfortable self*—displaying a confidence in the setting, oneself, the students, and presenting self as a relaxed, contented individual.
10 *Nonverbal immediacy*—smiling, making frequent eye contact with students, exhibiting forward leans and other nonverbal cues indicating interest.
11 *Altruism*—attempting to be of assistance to the student by doing things for her or him, giving advice.
12 *Present interesting self*—highlighting of past accomplishments, positive qualities, and demonstrating one's knowledge; and trustworthiness—letting the student know that as a teacher he or she is responsible, reliable, fair, honest, sincere, consistent in beliefs, and behaviors, and will fulfill promises.

Collectively these behaviors appear to shape a global judgment that a teacher is both knowledgeable and caring.

Teven and Hanson (2004) conducted two studies that were designed to assess the effects of teacher caring, and teacher immediacy on teacher credibility. Subjects were asked to respond to four hypothetical scenarios that manipulated immediacy and caring: (1) high immediacy/high verbal caring; (2) low immediacy/high verbal caring; (3) low immediacy/low verbal caring; and (4) high immediacy/low verbal caring. They found that credibility was positively related to teacher immediacy. The authors argued that the findings strongly indicate that teachers who display caring and immediacy will be perceived as more competent and trustworthy.

Summary

The classroom is a context full of interpersonal challenges. Effective teachers need to understand that learning goals are embedded in relational dynamics. The research suggests that the path to learning is less rocky and contains fewer hairpin turns when there is a positive relational foundation. It is important to stress that at risk students appear to gain the most from positive relationships with their teachers. We want teachers to reflect on the role of the teacher–student relationship and the approaches they take to build and manage them. We also want teachers to think about the way in which diversity influences their approach to students. Are teachers more willing to display immediacy to students who are similar to them in ethnicity and socio-economic circumstances? The data on impact of positive teacher student relationships are clear. By studying the stages and dialectical processes involved in relationship development and by utilizing the strategies that enhance relationships, teachers will be in a better place to accomplish instructional goals and objectives.

Learning Activities

- Analyze the dialectical tensions in a current teacher–student relationship. Which tension do you find most difficult to manage? What strategies do you use to manage the various tensions?
- Write a five-page position paper on Rawlins' perspective on Teaching as a Mode of Friendship. Explain the pros and cons of this framework.
- Think about a teacher that you currently have. Describe this teacher's verbal and nonverbal immediacy. How does this particular behavior serve the academic goals of the teacher?
- Which types of teacher humor promote positive teacher–student relationships?
- Identify three affinity-seeking strategies you typically use. Explain how you would use these strategies to build positive teacher–student relationships.

Resources

- Forming positive student–teacher relationships
  www.cedu.niu.edu/~shumow/itt/StudentTchrRelationships.pdf
- Tips for developing a positive teacher–student relationship
  www.jamaica-gleaner.com/gleaner/20090518/news/news10.html
- Send in the clowns
  www.reacheverychild.com/feature/humor.html
- A funny thing happened …
  www.teachersfirst.com/humor.shtml

Chapter 7

Building a Community of Learners in Diverse Classrooms

Mr. Kiyuna is a first-year science teacher at Mark Twain Middle School. He enters his classroom on the first day of the new semester to find some students slumped in their chairs, staring into space. Others are sitting on top of the desks, chatting with friends. Mr. Kiyuna knows he has a challenge ahead as many of his students have serious academic and social problems. Chung has a learning disability in reading. He is reading on the third grade level and has a great deal of difficulty comprehending what he has read. Mateo has an attention deficit hyperactivity disorder (ADHD) and has difficulty with impulsiveness. Other teachers have told Mr. Kiyuna that Mateo is capable of disrupting his entire class. Irene is an adorable girl who has autistic-like tendencies and is nonverbal. Her intelligence is above average. As you read through this chapter, put yourself in Mr. Kiyuna's shoes and think about how you would go about addressing some of the special needs his students present.

Teachers can easily become discouraged when faced with the challenges we have described for Mr. Kiyuna. Unfortunately, traditional approaches such as punishment, failure, and exclusion have become preferred practices for dealing with students who do not fit the "norm." Students who have special needs often fail to experience a sense of belonging and academic achievement in school. The focus on exclusion has, in recent years, been replaced by research suggesting that creating classroom communities in which students' academic and social needs are met reduce the need for discipline. According to Elias et al. (1997):

> when schools attend systematically to students' social and emotional skills, the academic achievement of children increases, the incidence of problem behaviors decreases, and the quality of the relationships surrounding each child improves. And, students become the productive, responsible, contributing members of society that we all want.
>
> (pp. 1–2)

Addressing their needs may improve students' motivation, behavior, and learning. In this chapter we will define social and emotional learning and discuss the concepts of community and belongingness. Teacher support, peer mediated learning, classroom meetings, and service learning will be discussed as strategies for increasing students' sense of community.

Social and Emotional Learning

Over the years educators have been bombarded with programs designed to counter the negative effects of poverty, drugs and alcohol, violence, etc. Many of these programs have come and gone as fads do in education. Teachers have reported that these programs have many positive components but seem to be tried for only short periods of time, and are then put on the shelves in the materials center to collect dust.

Elias et al. (1997) contended that social and emotional development and the recognition that learning is relational form a missing piece in our educational system. They defined social and emotional competence as:

> the ability to understand, manage, and express the social and emotional aspects of one's life in ways that enable the successful management of life tasks such as learning, forming relationships, solving everyday problems, and adapting to the complex demands of growth and development.
>
> (p. 2)

Social and emotional competence includes such skills as self-awareness, understanding communication processes, working cooperatively, self-management, problem solving, and decision-making. In Chapter 2 we discussed the work of Gardner (1983) and Goleman (1995) who stressed that emotional and interpersonal competences play dramatic roles in the learning process.

In *A Celebration of Neurons*, Robert Sylwester (1995) also discussed the importance of emotion in student performance: "We know that emotion is very important to the educative process because it drives attention, which drives learning and memory" (p. 72). Social and emotional issues may very well be at the core of many problem behaviors exhibited by children today. A student who is hungry and traumatized over a recent violent episode at home may not be enthusiastic about a math assignment. Such a student, when asked by the teacher to "get busy," may get angry instead and throw books on the floor. Goleman (1995) referred to this type of response as the thinking brain being "hijacked." A teacher who has very little understanding of the ways emotions direct learning may respond to the student with harsh discipline. Unfortunately, many students and teachers experience "hijacking" as they attempt to deal with complex issues presented in today's classrooms. Much has been written about the importance of developing classroom communities to meet the academic, social and emotional needs of today's students.

Defining Community

The term community has many definitions in the literature. McMillan and Chavis (1986) identified four elements of community. The first element is membership (the feeling of belonging or personal relatedness). The second element is influence: members make a difference to a group and the group matters to its members. The third element is reinforcement, the feeling that members' needs will be met by the resources received through their membership in the group. The last element is emotional connection, which occurs when members share history, common places, time together, and similar experiences. Communication is central to building community. Kohn (1996) defined community as:

> a place in which students feel cared about and are encouraged to care about each other. They experience a sense of being valued and respected; the children matter to one another and to the teacher. They have come to think in the plural: they feel connected to each other; they are part of an "us." And as a result of all this, they feel safe in their classes, not only physically but emotionally.
>
> (pp. 101–102)

Dewey (1963) reflected on the social nature of schooling, observing that most children are "sociable." He stated:

> A genuine community life has its ground in this natural sociability. Community life does not organize itself in an enduring way purely spontaneously. It requires thought and planning. The educator is responsible for a knowledge of individuals and for a knowledge of subject-matter that will enable activities to be selected which lend themselves to social organization, an organization in which all individuals have an opportunity to contribute something, and in which the activities in which all participate are the chief carrier of control.
>
> (p. 56)

In this type of community, the teacher maintains the position of leader of group activities instead of boss or dictator.

Watkins (2005) outlines four defining characteristics of a classroom learning community: agency, belonging, cohesion, and diversity. Agency means that students make choices and take actions that promote individual and class goals. This requires that students recognize that personal and class goals are accomplished through interdependent actions. A second characteristic is belonging. A sense of community is promoted when students feel respected, liked, supported, and appreciated. The third characteristic is cohesion. As students increase their connection to the class, they move away from an "I" to a "we" orientation. The final characteristic consists of diversity. In a community, diversity is not viewed as threat but as strength. Watkins (2005) argues that the ability to embrace difference and positively view diversity leads to reduced stereotypes and more productive interdependent relationships among all members.

Watkins also explicates several processes that undergird community. First is acting together. Activities in a classroom community require coordinated action that leads to a desired outcome or goal. Second is bridging. This refers to the connections that are created through interpersonal communication. Through communication, identities and experiences are negotiated and redefined. Individual strengths and limitations are revealed and understood. Third is collaboration. Collaboration is closely related to bridging. Through collaboration, students seek to find a common ground or discover new ways of viewing academic and non-academic tasks. Fourth is dialogue. Students engage in dialogue when they exchange meaningful ideas and thoughts. Dialogue is also central to the creation of new meanings and understandings.

Watkins and other researchers also point out that learning communities also serve to support the basic social psychological needs of students. For example, several theorists (Baumeister & Leary, 1995; Deci & Ryan, 1985; Solomon, Battistich, Watson, Schaps, & Lewis, 2000) have suggested that an effective school environment supports a student's basic psychological needs to (a) belong to a social group whose members are mutually supportive and concerned; (b) have age-appropriate opportunities to be autonomous, self-directing, and influential; and (c) feel competent and effective in valued activities. Unfortunately, many students, especially those of color and those with learning and emotional and behavioral problems, continue to feel isolated and lonely as most schools focus on academics and pay little attention to students' affective or social-emotional needs.

Students' Need for Belonging

According to some researchers, belonging is one of several basic psychological needs that is critical to academic and social growth and development (Brendtro, Brokenleg, & Van Bockern, 1990; Deci, Vallerand, Pelletier, & Ryan, 1991; Ryan, 1995). Brendtro et al. (1990) in a true story of an orphan, described the tragedy of a young man who was abandoned, living in shelters, group homes, and treatment facilities. "Each time he was moved was like pulling a piece of used tape from the wall and trying to fasten it again," the authors explained. This young man, failing in school and desperate to belong, hanged himself suspended from two trees at his last foster home. This story typifies the loneliness and feelings of worthlessness that so many youth feel. Unfortunately, the needs for belonging and connectedness are often ignored in schools.

In an extensive review of literature, Osterman (2000) found many positive outcomes associated with feelings of belongingness. Children who experience a strong sense of belonging or relatedness have more positive attitudes toward school, teachers, and peers. They are more likely to enjoy school and be engaged in learning. Children who experience a lack of belonging, who feel rejected and alienated, are more likely to display problem behavior (aggression or withdrawal) in the classroom, show less interest in school, have lower achievement, and may drop out of school. Other research suggests that many psychological and behavioral problems, such as drug use, eating disorders, depression, dropouts, teen pregnancy, etc., exist as a result of "lack of belongingness" (Baumeister & Leary, 1995).

Much has been written about bullying, a serious problem involving one student or group of students harassing a victim verbally or physically without provocation (Barone, 1997; Batsche & Knoff, 1994; Horne & Socherman, 1996). There are serious and devastating consequences for both bullies and their victims. Bullies often have problems with the law in adulthood and are likely to continue the cycle of abuse with their spouses and children (Batsche & Knoff, 1994; Lochman, 1992). Victims of bullies often experience high levels of anxiety, have low self-esteem, and are without friends at school (Lane, 1989; Slee, 1994). Schools and teachers can make a difference by providing students with positive environments that encourage a sense of community and belonging.

A significant body of literature regarding students' sense of community comes from the Child Development Project in which researchers were assigned to help school districts become communities of support that address students' needs for belonging. A goal was to help students experience the classroom as a supportive and caring environment, in which students were involved in decision making and goal setting. This was the first comprehensive, longitudinal, school-based project that focused on prosocial education. In two separate longitudinal studies, researchers found a positive relationship between students' sense of community and intrinsic academic motivation (Battistich, Solomon, Kim, Watson, & Schaps, 1995; Solomon et al., 2000). These studies also found that belongingness is associated with positive feelings about school, class work, and teachers.

Battistich and Hom (1997) found that increases in school-level sense of community were associated with lowered levels of drug use and delinquent behavior among fifth- and sixth-grade students. Other studies reported positive effects of peer support or acceptance on students' academic behavior and interest in school (Ladd, 1990; Ryan, Stiller, & Lynch, 1994; Wentzel & Asher, 1995). The absence of peer support—feeling rejected or alienated—was linked to students' emotional distress, behavior problems in the classroom, disliking for school, lower achievement, and dropout.

In a review of literature regarding gender differences and belongingness, Wentzel and Caldwell (1997) found that boys are less likely to experience a sense of belongingness than girls. Girls experienced higher peer acceptance rates and had more friends, whereas boys experienced more negative relationships. Problem behavior may indeed be an indicator that students' needs for belongingess and relatedness are not being met.

Solomon, Watson, Battistich, Schaps, and Delucchi (1996) identified teacher interventions utilized in the Child Development Project to enhance students' sense of community. Several elements were found to contribute positively to students' sense of community: (1) cooperative learning; (2) developmental discipline; (3) use of literature to promote interpersonal understanding and discourse about prosocial values; (4) helping/prosocial activity; (5) school-wide and parent activities; and (6) promoting non-exclusionary attitudes. Developmental discipline involved building trusting relationships between teachers and students, providing students opportunities for autonomy, and teaching appropriate social skills. Students were actively involved in classroom governance. Classroom meetings and discussions encouraged students to take responsibility for their own behavior. Literature was used to help students gain an understanding not only of what they read but also the needs of others. Inclusion was promoted through various cooperative groupings and noncompetitive science fairs and service projects across grade levels. Most of the research cited suggested many positive academic and social outcomes for students who experience a sense of belonging and community in their schools and classrooms.

Teacher Support

How students feel about school and their classes is in large part determined by the quality of relationship they have with their teachers. That relationship is supportive for the student when the teacher is caring, friendly, helpful, understanding, and dependable (Goodenow, 1993; Skinner & Belmont, 1993). Refer to Chapter 6 for additional information on student–teacher relationships and teacher immediacy. Caring teachers are important to the development of classroom communities (Kohn, 1996; Noddings, 1995; Osterman, 2000). Noddings (1995) suggested that "we should want more from our educational efforts than adequate academic achievement and . . . we will not achieve even that meager success unless our children believe that they themselves are cared for and learn to care for others" (pp. 675–676). Noddings argued that spending time developing relationships with students, talking to them about their problems, and guiding them toward sensitivity and competence are legitimate teaching activities. Noddings supported the integration of themes of care into the core curriculum because it fosters teacher/student connections and encourages learning that may not occur otherwise.

Kohn (1996) noted that:

> Caring teachers converse with students in a distinctive way: they think about how what they say sounds from the students' point of view. They respond authentically and respectfully rather than giving patronizing pats on the head (or otherwise slathering them with "positive reinforcement"). They explain what they are up to and give reasons for their requests. They ask students what they think, and then care about the answers.
>
> (p. 112)

Teachers demonstrate caring by empathizing with students' feelings and dilemmas and by protecting students with clear boundaries (Elias & Tobias, 1996). They communicate caring in their teaching by showing enthusiasm for the subject, by teaching to students' strengths and abilities, and by providing opportunities for students to be challenged yet successful. Caring teachers express optimism about their students' educational futures.

Bosworth (1995) interviewed middle-school students regarding their ideas of what it means to be a caring teacher. Helping with schoolwork was the frequently mentioned characteristic of a caring teacher. Valuing individuality and recognizing different learning styles were important to seventh- and eighth-graders and among males. Providing guidance and helping with problems outside of school time was the second most frequently mentioned characteristic.

Noddings (1995) noted that caring teachers model appropriate behavior; provide dialogue in which students can affect decision making in the classroom; arrange opportunities for students to demonstrate caring through such activities as community service; and validate student growth in their development of caring.

Many students come to school facing what seem to be insurmountable odds to becoming successful. Much has been written about the resilient child who, despite many difficult challenges, is able to bounce back. Resilient children usually display such qualities as social competence, problem-solving skills, autonomy, and a sense of optimism about the future (Bernard, 1993). Sagor (1996) talked about the need for educators to provide all students, and especially those at-risk, with a "resiliency antibody." Teachers must provide opportunities in each child's daily routine to experience feelings of competence, belonging, usefulness, potency, and optimism. Sagor suggested that certain activities can help students develop resilience (e.g. mastery learning, authentic assessment, learning style of friendly instruction, cooperative learning, service learning, problem-solving approaches to discipline, goal setting). One of the most protective factors identified in resilient children is that of a trusting relationship with an adult who accepts them unconditionally (Werner & Smith, 1982). The adults could be a teacher, counselor, or other adult who serves as a role model.

Good (1983) indicated a relationship between teacher expectations and student achievement and behavior. Good and Brophy (1997) cautioned that teachers' expectations can become self-fulfilling prophecies and affect outcomes such as student achievement, class participation, and social competence. Teachers prefer and have higher expectations for students who are high achievers and engaged over those who are perceived to be less capable (Ladd, 1990; Swift & Spivack, 1969; Wentzel & Asher, 1995).

Perceived teacher support has been found to be related positively to student engagement, liking for school, and motivation (Goodenow, 1993; Skinner & Belmont, 1993). Ryan and Patrick (2001) found that students who perceived their relationships with their teachers to be positive engaged in more self-regulated learning and in less off-task or disruptive behavior. Positive teacher–student relationships often serve as a buffer against developing social and academic problems. Deci et al. (1991) found that, in classes where teachers encourage autonomy, children were more intrinsically motivated and had higher self-esteem than in classrooms where teachers were more controlling.

Good and Brophy (1973) identified four personal qualities that teachers must acquire in order to manage the classroom successfully:

1   They must have the respect and affection of the students.
2   They must be consistent, credible, and dependable.
3   They must assume responsibility for the students' learning, seeing their responsibility as teaching, not mothering, babysitting, or entertaining the students.
4   They must value and enjoy learning and expect the same from their students.

Jones and Jones (2007) discussed the importance of establishing and maintaining "positive relationship bank accounts" with students. They noted that teachers can build positive relationships by getting to know their students, maintaining a high ratio of positive to negative comments, communicating high expectations, and creating opportunities for personal discussions. For example, Ms. Gonzales, a high-school teacher, has "Teach Me Tuesdays" every week, when students are allowed to talk for about 10–15 minutes about what they did over the weekend or to teach Ms. Gonzales something new about current trends in music or dress. Ms. Gonzales is amazed how much she learns about her students. Her students really look forward to Tuesdays. This time is validating to the students and also gives the teacher information that helps in planning instructional activities.

Reflection

♦ Observe a classroom teacher or, if you have your own classroom, have a peer observe and document your positive and negative comments to students in the classroom. What did you learn from this observation?

♦ Identify some specific ways that teachers can build positive relationships with their students.

Peer-Mediated Learning

We all know that peers can be powerful influences, both positive and negative, on the ways people behave. Researchers have found the heavy reliance on peers to be one of the strongest predictors of problem behavior in adolescents. Bronfenbrenner (1986) noted that adolescence is a time of challenge when young people seek creative outlets for their energy. When constructive challenges are not available to them, they find their challenges in such peer group-related behaviors as poor school performance, aggressiveness or social withdrawal, absenteeism or dropping out, drug abuse, promiscuous sexual activity, and delinquency. Two studies found that peer acceptance and group membership were related to academic achievement (Ladd, 1990; Wentzel & Caldwell, 1997).

Most teachers start the school year with their academic agendas in mind while students begin the school year with their social agendas in mind. Brown and Bauer (1994) suggested that students demonstrate their need to connect through visual, verbal, and physical behaviors. Visual behaviors include watching another student, making eye contact, and looking and smiling at another student. Verbal behaviors consist of using the same phrase as another student, making a similar comment or agreeing with another student, making parallel statements, or making a statement referring to gender (i.e. "we're sisters"). Finally, students attempt to connect with others through touching, mirroring another students' movements, or moving closer to another student. Many times teachers misperceive students' need to connect socially as purposeful disruptive behavior. Teachers must learn to harness peer support in the classroom in ways that improve student achievement and conduct.

Peer-mediated learning includes strategies such as observational learning, cooperative learning, and peer tutoring. Montagu, Mecham, and McLaughlin (1991) identified the advantages of peer-mediated learning to both students and teachers. Peer-mediated strategies can do the following:

- Foster positive peer relationships that can lead to a greater appreciation for all students' strengths and weaknesses.
- Help develop cooperative attitudes and mutual respect among students.
- Individualize instruction and allow students time for practice and repetition. This can be particularly helpful to students with learning problems.
- Provide more opportunities for students to make relevant academic responses and allow opportunities for informal talk as well.
- Give students immediate feedback.
- Allow the teacher to move ahead when students are ready.
- Be cost-effective.

When students spend more time on academic tasks and have more opportunities for response and engagement, they are generally more motivated to complete their work. Ryan and Patrick (2001) found students to be more engaged in learning when their teachers supported peer interaction in academic work, when their ideas were shared and respected, and when their performance was not compared to that of others.

Observational Learning

Children and adolescents observe and learn from one another and from the teacher in the classroom. Teachers must be aware that all of what they say and do will be observed and perhaps modeled by their students. Practicing what we preach becomes of paramount importance. Teachers who are keenly aware of the influence of peers in the classroom can use modeling to improve student behavior.

Kauffman, Mostert, Trent, and Hallahan (1998) recommended that a student who is chosen as a model be seen by the target student as attractive and influential. If you are looking for a model to help a target student become less anxious about word problems in math, the model should be someone for whom the student has respect and who does well in solving math problems. If you are trying to involve a withdrawn student in class discussion, a model student may be one who enjoys class discussion and is encouraging to the target student. The model should exhibit a competence level in the desired behavior just above that of the target student. Kauufman et al. cautioned that teachers often choose models who are "too good" to be encouraging to the target student. Mica, a student with Downs Syndrome included in a regular education elementary classroom, spent the first few weeks of school hitting other students. The teacher worked with the students to teach them to teach Mica other ways of getting positive attention. A few weeks later and after a few more knocks on the head, Mica was learning to work cooperatively. Teachers should remember to praise models and target students for attempting new behaviors.

Cooperative Learning

In Chapter 9, we discuss the benefits of cooperative learning and specific cooperative learning strategies. Just to reiterate, cooperative learning has been touted as providing many benefits to students of all ethnic backgrounds and ability levels. As discussed in Chapter 3, African-American learners, Asian and Latino students, Central Americans, Native Americans, and Hawaiian-American children prefer cooperative learning activities to teacher lectures. Mainstreamed students with disabilities learn more in cooperative groups compared to those in controlled classes and also develop friendships with their non-disabled peers (Johnson & Johnson, 1986; Madden & Slavin, 1983).

Cooperative learning provides students with opportunities for social and emotional growth as well as academic achievement. Students practice appropriate social skills as they learn to take turns, listen, and provide feedback to their peers. Cooperative learning groups are effective for increasing student interaction and mutual respect. Students learn perspective-taking and problem solving. All of these strategies help to build a student's sense of belonging and community in the classroom.

Peers can be very powerful in their influence to modify student behavior. For example, group-oriented contingencies or peer pressure can be used to encourage positive interaction and productivity among group members. Kauffman et al. (1998) identified several types of group contingencies. Independent group contingencies apply to the entire class regardless of the performance of the group. All students who finish their work are allowed free time on the computer. In a dependent group contingency, the performance of one peer may determine the consequences received by the entire group. If one student does not complete an assignment necessary for a group presentation, each student in the group may receive a lowered grade. This works best when group members are responsible and not as well when the behavior of the group is generally disruptive. Interdependent group contingencies apply when a reward is given for the performance of individual group members as well as for the performance of the group. Team sports are a good example of this type of contingency.

There are advantages and disadvantages in using group contingencies. Sarafino (2001) identified several advantages of group contingencies over individual contingencies. Monitoring and dispensing reinforcers is easier with a group than with individuals within the group. Group contingencies have built-in incentives encouraging group members to discourage inappropriate behavior. Also, group contingencies increase cooperation. Problems can occur when using any of these contingencies when peers threaten or harass a student who does not perform as directed. To avoid negative peer pressure, Kauffman et al. (1998) recommend the following guidelines when choosing group contingencies:

1   Be certain that the performance standard is not too high.
2   Emphasize reward for appropriate performance rather than punishment for undesirable behavior.
3   Keep the competition fair. Kohn (1998) reminded us that competition or win/lose structures undermine the spirit of cooperation and diminish the goals of developing caring communities in which students learn empathy, perspective taking, and generosity.
4   When using interdependent group contingencies, encourage everyone to participate, but do not require it. Allow those who do not want to be team members to "sit out."
5   Make allowances for those who do not work well as part of any group you can construct. Set up individual contingencies for them, and allow them to rejoin the group when they are ready to work cooperatively.

The use of group-oriented contingencies is an indirect way of involving peers in encouraging appropriate behavior and participation. Teachers must be aware of the needs of individual students and group goals if they are to maximize the effectiveness of these strategies. A more direct way of involving peers is through the use of peer tutoring.

Peer Tutoring

Jenkins and Jenkins (1985) defined peer tutoring as "a system of instruction in which pairs of students help one another understand and learn by teaching." A synthesis of the literature highlights the benefits of peer tutoring: (1) peer tutoring is academically and socially beneficial for tutees and tutors alike; (2) benefits for tutors and tutees occur frequently and at consistently high rates; (3) students with disabilities can function effectively as tutors for other students; (4) the effects of peer tutoring interventions are aligned closely with the subject matter and reveal significant improvements in academic subjects; (5) social benefits are restricted to attitudes toward school, the academic content taught, and social interactions between tutors and tutees; and (6) the outcomes of peer tutoring strategies are related to the research design, experimental-control group comparisons, and pre-post treatment only group designs (Utley, Mortweet, & Greenwood, 1997, p. 350).

Peers can be used to tutor students in specific skills, teach appropriate social skills, encourage student involvement, reinforce positive behavior, and mediate student conflicts. Peer tutors can be especially helpful to second-language learners and to students with disabilities. Cross-age tutoring in which older students tutor students one or more years younger than they are has become increasingly popular, especially with "typical students" tutoring students with disabilities or older students with disabilities tutoring younger students with similar problems. Tutors may or may not be from the same school as their tutees. These types of arrangements allow teachers to attend to the individualized learning needs of students.

Peer tutors must be chosen carefully and trained to perform their role. Peer tutoring can create more problems than it can resolve if not carefully implemented and monitored. A student who has significant problems with attention may become more manageable when tutoring a peer. However, if not properly trained, this student may carry his inattentiveness into the tutoring situation and disrupt the other student's focus on a task. The best peer tutors are those who attend school regularly, have good relationships with their peers, can follow directions, and have the skills teachers have deemed desirable for target students to obtain. Training peer tutors requires a time commitment on the part of teachers to teach trainees the specific skills needed.

Peer Mediation

Peer mediation has become a popular response to increased school violence. There are many types of peer mediation programs available. One program, developed by Myrick and Erney (1984, 1985), was piloted at Bucholz High School in Gainesville, Florida. Initially the program focused on training high-school students in basic counseling skills and providing them with information about substance abuse prevalent in their community. After completing the training, the high-school students worked as peer facilitators with children in elementary schools. The program was broadened to include elementary and middle-school students in the training. These students learn to be good listeners, group leaders, and role models for one another. Training focuses on student achievement, parental issues, making friends, and career choices.

Peer mediation, or what is often referred to as conflict resolution programs, are becoming part of school-wide efforts to curb student violence. The process involves training student volunteers or students who have been nominated by their teachers to mediate conflicts between their peers and to help their peers find reasonable solutions to their conflict. The goal is to provide students an opportunity to share their feelings and their account of the conflict with their peers. The hope is that this process will teach students ways of handing conflict other than violence. The mediation process as outlined by Conboy (1994) proceeds as follows:

1   The peer mediator asks all parties involved to agree to listen to the others' points of view without put-downs or name-calling.
2   Conflicting parties are guided to define the problem, what happened, and how they responded or felt.
3   The mediator paraphrases what has been said to ensure that everyone feels their points of view and their feelings about the conflict has been correctly reflected.
4   The mediator asks participants to brainstorm solutions that would be fair to both sides.
5   Once the participants have agreed to a solution, a written contract is developed and signed by both parties.

Conboy suggested that peer mediation offers administrators and teachers a positive alternative to resolving conflict, prevents conflicts from escalating, helps create a more positive school climate, and encourages students to think of alternative solutions to solving problems with their peers. Peer mediation programs focus on such topics as gossip, theft, harassment, and fighting. Several high-school programs offer anger management classes. Research points to the effectiveness of peer mediation programs in reducing violence and increasing cooperation among students (Johnson & Johnson, 1996). Students learn alternatives to conflict and become more responsible for their own behavior (Thompson, 1996). When students are involved in solving their own conflicts, teachers report less stress as they have more time to spend on academics. Mediators report improved attitudes toward school and better academic performance. Even after they leave school, mediators report the benefits of their training in solving their own problems (Carruthers, Sweeny, Kmitta, & Harris, 1996).

Reflection

♦ **Armando and Hector are two students in Mr. Kiyuna's class, who are always arguing. Today, Hector slapped Armando on the side of the head in response to a comment he claims that Armando made about his nose. How would you go about responding to this situation? How would you facilitate a workable relationship between these two boys?**

Classroom Meetings

Many teachers use class meetings as a tool for building a sense of community and belonging. Zionts and Fox (1998) noted that the goal of classroom meetings is to teach students to communicate, to solve problems, and to accept and appreciate diversity. Kohn (1996) suggested that classroom meetings are the best places for sharing, deciding, planning, and reflecting on a myriad of issues—from what the students did over the weekend to what kind of place the classroom should be. Kohn (1998) noted that structured opportunities for class members to meet help children feel respected, build a sense of community; and contribute to the development of such skills as perspective taking and problem solving.

Perhaps the guru of classroom meetings is William Glasser. In his 1969 book, *Schools Without Failure*, Glasser discussed three types of meetings: (1) social-problem-solving; (2) open-ended; and (3) educational/diagnostic. Social-problem-solving meetings attempt to solve individual and group problems that involve problems of the class and the school. Students identify problems, propose alternative solutions, and commit themselves to a plan of action. In open-ended meetings, children are asked to discuss any topic relevant to their lives including classroom curriculum. Glasser gave the example of an incredible discussion that evolved around the children's' interest in what it would feel like to be blind. Glasser noted that "a class that is involved, thinking, and successful will have few disciplinary problems." The third type of meeting is the educational/diagnostic one, in which the topic is directly related to what the class is studying. This type of meeting gives the teacher the opportunity to determine students' prior knowledge of a topic and to evaluate the extent to which information presented is understood and generalized to other areas. For example, a teacher who is teaching about HIV/AIDS may want to use an initial meeting to determine what students know about the topic. A meeting held after information has been taught could determine whether students would be willing to design a group project focused on HIV/AIDS awareness.

The goals of classroom meetings may vary by grade level. In elementary classrooms teachers often use classroom meetings to teach social skills. In secondary classrooms teachers see several different groups of students and the focus may be more specific to projects or small and whole-group concerns. One teacher at the middle-school level used class meetings to discuss group projects, to identify group roles and rules, and to evaluate process. Another teacher used a "solutions box" to encourage to identify topics or issues they wanted to discuss during class meetings.

One teacher of a self-contained class for students with emotional and behavioral problems held class meetings three times a week. The meetings usually focused on problem solving for interpersonal issues but were also used to plan field trips and class projects. The teacher described one class meeting that "saved the melodrama." The principal was on her way to the class to see the students who were not exactly her favorites, perform, when two students who were having a relationship issue walked out of the class. Several peers were successful at getting the students to return to class. A brief classroom meeting was held to resolve the conflict and the show went on. Students are much more likely to take responsibility when they are allowed to solve their own problems.

Jones and Jones (2007) provided the following guidelines for organizing classroom meetings:

1   Class meetings will be held in a tight circle with all participants (including the teacher) seated in the circle. The circle must not be too large or it will detract from students' involvement and encourage off task-behavior.

2   All problems related to the class as a group can be discussed. Problems involving two or three individual students may be discussed outside the class meeting unless the problem affects the class as a whole.

3   An agenda that is created by students will be written on a clip board. Students must sign their names behind the agenda item. Students do not list other students' names but merely the issue to be readdressed. (The items will be discussed in the order in which they appear on the board. If an agenda item no longer applies when the meeting is held, however, it will be deleted from the list.)

4   Discussions during class meetings should be directed toward arriving at a solution that is not a punishment. The goal of class meetings is to find positive solutions to problems and not to criticize people or occurrences in the classroom.

5   If an individual student's behavior is on the agenda, the item will not be discussed without the student's permission. If the student agrees to have a behavior discussed, you (instructor) should emphasize that the goal of the meeting is to help the student. Be sure that students' statements focus on the youngster's behavior and are presented as I-messages rather than as judgmental statements about the youngster or the behavior. The focus should always be on providing the student with sensitive, thoughtful feedback and positive suggestions for altering behavior.

6   Students' responsibilities during class meeting include: (a) raising hands and being called on to speak; (b) listening to the speaker and not talking while someone else is speaking; (c) staying on the topic until it has been completed; (d) being involved by sharing ideas that will help the group; and (e) using positive, supportive words to discuss the problem and solutions.

7   The teacher will initially serve as facilitator for the class meetings. (pp. 375–376)

Zionts and Fox (1998) identified several basic interpersonal skills that teachers must possess to be effective leaders. They must be good listeners able to reflect the thoughts, perceptions and feelings of others. They must seek clarification by asking questions and summarizing concisely. They must be able to give information to the group in order to ensure the flow of the conversation, a sort of "guide on the side," and communicate encouragement and support. They can use self-disclosure, which is "leading by example." We caution that teacher self-disclosure should not include too much personal information. The meeting should be focused on students' needs.

Zionts and Fox also suggested that class meetings be organized ahead of time. Rules should be developed by students and the teacher. Meetings can be held one to five times a week and last from 30 minutes to 1 hour. Length may depend on the students' attention spans. Glasser (1969) recommended 10 to 30 minutes for the lower grades and 30 to 45 minutes for the upper grades. It is important to determine the purpose(s) of class meetings. For students with emotional and behavioral disorders, a meeting format may include solving problems of a member or members, teaching new skills, and evaluating the results. Nelson, Lott, and Glenn (1993) offered guidelines for effectively using classroom meetings in their book *Positive Discipline in the Classroom*.

Jones and Jones (2001) noted:

> Whenever people live close together for many hours each day, it is mandatory that time be taken to resolve minor conflicts openly. Like an automobile engine that may appear to run smoothly but will suddenly boil over unless properly lubricated, classrooms require proper maintenance checks and minor tune-ups. When implemented in a positive, supportive atmosphere, class meetings serve as the lubricant for a smoothly running classroom.
>
> (p. 342)

Reflection

♦ **How could Mr. Kiyuna utilize classroom meetings to build a sense of belonging?**

Service Learning

Ms. Buckman involved her students, all diagnosed with learning disabilities, in a project with senior citizens. The seniors, from a convalescent hospital, and the special education students joined forces once a week to make cards and craft items to donate to homeless children at a local shelter. The students were involved in service learning.

Students from elementary school through college benefit from service learning projects. Projects can range from advocating for animal rights to adopting grandparents in a nursing home, planting a garden and donating the food to needy families, cleaning up graffiti, recycling, and raising money for survivors of disasters.

Damon (1995), in his book *Greater Expectations*, described the need for children to experience a sense of purpose. He stated: "The surest antidote to youthful demoralization is a sense of purpose: acquiring, that is, a belief in (and dedication to) something larger than oneself" (p. 240). Damon suggested that schools and communities must offer children opportunities to contribute to the welfare of others.

Brendtro et al. (1990), agreed that young people cannot develop a sense of their own value unless they have opportunities to be of value to others. Brendtro and colleagues argued that today's youth at risk have become alienated, discouraged, and self-centered. Service learning projects bring young people beyond the "narcissism of self-absorption." As young people find that they can make a difference in the lives of others, they validate their feelings of self-worth. Kohn (1991) suggested that schools would best serve students and our society by focusing on teaching students to be not only good learners, but also good people. He noted that schools are ideal places to teach children about generosity and caring.

Serving others takes on many forms. Volunteerism, for example, is contributing time without being paid. Community service is helping the community by choice or by court order, also without pay. Volunteerism and community service do not necessarily involve the integration of academics, curriculum, or reflection. Service learning is a philosophy and teaching methodology that integrates service experiences into the curriculum and connects schools with their communities to enrich students' learning and facilitate their academic, social, and emotional growth.

Service learning was defined in the National and Community Service Act of 1990, signed into law by President George Bush, and reauthorized in 1993 under President Bill Clinton. America's Promise—The Alliance for Youth, led by Colin Powell—has mobilized the nation to provide young people opportunities to give back through community service. In May 1993, the Alliance for Service Learning in Education Reform defined service learning and set forth standards of quality for its use in school-based programs. Service learning is defined as a method by which young people learn and develop through active participation in thoughtfully organized service experiences that:

- meet actual community needs;
- are coordinated in collaboration with the school and community;

- are integrated into each young person's academic curriculum;
- provide structured time for young people to think, talk, and write about what they did and saw during the actual service activity;
- provide young people with opportunities to use newly acquired academic skills and knowledge in real-life situations in their own communities;
- enhance what is taught in the school by extending student learning beyond the classroom;
- help to foster the development of a sense of caring for others.

The Standards set by the National and Community Service Acts are as follows:

1   Effective service-learning efforts strengthen service and academic learning.
2   Modeling service learning provides concrete opportunities to learn new skills, to think critically, and to test new roles in an environment, which encourages risk-taking and rewards competence.
3   Preparation and reflection are essential elements in service learning.
4   Students' efforts are recognized by their peers and the community they serve.
5   Youth are involved in the planning.
6   The services students perform make a meaningful contribution to the community.
7   Effective service learning integrates systematic formative and summative evaluation.
8   Service learning connects school and its community in new and positive ways.
9   Service learning is understood and supported as an integral element in the life of a school and its community.
10 Skilled adult guidance and supervision are essential to the success of service learning.
11 Preservice and staff development, which includes the philosophy and methodology of service learning, best ensure that program quality and continuity are maintained.

There are several different types of service learning experiences: direct service, indirect service, and advocacy. In direct service, students have personal contact with those they are serving. Projects such as mentoring, tutoring, and working with senior citizens in retirement homes are all examples of direct service. Indirect service requires the students to addresses a problem in the community rather than having direct contact with others. Examples are raising money, sorting clothes at a homeless shelter, and writing letters to hospitalized children. Advocacy service learning projects allow students to lend their voice to increase public awareness of a problem such as teenage smoking by writing letters to legislators or tobacco companies, or by creating fact posters and presenting them to young children.

Kaye (2000) identified four steps in service learning. The first step is preparation, which requires the teacher to guide students in identifying a need in the community. Students learn new information and collaborate with community partners. A plan is developed that encourages student responsibility and focuses activities on the integration of service and learning. The project should help students master their subject matter.

In step two, students take action through direct service, indirect service, or advocacy. The integration of action and service provides students with opportunities to actively apply knowledge and skills and simultaneously contribute to the community. A well-known Chinese proverb applies to this step: "I hear and I forget. I see and I remember. I act and I understand."

The third step involves a systematic and ongoing process of reflection through role-play, discussion, or journal writing. This is a guided experience in which students are asked to think critically about their service experience. Reflection activities have been found to increase student self-confidence, autonomy, risk-taking, self-respect, and sense of usefulness and purpose (Cairn & Kielsmeier, 1991). In their review of research on service learning, Conrad and Hedin (1991) found that reflection afforded students the opportunity for social and personal development.

The last step requires students to demonstrate their learning through presentations and performances; visual art forms; or written articles or letters to their peers, parents, and/or community members. Students may choose to extend their activities to developing other projects that may be of benefit to the community. Others have added a fourth step: celebration. This component recognizes students for their accomplishments through special assemblies, certificates, parties, and sometimes media coverage. Service providers and recipients may participate.

Benefits and Barriers

Service learning has proven to be beneficial to both general education and special education populations. Studies on the effects of service learning for typical children have reported improved academic and social skills (Brugh, 1997; McPherson, 1997; Wade, 1994). Dundon (1999) wrote about the value of service learning: "The most enduring value comes with the connection to our own deepest selves—to the place where empathy and compassion live. Once we have tapped that core being, once we know what that feels like, we will want to go there again" (p. 37).

Many students with special needs have significant difficulties in both academic and social domains and have experienced continual failure leading to feelings of inadequacy and helplessness. Students with disabilities are often the recipients of service and seldom have an opportunity to view themselves as valuable to others. Studies that involved students with disabilities pointed to positive gains from service learning in behavior, academics, attitudes, functional skills, social skills, attendance, and relationships with non-disabled peers (Brill, 1994; Malmgren, Abbott, & Hawkins, 1999; Muscott, 2000; Wade, 1994; Yoder, Retish, & Wade, 1996). Curwin (1993) noted the benefits of service learning for at-risk students: "Opportunities to help others may provide a way to break the devastating cycle of failure—to substitute caring for anger and replace low self-esteem with feelings of worth" (p. 36).

Service learning projects can be labor-intensive. According to Rockwell (2001), service learning projects require: (1) an understanding of the benefits; (2) a method of incorporating state standards into the service learning experience; and (3) an evaluation of resources. She warned of the difficulties in scheduling, integrating curricular content, and acquiring resources (e.g. time, money, and transportation).

Although there are many positive outcomes of service learning programs, Muscott (2001) suggested that we view these outcomes with "cautious optimism." Many of the service learning programs involving students with emotional and behavioral problems, for example, have been assessed qualitatively using anecdotal information from teacher observation, questionnaires, and students' interviews. Muscott stressed the need for more rigorous research to support the claims of service learning programs.

Kaye (2000) published *The Service Learning Bookshelf*, a collection of book titles to aid teachers and family members in connecting student learning with service to the community. Kaye recommended that books be used as "catalysts" allowing readers to consider what they have in common with the characters, to understand how the actions of the characters make a difference in the lives of others, and to identify and address problems in the neighborhood and community. *The Service Learning Bookshelf* lists categories commonly selected for service learning experiences, from AIDS awareness and education to special needs and disabilities.

Summary

Educational philosopher John Dewey (1971) began working for educational reform in the late 1800s. He believed that education should involve the whole child in a variety of activities that would prepare students to be productive citizens of the community. He wrote:

> When the school introduces and trains each child of society into membership within such a little community, saturating him with the spirit of service, and providing him with the instruments of effective

self-direction, we shall have the deepest and best guarantee of a larger society which is worthy, lovely, and harmonious.

(p. 29)

In this chapter we have discussed the importance of community building in and out of school, including establishing healthy relationships with peers and adults to promote students' social-emotional and academic growth. Students learn best when they are motivated and actively involved in the learning process. Teacher support and peer-assisted strategies such as cooperative learning, classroom meetings, and service learning all serve to give students a sense of ownership in their learning. Students learn to work together to serve others or to solve real problems in the school or community. We hope that you will move beyond what we have referred to as the "curriculum of control" and consider the affective needs of your students when designing your classroom.

Resources

- Building a learning community: crafting rules for the classroom
  www.readwritethink.org/lessons/lesson_view.asp?id=991
- The classroom as a learning community
  www.stenhouse.com/pdfs/8198ch01.pdf
- Creating a classroom community
  www.youthlearn.org/learning/teaching/climate.asp
- Youth Service America
  www.SERVEnet.org
- Service learning
  www.servicelearning.org

Chapter 8

Behavioral Management

Professor Donovan's students are studying to be teachers. In one assignment he asked his students to observe in a classroom with children who have been identified with emotional and behavior problems. Four students zeroed in on Julius, a 12-year-old African-American boy mainstreamed into Ms. Zimmer's seventh-grade history class. The students observed Julius' behavior over a 30-minute period. After a brief discussion, together, students noted the following:

Juilus walked in after the class period started and announced, "I'm here, let's party!" Most of the students in the class laughed and then continued their work. Students were working on a map activity at their desks. Written instructions were on the board. Julius began tapping his pencil on his desk and rapping a song, inappropriate for the classroom. Several students decided to rap with him. Ms. Zimmer asked the students in the class to get back to the assignment.

Under the pretense of sharpening his pencil, Julius walked down the aisle greeting each of his buddies with "Wasssup!" and a high-five. Ms. Zimmer commented, "Julius, you are always moving. Get back to your seat."

Julius muttered under his breath, "I'll show you a few moves." A few minutes later, with a smile and a wink, Julius shouted out, "Ms. Zimmer, this class is boring and not exactly meeting my needs."

Ms. Zimmer made the mistake of asking Julius how she could meet his needs. He muttered a few explicit sexual suggestions under his breath. Ms. Zimmer replied, "Julius, your smart mouth is not going to help you pass this class."

Julius then got up from his seat and headed toward the front of the class. With the entire class focused on him, Julius said, "Why don't we have a discussion about why this class is so boring?"

Ms. Zimmer, looking quite flustered, responded, "Julius, I need to talk to you privately." Julius shouted a few obscenities, overturned a desk, and left the classroom.

After class ended, Ms. Zimmer explained that Julius lives with his grandmother and 2 younger siblings. His mother left the family when

Julius was 2 years old. His father's whereabouts are unknown. Julius' achievement scores place him at approximately fifth-grade level in reading and comprehension. His verbal scores, however, are quite high. Julius has been diagnosed as inattentive, easily distracted, and hyperactive. His peers admire him because of his quick wit. He is very athletic but misses too many classes to be involved in any team sport.

Professor Donovan asked each student in his classroom management course to reflect on why Julius misbehaved. Their comments about Julius' behavior are as follows:

> Julius is behaving poorly because he has an attention problem. He needs to be on medication. That would probably rein him in.

> Julius has a definite anger problem. It's important to help Julius find out what's driving his anger.

> Julius doesn't know how else to behave. He needs to be taught appropriate classroom behavior, not just told to get back to work.

> I think there's a lot going on with Julius. His family situation, his learning problems, and the fact that the teacher's instructional style doesn't fit his need for activity all contribute to his acting out behavior.

Classroom and Behavior Management

Classroom management is a major concern of school administrators, teachers, students, and the public. Administrators want classes that are free from disruptions so that academic standards can be met and target performance goals achieved. Teachers want students who require few interventions to achieve academic tasks. Students want to be in classrooms where they feel safe to navigate their intellectual and social worlds. Finally, parents want to send their children to schools that are free from violence or other forms of harassment.

We all know that numerous factors (e.g. society, culture, school, teacher) influence students' behaviors. Fisher and Smith-Davis (1990) pointed to pervasive poverty, substance abuse, child abuse and neglect, the effects of divorce and single-parent homes, teenage pregnancy, school dropout, delinquency rates, increasing need for mental health services, and homelessness among other factors making the teaching-learning process far more difficult for teachers and school personnel. These out-of-school factors have become significant predictors of school behavior (Levin & Nolan, 2007).

As we argued in Chapter 3, culture is another factor influencing both student behavior and teacher responses to it. Since 1980, there has been a significant increase in the Asian and Pacific Islander, Hispanic, and Native-American populations in the U.S. McLaughlin (1995) reported that one-fifth of American school children come from homes in which a language other than English is spoken. The enrollment of these students is growing at 2.5 times the rate of students whose first language is English.

Linguistically and culturally diverse students find themselves in a vulnerable position on entering U.S. schools (Garcia, 1999). These students often experience conflicts in school when educators are not sensitive to their culture, family background, language, and learning styles (Baca & Cervantes, 2004). Encouraging, however, is the fact that educators are becoming more aware of the importance of multicultural education, respecting each child's cultural background, and choosing curricula and strategies that motivate and enhance learning.

Even though student behavior is influenced by many factors outside the control of the school, teachers and schools also have a major impact on student learning and behavior. Student behavior is more positive in schools where students experience a sense of belonging and support and in which instructional activities engage them in ways that connect to what is meaningful in their lives and cultures. Teachers' expectations about student behavior, their organization and management skills, and their use of instructional strategies all influence students' behavior. Unfortunately, very few teachers understand the connection between teaching effectiveness and student behavior.

This chapter covers theoretical perspectives of behavior including etiology and educational application. Cultural influences that may relate to interpreting problem behavior in the classroom are addressed. This chapter explores the use of punishment and suggests effective strategies for dealing with disruptive behavior.

Theoretical Perspectives on Behavior

Educators' perceptions about the behavior children exhibit affect the way they instruct and manage students in their classrooms. Teachers constantly struggle with understanding the factors influencing behavior. Although numerous theoretical models have been developed to explain problem behavior, five major theories prevail: behavioral, biophysical, psychoeducational, ecological, and needs-based theories. "For purposes of explanation and control of behavior, humans have been variously conceptualized, for example, as spiritual beings, biological organisms, rational and feeling persons, and products of their environments" (Kauffman, 1997, p. 193). The descriptions of these perspectives on behavior presented here are cursory, and much additional reading is required to fully understand each theory.

Behavioral

The roots of behaviorism can be traced to a philosophical movement called "positivism" popular in the 19th century (Maag, 1999). Positivism supported the notion that the only real knowledge is observable. The behavioral model includes a number of theories and points of view about human behavior (Bandura, 1977a; Skinner, 1971; Wolpe, 1961). Problem behaviors are considered learned and maintained by interactions within the environment. Events in the environment can reinforce behavior either positively or negatively (Cullinan, Epstein, & Lloyd, 1991). Because behavior is learned, it can be "unlearned" and new behaviors can be taught.

Behavioral techniques are the most commonly used interventions in classrooms today and are based on the use of positive reinforcement, negative reinforcement, and punishment. Before we explain these principles it is important to understand why challenging behaviors occur according to a behavioral perspective. There are two major reasons for misbehavior (Chandler & Dahlquist, 2010; Hardin, 2008). Students either try to obtain something that is desirable or escape from something that is undesirable. Positive reinforcement serves to strengthen a desired behavior. Teachers, who give rewards such as tokens, tickets, and extra time on the computer, believe that these reinforcements will encourage students to stay on task or engage in socially desirable behavior. Negative reinforcement strengthens an undesired behavior. In order to effectively use positive and negative reinforcement, it is important for teachers to consider the student. What is positive for one student may be negative for another. For many students, academic instruction is negative. Inappropriate behavior is displayed to avoid the task. To illustrate, Nu is a second-grade student who has difficulty with simple math concepts, adding and subtracting. Every time the teacher asks him to work at the board, he resists and becomes angry. Nu's behavior is likely to be an attempt to avoid doing math. The teacher sends him to time-out to think about his behavior. In this case the student has managed to escape the task he feared. If avoiding the task is the purpose of Nu's behavior, the teacher needs to spend time teaching him math skills. Nu needs to experience some level of comfort and competence with the math concepts before being asked to work at the board. Teachers must have an understanding of the function of the student's behavior in order to respond in a way that helps him/her learn to behave appropriately.

The third principle of the behavioral paradigm is punishment. According to Hardin (2008), punishment is the application of something unpleasant or the removal of something rewarding. For many teachers, controlling children seems to be the focus of their entire day. This "control mentality," says Maag (2001), is pervasive throughout education. Knitzer, Steinberg, and Fleisch, in their 1990 book, *At the Schoolhouse Door: An Examination of Programs and Policies for Children with Behavioral and Emotional Problems*, used the term "curriculum of control" to characterize classrooms for students labeled emotionally or behaviorally handicapped. They reported that, in such classrooms, "too often the dominant curriculum is not the traditional academic curriculum, nor is it about concepts, thinking, and problem solving. Instead the curriculum is about controlling the behaviors of children (p. 5)." Brophy and Rohrkemper (1981) found that when teachers felt threatened, angry, or frustrated by student behavior, they selected more punitive interventions (e.g. reprimand, time-out, detention, suspension, or expulsion). Problems with student behavior are among the main sources of teacher stress and often given as a reason for leaving the profession.

Let's return to our scenario about Julius from the beginning of the chapter. Many teachers would be frustrated by Julius' behavior. Remembering that Julius is an African-American male student with learning disabilities and an attention deficit disorder, how do you think most teachers would have responded to his behavior? Chances are they would respond with some type of punishment. Unfortunately, punishment has not proven effective in addressing problem behavior in the schools (Skiba & Peterson, 2000). In fact, physical and verbal punishment can increase the very behaviors that teachers wish to suppress (Kazdin, 2001).

Miltenberger (2007) identified a number of undesirable side effects associated with punishment:

- Punishment may produce elicited aggression or other emotional side effects.
- The use of punishment may result in escape or avoidance behaviors by the person whose behavior is being punished.
- The use of punishment may be negatively reinforcing for the person using punishment and thus may result in the misuse or overuse of punishment.
- When punishment is used, its use is modeled, and observers or people whose behavior is punished may be more likely to use punishment themselves in the future.
- Punishment is associated with a number of ethical issues and issues of acceptability (p. 114).

Although punishment has many undesirable side effects, it may be an appropriate response when the undesirable behavior is physically dangerous or when, along with punishment, an alternate behavior is taught to replace the negative behavior. A student who is suspended for fighting will likely continue fighting to resolve conflict. The student may need to learn more appropriate ways of dealing with anger. If a student shouts out answers during classroom discussions, he needs to be taught to raise his hand and wait to be called upon. Reprimanding the student in front of the class, ignoring the student, or taking away privileges do not teach the student what you want him to do. Although punishment may bring about a change in behavior, that change is usually temporary. Punishment teaches children what *not* to do, not what to do.

Why the over-reliance on control? The answers may be deeply rooted in the assumptions that we make about why children behave the way they do. If we think children are acting out because they have poor skills in reading, we may react in one way; if we think they are acting out to be defiant, we may react another way. If we believe certain children are unable to perform because they come from a low socio-economic background and from a culture other that our own, we may not be willing to find strategies that will help them be successful.

The choice of punishment over other strategies may be more of a symbolic gesture to appease administrators, parents, and other teachers. It suggests that strong action is being taken in response to a perceived breakdown of order in the schools (Noguera, 1995). Glasser (1969) demonstrated this with the "gun" analogy. He suggested that when we punish we may as well be threatening with a gun, as most punishments are poor motivators for changing behavior and only work as long as the gun is pointed and as long as the person is afraid. Although guns do not work, Glasser observed schools' attempts to solve their problems by resorting to bigger guns, more threats, more control, and punishments. Schools do this instead of finding ways to involve students and teachers in a rich curriculum of thinking and problem solving.

Maag (2003) suggested that punishment continues to be used because it works for about 95% of students attending public schools. Mild forms of punishment, such as verbal reprimands, loss of privileges, or removals from the classroom, control most students' behaviors. These strategies do not work for the 5% of students who display the most challenging behaviors. Maag cautioned that teachers start to think that the 5% need to be punished using the same strategies, more severely and more often. Of course, if the punishment worked in the first place, it would be used less rather than more frequently. Punishment does not teach alternative behaviors.

Teachers use punishment because it is quick and easy and works in the short term. For example, a teacher sends a student to the principal's office for talking back and refusing to read aloud. The teacher is reinforced because the student is no longer disrupting the class and the teacher is able to return to the reading assignment. If this student has low reading skills and is afraid to read aloud, getting out of class has reinforced the student. This is referred to as negative reinforcement. Teachers feel they are expected to have good classroom control. A quiet classroom is regarded highly by administrators and parents.

Many teachers, ill prepared in the area of classroom management, choose an authoritarian approach when dealing with students with problem behaviors. This may be because being controlling is part of their personality or it may be because they are afraid of the student(s). Kohn (1996) suggested that we punish because it makes us feel powerful; we think we need to win the battle. In any case, this approach often leads to power struggles that escalate the problem. Brendtro, Brokenleg, and Van Bockern (1990) observed that when adult strategies are in vogue, two opposing cultures arise: controlling adults and counter-controlling youth. Adult control becomes self-perpetuating: the more one controls the more one needs to control.

Social Learning Theory

Social learning or modeling is one principle proposed by behaviorists. According to Bandura (1977a, 1977b), children learn behaviors by observing the actions of siblings, parents, teachers, friends, and others. Behaviors, both negative and positive, can be learned through exposure to a model. Aggression, fear, and phobias can be learned vicariously. An individual's identification with the model, his thoughts and feelings about an event, may override reinforcements in the social environment. Educators use social skills training programs to teach new behaviors. Training programs involve direct instruction, modeling, behavioral rehearsal, and social reinforcement (Goldstein & McGinnis, 1977).

Cognitive-behavior modification

The melding of behavioral and cognitive research has brought about intervention strategies called *cognitive-behavior modification* (Bandura, 1986; Meichenbaum, 1977, 1980). These strategies support the notion that how individuals think and feel about events as well as environmental influences must be taken into consideration when modifying behavior. According to Zirpoli and Melloy (2007), interventions common to this approach include self-management strategies such as self-instruction, self-monitoring, self-reinforcement, and cognitive-interpersonal problem solving. Self-management interventions are all focused on giving more control and learning to the student. Alberto and Troutman (2006) identified some advantages to using self-management. Self-management procedures place the responsibility for change on the student: newly learned behaviors are more likely to generalize to other settings and students learn to be more independent.

The goal of cognitive-behavior modification interventions is to help individuals become more aware of their reactions to difficult events and to actively engage them in taking control of their own responses. Proponents of this model believe that externally oriented behavior interventions do not teach students new behavior and make students overly dependent on a teacher to monitor their behavior.

Understanding behavioral psychology is critical to implementing these strategies appropriately. Teachers need to learn how to observe behavior, collect data, design interventions, and evaluate results. For a thorough understanding of principles and procedures of behavior modification see Alberto & Troutman (2006); Maag (2003); and Miltenberger (2007).

Biophysical

The biophysical theory is basically a medical model placing an emphasis on organic origins of behavior. According to this perspective, problem behavior lies within the individual. Proponents of this model believe that physical defects, malfunctions, and illnesses directly affect an individual's behavior. Disorders such as autism, schizophrenia, hyperactivity, and depression are considered to have biophysical causes.

Biophysical interventions (e.g. drug therapy, surgery, biofeedback, and nutrition therapy) require the services of physicians, psychiatrists, neurologists, etc. The role of the teacher is that of liaison to the specialists and parents. For example, a teacher may have a student who is depressed and on medication. A goal of the medication may be to help the student be more alert and receptive to the classroom environment. Another goal, less often discussed, may be to move the student to behavior of a normative expectation. Teachers should be aware of the purposes and benefits of various medications prescribed to students and the potential side effects these drugs may have on academic performance and behavior. A teacher's observations can provide valuable information to parents and physicians. In addition, Walker and Shea (1999) suggested the supportive role of the teacher might also include referral, modifying the classroom environment and curriculum to meet students' unique needs, and obtaining permission for administering medication to the child in school.

Psychoeducational

The psychoeducational approach is an educationally focused version of the psychodynamic approach evolved from the original theoretical formulations of Freud (1935). Proponents of the psychoeducational approach (Glasser, 1969; Gordon, 1974; Long, Morse, & Newman, 1965) stressed the importance of teachers understanding the meaning of children's behavior. Behavior is seen as a symptom of inner thoughts and feelings. The underlying belief is that children have the primary responsibility of controlling their own behavior.

A teacher's responsibility in this approach is to help children deal with the thoughts and feelings that motivate the disruptive behavior. The education process should be less repressive, more encouraging of children's emotional expression, and more sensitive to crisis situations (Rezmierski & Kotre, 1974). Teachers might use conferencing and good communication skills, such as reflective listening and questioning, to help students solve problems. Other creative activities (e.g. play therapy, puppetry, role-playing, dance and physical activities, music, art, photography) are interventions that encourage students to express their feelings and emotions (Walker & Shea, 1999). Helping students gain control over their own behavior is seen as a long-term goal rather than a quick-fix solution.

These strategies probably work best for students who are self-directed and mature. Unfortunately, classroom teachers do not use this strategy as often as they should. Students are not often given opportunities to be expressive and to work toward solving their own problems.

Understanding problem behavior from this perspective helps educators understand the importance of providing a supportive, caring environment that encourages students to express their feelings openly and appropriately. This theory highlights the importance of social-emotional issues as they relate to learning. It also emphasizes the resource that counselors, psychologists, psychiatrists, and social workers provide outside the school setting.

Ecological

From an ecological perspective, behavior is seen as the expression of the relationship between an individual and the unique environment in which that individual functions (Brofenbrenner, 1979). In order to understand inappropriate behavior one must understand the context in which the behavior occurs. The ecological approach considers many variables in the family, classroom, school, and community. It is meaningless to discuss problem behaviors in isolation from the contexts in which the behaviors exist, since it is the contexts that define the behavior as a problem. From an ecological perspective, problem behavior is viewed as a problem within the system; therefore, the child can be viewed as part of the problem rather that the sole owner of the problem. Ecological interventions focus on changes not only in the child, but also in systems in the child's environment.

According to Rhodes (1967, 1970), problem behavior often lies in the expectations of those with whom the child interacts. Kauffman, Pullen, and Ackers (1986) identified several factors that teachers contribute to students' problem behavior: inconsistency in management strategies, reinforcement of inappropriate behavior, unrealistic expectations of students, a lack of responsiveness to individual differences, irritability with children, and reliance on punishment to manage behavior. Montgomery and Paul (1982) also noted conditions within the classroom that may contribute to problem behavior: unfair competition, autocratic or permissive teaching style, excessive structuring or lack of structure, over-stimulation or under-stimulation. Teachers can have a major influence on the way students approach their academic work and the way they behave in the classroom.

Peer groups are also a major influence on students' behavior in school. Children are likely to imitate the behavior of those who are socially popular, physically powerful, attractive, and in command of important reinforcers (Bandura, 1986). Students who act out are likely to gravitate toward peers that are also disruptive (Kauffman, 1997). Rejection by peers can cause aggression or depression in some students. Teachers need to be aware of peer influence when planning seating arrangements, assigning cooperative projects, and designing behavioral consequences or rewards.

In addition to classroom pressures, students may be dealing with problems at home (e.g. divorce, illness, death, or loss of employment) that make it difficult for them to attend to school tasks. A student who is angry over a family dispute the night before may not be available for math instruction. We must remember that parents and teachers hold certain values and beliefs and set behavioral expectations based on the cultures in which they live and work. Students come to school with their own beliefs, values, skills, and expectations about how things should happen. They may react negatively or withdraw when things do not go as expected.

From an ecological perspective, the classroom must be organized to facilitate student learning and behavior management. Among the factors that must be considered are the use of space, materials, and equipment; procedures for classroom routines; and rules for guiding student behavior. Classroom interventions may include the use of group discussion and class meetings to support students' working through conflicts and seeing those conflicts from another's point of view.

Understanding problem behavior from an ecological perspective requires teachers to consider their own behaviors, classroom routines, and other factors that may influence a child's behavior. The teacher role is that of liaison among the numerous individuals and agencies that are involved in the lives of their students. All systems must be analyzed for factors that may contribute to a child's problem behavior and, then, possible solutions can be determined and implemented.

Needs Theories

Another approach to understanding children's behaviors suggests that problems occur when children's needs are not met in the classroom environment. Many times students act out because they did not understand the instructions, the work is too hard or too simple, or peer or teacher interactions are difficult. Some may not have the academic or social skills to be successful. Students may have problems at home that interfere with their ability to concentrate on schoolwork. Some students would prefer to act out rather than look stupid. Teachers may be able to minimize problem behavior by determining student needs, modifying instructional strategies, and/or teaching new skills.

A number of researchers have written about students' basic psychological needs and how those needs influence behavior in the classroom (Brendtro et al., 1990; Coopersmith, 1967; Dreikurs & Cassel, 1972; Glasser, 1969, 1990; Kohn, 1993; Maslow, 1968). Each of these authors resonates with our discussion of culturally responsive teaching. For example, Brendtro et al., drawing on European tradition and Native-American philosophies of child rearing, indicated that students need to feel a sense of belonging, experience mastery and interdependence, and have an opportunity to be generous to others in order to be successful in school. Native-American child rearing practices focus on educating and empowering children.

Maslow (1968) suggested that students' needs fall within a hierarchy beginning with the basic physiological needs for shelter, sleep, food, and water. Many children come to school without these basic unmet needs. Problem behavior is viewed as a child's reaction to the frustration of not getting his/her needs met. It is difficult to focus on math when you have not eaten or have not had adequate sleep. Physiological needs are followed by safety needs (e.g, freedom from danger), love needs (e.g. acceptance from teachers, peers), esteem needs (e.g. competence, mastery), and ultimately the need for self-actualization (e.g. creative self-expression, satisfaction of curiosity).

Glasser (1969) maintained that all behavior is an attempt to meet five basic needs: survival (food, shelter, freedom from harm), belonging (security, comfort, group membership), power (sense of importance, consideration by others), fun (enjoying emotional and intellectual endeavors), and freedom (exercising choice and responsibility). In his book *The Quality School*, published in 1990, Glasser further identified the needs for love and self-worth.

Glasser further suggested that our current school system is based on a philosophy of noninvolvement and a limited emphasis on thinking, which is a formula for school failure. In order to achieve self-worth, students must learn to think and solve problems. Love and self-worth lead to the most important need: self-identity. It is the responsibility of schools and teachers to help children find a successful identity. Some students who have not learned to think and solve problems may develop an identity that is delinquent or non-productive. This identity leads to failure. A good teacher–student relationship is especially critical for those children who are unable to fulfill their needs at home.

Other theorists argue that teachers need to understand the underlying goals that students seek to achieve in the classroom. Research (Albert, 1996; Hardin, 2008) has identified four goals: attention seeking, power seeking, revenge seeking, and failure avoiding. According to Hardin (2008), most student misbehavior is a function of attention seeking. For these students, their self-worth is connected to the attention, positive and negative they receive, from significant others. This student may be very participative and attentive in class but if these behaviors do not produce sufficient attention, he or she may act out in more problematic ways.

A second goal is to gain power. Students with this goal may react very negatively when a teacher tries to redirect their behavior. The locus shifts from gaining attention to controlling the adult. This student may throw a "temper tantrum," claim that the teacher is picking on him or her, or challenge classroom assignments or activities.

Revenge seeking is a third goal underlying student misbehavior. According to Hardin (2008), revenge seeking results from a series of discouragements which leads the student to believe that they are not capable of attaining positive attention. The anger that the student has may be a function of exogenous factors such as a broken home or endogenous factors such as prejudice, bullying, or academic failure. The way to get attention then is to get back at students, and teachers. The most striking example of revenge seeking occurred at Columbine High School in 1999. Hardin states that revenge seeking is pathological and requires interventions from professionals (p. 86).

The final goal is avoiding failure. These students are discouraged and helpless. They do not believe that any amount of effort will result in academic success. These students may not act out but they do not try to be successful. Our discussion of self-worth theory in Chapter 2 is relevant here. Some students would rather fail as a result of low effort than put forth effort and fail. These students may not be disruptive; they tend to remove themselves from investing much energy in academic tasks.

Kohn (1993) suggested that, to be motivated to learn, students need what he called the three Cs: content, community, and choice. Students need to be taught content that has meaning to their lives. Kohn believed that cooperative learning helps children feel they are part of a safe community. Kohn felt that "kids learn to make good choices not by following directions but by making choices." Kohn argued that teachers spend too much time manipulating student behavior instead of providing students with an engaging curriculum and a caring atmosphere.

The theoretical perspectives discussed provide a way for educators to think about, understand, and manage student behavior. Each perspective focuses on different issues, emphasizes different etiologies, and arrives at different conclusions regarding intervention. No one theory will suffice to fully explain student misbehavior. Rather, we hope that prospective teachers will draw upon the theoretical approaches, their own experience, and the experiences of others to diagnose behavior problems and choose interventions that best meet the needs of individual students.

Reflection

♦ Discuss Julius' behavior from each theoretical perspective.
♦ What intervention strategies would you choose for Julius and why?
♦ Which theoretical perspective(s) best fits your view of problem behavior?
♦ Brainstorm activities to meet each of these basic needs of students in a classroom: Safety, Belonging, Power, Fun, and Freedom.

Cultural Influences

Culturally and linguistically diverse students are likely to experience conflicts when schools and teachers are not sensitive to their culture, language, family background, and learning styles (Baca & Cervantes, 2004). Cartledge and Talbert-Johnson (1998, cited in Utley & Obiakor, 2001) noted that:

> We are all products of our environment, and [our] experiences greatly determine how we perceive the world and respond to environmental events. With a largely White female teaching force, cultural discontinuities enter in when the student population consists of racially/ethnically diverse youngsters who are disproportionately impoverished. When teachers and students are out of sync, they clash and confront each other, both consciously and unconsciously in matters concerning proxemics (use of interpersonal distance), paralanguage (behaviors accompanying speech such as voice tone and pitch and speech rate and length), and verbal behavior (gesture, facial expression, and eye gaze). Examples of these transactions are the ways status in the classroom is determined, the degrading connotations attached to the use of other languages and dialects, and the ways we differentially affirm group membership and cultural identity. The resulting dissonance in communicative processes contributes to the development of communication gaps and misunderstandings.
>
> (pp. 8–9)

Zirpoli and Melloy (2001) contended that cultural influences on behavior have been largely ignored in the field of behavior management and must be addressed. Teachers must understand that selected behavioral interventions can be influenced by the students' cultural backgrounds and by their own beliefs and backgrounds (Ishii-Jordan, 2000). Grossman (1995) pointed out that:

> Even well meaning teachers can misperceive and misunderstand students' behaviors when they interpret them from their own perspective. They can

perceive problems that do not exist, not notice problems that do exist, misunderstand the causes of students' behaviors, and use inappropriate techniques to deal with students' problem behaviors.

(p. 358)

Boutte (1999) suggested that teachers enter the teaching profession to help children and often do not think that they have biases, a situation that may be harmful to students. Boutte noted that negative attitudes are not unique to white teachers. Because our society has traditionally been viewed from a Euro-centric perspective, teachers of color are equally as likely to hold negative attitudes about children of color. These attitudes may not be intentional or even recognized by teachers but can have serious consequences for students.

As the student population becomes more diverse, teachers must become knowledgeable and sensitive about different ethnic and cultural groups. As we view cultural information, it is important to avoid stereotyping and to remember that within any cultural group there is a great deal of diversity and individualism.

African-Americans

Grossman (1991, 1995) reported that educators tend to maintain more prejudicial behavioral expectations for minority students than for non-minority students. For example, teachers tend to have lower expectations for poor African-American students, criticize them more often, and use more punitive disciplinary strategies with them. In a recent study of urban school districts, African-American male students were sent to the office more often and were suspended more often than any other ethnic group (Skiba, Peterson, & Williams, 1997). African-American students were suspended for physical aggression, noncompliance, and insubordination. Other related data indicated that African-American male students with disabilities are more likely to be suspended at an early age and for a longer period of time (Forness & Kavale, 1988). These practices exclude African-American students from opportunities to learn.

Townsend (2000) identified several cultural conflicts in the classroom that may pose a threat to African-American students. One is the ability of African-American students to engage in multiple tasks simultaneously. The need to socialize while working on assignments may be perceived as defiance when tasks require individualized work. African-American students also have a need to "prepare" to work, which has been referred to as "stage-setting" behavior. This entails socializing with others, sharpening pencils, and getting out the right notebook before beginning a task.

Townsend identified language differences that lead to misinterpretation. He referred to the use of nonstandard English and slang spoken by African-American students and unfamiliar to most school personnel.

Nonverbal communication is also misinterpreted. The example Townsend gave is of African-American girls who act in a very "impassioned" and "emotive" manner. Teachers may choose to punish students for what they perceive as combative or argumentative behavior. Julius, our student at the beginning of the chapter, demonstrated some of these behaviors typically exhibited by African-American students. Townsend recommended that educators examine their own attitudes and expectations regarding African-American students. Instruction should involve active learning, including opportunities for physical movement, and opportunities to work collaboratively with peers. Teachers should "get to know" their students and their families.

Asian-Americans

Although it is difficult to ascribe general behavioral characteristics to specific cultural influences, teachers do tend to describe the behavior of Asian-American students as highly motivated, respectful, obedient, and modest. Fewer problem behaviors are reported for Asian-American students than for other minorities.

Schwartz (1996) offered the following suggestions for teachers working with Asian-American students:

- Reject the stereotype that most East Asian children are gifted and are generally docile.
- Distinguish between behavioral or physical disorders and communication difficulties. Communication problems may be related to language differences and culture.
- Pay particular attention to signs of hearing impairment, a highly prevalent disability among Southeast Asians.
- Understand that smiles or laughter may express confusion and embarrassment, not pleasure.
- Understand that emotional restraint, formality, and politeness may be considered essential for appropriate social behavior.
- Understand that when a teacher reprimands a student, the student may believe that he or she is bringing shame to the family.
- Understand that periods of silence may be important to communication.

Native Americans

Many Native-American children have not been exposed to their own tribal customs, but some of the subtleties of Native-American culture can be found in children regardless of their knowledge. Some teachers may misinterpret behaviors such as the lack of eye contact when talking to others as non-compliance. Many Native-American students may consider eye contact as an act of disrespect, hostility, or rudeness. Silence may be a way of expressing respect for the teacher.

Native Americans often emphasize generosity, sharing, and cooperation, which sometimes conflict with the competition that is a focus in the mainstreamed classroom. Native-American students should be given opportunities to work in teams or cooperative groups. Native Americans often have a different concept of time and may not be as concerned about being on time to class or turning in assignments on schedule. Teachers need to be careful not to perceive this as laziness or not caring. Native-American students may need time to assess a situation before responding to questions or may need more time to complete tests or assignments. LaFromboise (1982) advised educators to watch for visual clues from Native-American children as body language and movements can reveal a person's feelings and attitudes. Guild (1994) noted that Native-American students enjoy learning through visual imagery, perceive information globally, and have reflective thinking patterns. Teachers should provide a context when presenting new information and allow quiet times for reflection.

Hispanic-Americans

Undoubtedly, many of the problems Hispanic-American students experience stem from their difficulties with English. Hearing Spanish at home and being expected to communicate in English in school often results in academic and behavioral problems, lower self-esteem, negative cultural identities, and a general pessimism toward teachers and schools (Manning & Baruth, 2000). Some students are even punished for speaking Spanish. Second-language learners can receive academic support through bilingual programs, English language (ESL) programs, and other remedial programs.

Many Hispanic-American children enjoy working in cooperative groups and helping one another complete assignments. Sharing materials and personal belongings is common among these children, as is the expectation that others will want to do the same. Zirpoli and Melloy (2001) recommend that teachers working with Hispanic/Latino children establish personal rapport and encourage student group participation and discussion, as opportunities for socialization are important. Loyalty to family is also important and teachers should make every attempt to involve family members in school communication and activities.

Underachievers

Students with disabilities, students from lower socio-economic backgrounds, and students speaking minority languages or nonstandard dialects of English tend to be over-represented among the ranks of underachievers (Gollnick & Chinn 1994). Good and Brophy (1997) highlighted teachers' differential treatment of high- and low-achieving students. They found, for example, that teachers allow less wait time for low-achieving students, giving them the answers or calling on other students to respond. Some other responses to low-achieving students included: being more critical of student failure; interacting less often and giving them less attention; engaging in less "friendly" interactions (e.g. less smiling, fewer nonverbal signs of support); providing differential treatment in the administration/grading of tests and assignments; and providing low-achieving students with a poor curriculum (limited/repetitive content, emphasis on factual recall, recitation, and drill and practice).

Students from lower socio-economic backgrounds are also more likely to experience physical or verbal punishment and be excluded from the classroom. Students receiving these types of responses can become callous and turned-off to school. Acting out is often a response to not being successful in school and feeling that the teacher does not care.

Cultural differences affect the way children process information, the way they organize and learn material. Utilizing effective instructional strategies can produce positive academic and social outcomes for nearly all students, minimizing the occurrence of problem behavior. Generally, teachers who use a variety of approaches in instruction and assessment will meet children's needs. Banks (1999) recommended a multicultural curriculum be implemented:

> with teaching strategies that are involving, interactive, personalized, and cooperative. The teacher should listen to and legitimize the voices of students from different racial, cultural, and gender groups. Multicultural content is inherently emotive, personal, conflictual, and interactive. It is essential that students be given opportunities to express their feelings and emotions, to interact with their peers and classmates, and to express rage or pride when multicultural issues are discussed.
>
> (p. 111)

Banks and Banks (1989) warned that, "although membership in a gender, racial, ethnic, social class, or religious group can provide us with important clues about individuals' behavior, it cannot allow us to predict behavior" (p. 13). The information gleaned from a person's group affiliation allow teachers to begin thinking about their own beliefs, values, and prejudices and their effects on the teachers' responses to behaviors exhibited by children from cultures other than their own. Teachers are encouraged to recognize cultural diversity as a strength on which to build a positive educational foundation for students.

Reflection

♦ **As Julius' teacher, what cultural considerations might influence your planning to include him in classroom activities?**
♦ **What are some ways that teachers could make the classroom environment inviting to students from different cultural backgrounds?**

Proactive Behavioral Supports

Numerous factors influence a teacher's ability to effectively manage a classroom. Earlier in the chapter we discussed the importance of identifying the assumptions teachers make about behavior and the influence of students' cultural background on how teachers relate to students. Understanding one's own experience and biases as they relate to classroom goals and student behavior can be a starting point toward effective classroom management. Good and Brophy (1991) identified key principles in effective classroom management:

- Students are likely to follow rules they understand and accept.
- Discipline problems are minimized when students are regularly engaged in meaningful activities geared to their interests and aptitudes.
- Management should be approached with an eye toward maximizing the time students spend engaged in productive activities rather than from a negative viewpoint that stresses control of misbehavior.
- The teacher's goal is to develop self-control in students, not merely to exert control over them (p. 199).

Proactive behavioral supports refer to positive strategies designed to prevent or minimize problem behaviors. Proactive strategies minimize the occurrence of common classroom problems (e.g. talking, making noise, fidgeting, roaming). We agree with the key principles for effective classroom management identified by Good and Brophy and follow with guidelines for implementation.

Classroom Organization

One of the most important roles that the teacher plays is that of classroom manager. Learning is difficult to achieve without a well-organized classroom. Research on teacher effectiveness indicates that effective teachers organize their classrooms so as to prevent disruptive behavior (Jones & Jones, 2007). Spending time at the beginning of the year designing the physical environment and teaching and clarifying classroom rules and procedures minimizes the occurrence of problem behavior later.

Rules and Procedures

Rules and procedures are necessary if students are to work in a safe, caring environment. The way the rules are selected and implemented can impact students' classroom behavior greatly. In fact, the extent to which students know the rules and follow them are directly correlated with appropriate behavior (Brophy & Good, 1986).

Developing classroom rules requires, first, knowing the district and school rules in which you work. The rules you develop in your class may be different, but should not contradict the rules of your local campus or school district. Scheuermann and Hall (2007) suggest some guidelines for developing rules:

1 State rules in positive terms. Tell the students what you want them to do. "Walk in the classroom and halls" as opposed to "Don't run in the classroom or hall ways."

2 Keep the number of rules to a minimum, no more than five. When you have too many rules students tend to ignore them. It may seem to students that you are too authoritarian.

3 Set rules that cover multiple situations. "Be prepared for class." Instead of "Have paper, pencil, and materials ready when class begins."

4 Keep the rules appropriate for students' ages and developmental levels. "Keep your hands, feet, and objects to yourself," may be appropriate for elementary students but not for high school students.

5 Teach your students the rules. You can't expect that students know what the rules mean unless you show them they are able to demonstrate the behavior.

6 Set an example for rule-following behavior. A teacher might have a rule stating, "Students must turn in their work in on time," but then not return their graded papers in a timely manner. Or the teacher may have a rule, "Cell phones, Ipods, laptops are not to be used during circle time" and answer a cell phone call during circle time.

7 Be consistent in enforcing the rules. Perhaps the teacher has a rule, "Raise your hand for permission to speak or leave the classroom," but ignores the rule during a lively class discussion.

(pp. 175–177)

Teachers should remember to respond positively, i.e. "thank you for raising your hand" when the rules are followed. Consequences should be developed for non-compliance.

Glasser (1990) discussed the importance of students having a voice in determining the curriculum and the rules of their school. He believed that democracy and responsibility are learned by "living" them.

Students are involved in numerous classroom activities that require specific procedures if the classroom is to run smoothly. There are procedures related to equipment (e.g. desks, storage areas, learning centers, pencil sharpener), individual seat work (e.g. asking for help, participation, assignments), make-up work, group work (e.g. student roles, expected behavior), and out-of-class activities (e.g. lining up, fire drills, playground, cafeteria, library, bus). For example, students going back and forth to the pencil sharpener can be quite noisy and distracting. A procedure that would cut down on the noise and distraction might be as follows: (1) Raise your hand for permission to get up; (2) walk quietly to the counter; (3) place old pencil in the container and pick up a sharpened pencil; (4) return to your desk quietly. Teachers usually complain that most problem behavior occurs during transition periods, changing from one activity to another. Students who finish assignments early and have nothing else to do are likely to find something to do, not usually something the teacher had in mind. Planning for "down time" is critical to effective classroom management.

Procedures need to be clearly defined and taught to students. Again, the time spent clarifying classroom procedures and teaching those procedures to students will lessen opportunities for problem behavior to occur. Asking for student input in creating classroom rules and procedures empowers students and allows teachers to teach and monitor student learning.

Reflection

♦ Think about the grade level you teach or are interested in teaching and identify several rules that you think would be appropriate for your students. Justify your choice of rules.
♦ Describe how you will establish rules in your classroom and how you will teach the rules to your students.
♦ Identify five classroom activities that may discourage problem behavior and develop a procedure for each.
♦ Write a classroom procedure for the following: entering the classroom, participating in a small group activity, and independent work. Be sure the steps can be followed easily.

Student Engagement

Classroom management is often conceptualized as a matter of control of students rather than as a dimension of curriculum and instruction. The key to classroom management is what the teacher does ahead of time to engage students in learning and minimize the potential for problems to occur. Kohn (1993) suggested that the curriculum is part of the larger classroom context from which a student's behavior or misbehavior emerges. Kohn called upon teachers who were responding to behavior problems to ask the question, "What is the task?" Curriculum that is not relevant to students' needs and assignments that are boring, too difficult, or too easy may be antecedents for inappropriate behavior.

Glasser (1969) suggested that, when relevance is absent from the classroom, students would not be motivated to learn. He discussed the importance of emotion in learning. He noted, "Laughter, shouting, loud unison responses, even crying, are part of any good learning experience … "A totally quiet, orderly, unemotional class is rarely learning; quiet and order have no place in education as all-encompassing virtues" (p. 56). Glasser reminded us that every child has background experience and that it should be the business of the school to communicate with students by "plugging in to their background."

Failure has been the key school experience for many low-achieving students, including those with mild learning disabilities. Numerous strategies can be used to teach ALL students about the learning process, thereby engaging them in their own learning. Jones and Jones (2007) discussed variety of strategies for "demystifying" the learning process. Some of the strategies they recommended are as follows:

- Work with students to clearly and explicitly define learning.
- Write and verbally explain the goals and objectives for each lesson and why these have been chosen.
- Relate learning to students' own lives and interests.
- Have students establish learning goals.
- Teach students about types of special abilities (Howard Gardner's concepts).
- Use peer tutoring and teach students how to be tutors.
- Have students monitor their own learning gains and grades.

For many "at-risk" students, negative attention is better than no attention at all. Teaching students about the learning process and about their strengths and weaknesses and providing them with strategies to address learning tasks serve to reduce the occurrence of minor classroom disruptions. Once students experience academic progress, they are less likely to seek attention in a negative way.

Positive Reinforcement

As Good and Brophy (1973) pointed out, an effective approach to classroom management involves rewarding desirable behavior and utilizing techniques that prevent problems from emerging. Positive reinforcement, such as praise, increases the probability that the behavior it follows will recur. Wielkiewicz (1995) noted that the effectiveness of positive reinforcement is a universal principle that works regardless of gender, age, culture, or disability of a child. In fact, many strategies using positive reinforcement (e.g. praise, behavioral contracts, token economies, and group contingencies) have been empirically validated regardless of student characteristics.

Teacher praise has been found to be one of the most empirically sound teacher competencies (Brophy, 1981; Conroy, Sutherland, Snyder, Al-Hendawi, & Vo, 2009; Maag & Katsiyannis, 1999). Unfortunately, strategies using positive reinforcement have rarely been used, or used correctly, to manage students' behavior. Teachers respond more often to disruptive behavior than to on-task behavior. The expectation is that students will behave well and when they do, they are ignored. By acknowledging students' positive behavior, teachers encourage students to take responsibility for their own learning. Students are most drawn to teachers who are encouraging and supportive, recognize effort and achievement, and show genuine enthusiasm when students are successful.

Brophy (1981) outlined several characteristics of effective praise. Some of his recommendations are:

1   Effective praise is delivered contingently. Praise must immediately follow desired behaviors. One teacher said, " I can't find anything to praise this student for." She finally started with, "Jacob, it's great to see you here on time today." Another teacher was observed praising a student for sitting down, not talking, putting his pencil on the paper, and for just about everything else the student did that day. We know you have to start somewhere but too much praise is confusing and not useful as a motivator. Students with disabilities and other students at-risk have already experienced failure and may need to be encouraged for small steps toward their goals.

2   Effective praise specifies the particulars of the accomplishment. "Good job" does not always tell students what they have done to receive praise. "Your project report was well-written and addressed the critical issues of inclusion, and implications for teacher training." This statement more clearly identifies the specifics of the accomplishment.

3   Effective praise shows spontaneity, variety, and other signs of credibility. "I like the way you chose to solve that problem—very creative." Most secondary students know whether or not you are genuine in praising them. They may perceive praise given for easy tasks as an indication that the teacher had low expectations of them.

4   Effective praise rewards attainment of specified performance criteria, including effort criteria. "You followed all of the steps to get the right answer. Your persistence paid off."

5   Effective praise provides information to students about their competence or the value of their accomplishment. "Your presentation showed me that you have a good understanding of the impact of smoking on pregnancy. I would like to display the posters you developed in the library."

6   Effective praise orients students toward better appreciation of their own task-related behavior and thinking about problem solving. "I observed your hard work on this project, especially the way you brought your group members together. Great collaboration."

7   Effective praise uses students' own prior accomplishments as the context for describing present accomplishments. "This is the second week in a row that you've gotten 100% on your spelling test. Using mnemonics is really paying off."

8   Effective praise attributes success to effort and ability. Research indicates that those who link effort and achievement will become more internally motivated and academically engaged (Lam, Yim, & Ng, 2008).

9   Effective praise gives students immediate and specific feedback about their performance.

Praise provides students information about their progress on any given task and also communicates that the teacher is involved in helping them reach their goals. Teachers need to be careful not to praise inappropriate behavior and not to praise every desired behavior. The key to using praise effectively "lies in its quality rather than its frequency" (Good & Brophy, 1984, p. 193). Conroy et al. (2009) noted that praise is a "complex, reciprocal process" (p. 18). Effective praise is influenced by a number of factors such as the student's individual and cultural differences, the circumstances under which praise was previously given, and the characteristics of the praise that is given. When utilized appropriately and effectively, praise can be a practical means of affecting students' motivation to engage in behaviors associated with learning.

Positive reinforcement, including special privileges or tangible rewards, should always be accompanied by positive comments such as praise. Offering students rewards (e.g. extra points, food, stickers and stars, free time) for achievement gains can be positive for some students and counterproductive for others. What is reinforcing for one student may be punishing for another. For example, a student who is low in reading may prefer to have extra computer time as a reward for the successful completion of work. Another, who is reluctant to use the computer, may prefer reading as a reward.

In his 1993 book, *Punished by Rewards*, Kohn argued that rewards are ways of manipulating student behavior. He cautioned teachers that rewards could be most damaging when the task being rewarded is already intrinsically motivating to the student. A student who is praised every time they complete their math facts may lose interest in the task, especially if math comes easily for them.

Good and Brophy (1987) commented, "The quality of task engagement and of ultimate achievement is higher when students perceive themselves to be engaged in a task for their own reasons rather than in order to please an authority figure, obtain a reward, or escape punishment" (p. 227). We recommend that rewards be used sparingly, perhaps for end of the year celebrations or for individual and group successes that involve challenging tasks.

As discussed, students will be more likely to display fewer problem behaviors when the classroom is well organized and when rules and procedures are clearly defined. Effective managers involve students in classroom processes such as developing rules and procedures, teaching them about learning styles, engaging them in productive work, and providing feedback that is informational.

Responding to Minor Disruptions

Sometimes students' disruptive behaviors require intervention. Levin and Nolan (2007) presented a hierarchy of strategies to deal with what Redl and Wineman (1952) called "surface behaviors." Surface behaviors include verbal interruptions (talking, giggling, whispering), off-task behavior (day dreaming, sleeping, drawing), "busy" physical movement (roaming, fidgeting, touching others), and disrespect toward teachers and other students (arguing, yelling, profanity). The hierarchy consists of three tiers of intervention: nonverbal, verbal, and the use of logical consequences. Teachers are encouraged to move through strategies beginning with nonverbal interventions to more directive actions when earlier interventions have not led to appropriate student behavior.

The first level in the hierarchy is nonverbal intervention: planned ignoring, signal interference, proximity interference, and touch interference. Planned ignoring means intentionally not responding to problem behavior. Planned ignoring is most successful with behaviors that do not necessarily disrupt the teaching/learning process such as whistling, humming, and pencil tapping. Students may not even be aware of some of these behaviors. One teacher recalled a time when a female student expelled gas at the end of a class period and laughter exploded in the classroom. This was at a psychiatric school program, where points were deducted for such behavior. The teacher, with a blank face, simply deducted the points and handed over her point sheet. The teacher waited until the classroom was vacant to have a good laugh and breathe a sigh of relief that the incident had not happened during the lecture. If it occurred earlier in the period and if the student was intent on getting attention, ignoring may not have worked. Ignoring is also not appropriate with behaviors that may be dangerous, such as threatening other students or fighting. Generally, planned ignoring works when you are sure that others in the classroom will also ignore the behavior.

Signal interference provides nonverbal cues to the student that certain behavior is inappropriate. Providing cues to individual students or to the class can be an effective way of obtaining expected behaviors. Hoover and Collier (1986) suggested using nonverbal signals and cues that do not draw attention to individual students. Facial expressions, gestures, eye contact, ringing a bell, and clapping hands are examples of nonverbal signals. A teacher once said she practiced for hours in the mirror trying to perfect the "evil eye." She had a chance to try it out when a student in her class was caught eating a candy bar from his pocket. She started laughing when she tried to use the "evil eye," acknowledging to the student that she had been practicing her look at home and it was not working. The student laughed too and threw away the candy. This is an example of how signal interference and a little humor took care of a problem.

Proximity interference, moving toward the vicinity of the student or standing at the side or behind the student, is sometimes all that is necessary to reduce student distraction or to interrupt misbehavior. Teachers who frequently walk around the room, checking in with students, are practicing proximity control. Teachers, who stand at the door, greeting students in the morning or during transition periods, minimize opportunities for problem behavior to occur.

Touch interference is described as physical contact with a student that is nonaggressive. A teacher may take the hand of a wandering student to guide him back to his desk or may use a hand on the shoulder to redirect a student's attention or reassure a student who is frustrated. Hoover and Collier (1986) cautioned that touch interference can be a culturally insensitive form of nonverbal communication. Standing behind students to monitor behavior can convey messages different from those intended. Tapping a student on the head or shoulder could violate accepted norms of interpersonal contact for some students. Teachers need to be sensitive to the responses of students. Some students may find touch reassuring and others may respond with anger and aggression. Physically aversive strategies, such as hitting or grabbing students, are unacceptable.

Tier II consists of verbal interventions. Verbal interventions fall into three categories: hints, questions, and requests or demands. A hint is usually a public commendation of a student's appropriate behavior. If the teacher is angry with Melissa for shouting out the answer and not raising her hand, she can commend another student for displaying the appropriate behavior: "Marc, I really appreciate you remembering the rule to raise your hand." This strategy probably works best at the elementary level and when the teacher is highly regarded by most students. At the secondary level, when peer influence is generally more powerful, teacher praise may not be effective. Levin and Nolan suggested that reinforcement of the group, as a whole may be a more appropriate intervention at the secondary level. Verbal interventions should be private and brief. Stooping down right next to the student or asking someone to come to your desk is less embarrassing to students than criticizing or confronting them in front of the class. Using sarcasm, preaching, judging, and yelling are examples of verbal interventions that do not work.

Questions are used to determine if students are aware of how they are behaving and how their behavior is affecting others. For example, a teacher who is frustrated with Samuel for loudly humming a tune might say, "Samuel, that's a great tune but some students are complaining that they can't concentrate on their work. Could you keep it down?" This is best done privately at Samuel's desk so as not to embarrass him. Students often misbehave because they do not understand the assignment or they find the work too easy, too difficult, or not interesting. Asking questions gives the teacher information about what the student needs to complete the task.

Requests/demands are more direct responses to inappropriate behavior. A student who calls out answers instead of raising a hand may be responded to by the following request: "Roberto, what is the rule about raising your hand?" Another demand that might be used would be: "Roberto, I will call on you as soon as you raise your hand."

Finally, Tier III involves the use of logical and natural consequences for managing problem behavior. Natural consequences result directly from the student's misbehavior. A student who fails to turn in a homework assignment receives no grade (a natural consequence). The natural consequence of forgetting lunch money is not eating lunch. Logical consequences require teacher intervention and are more closely related to student behavior. A student who continues to blurt out answers instead of raising his or her hand should be reminded that he/she has a choice: "Michael, you have a choice, you can either raise your hand and continue to participate in the discussion, or choose not to participate by remaining quiet." According to Elias and Schwab (2006), three conditions must be met if logical consequences are going have maximum effect. In order to be effective, the consequences must be related, reasonable, and respectful. A consequence is related when it is connected to the misbehavior. If a student throws paper on the floor, then asking him/her to clean the floor is appropriate. A consequence is reasonable when it is "mild." If a student takes another student's crayons, he/she may be asked to buy a new box of crayons for the student. A consequence is respectful when it is delivered calmly without demeaning the student. A student who has a temper tantrum that disrupts the class may in a classroom meeting apologize to the class for the disruption. One of the potential benefits of implementing logical consequences is the promotion of social skill development. Our discussion is introductory and we encourage you to read further on this topic (i.e. Albert, 1996; Dreikurs, Grunwald & Pepper, 1982; Hardin, 2008; Nelson, Lott, & Glenn, 1993).

Levin and Nolan (2007) also discuss what they call "contrived" consequences. These consequences are imposed by the teacher, but have no real connection to student misbehavior. Here's one you've all heard, "Michael, you continue to not raise your hand, so I want you to write 100 times, "I will raise my hand to be called on." Students rarely see the connection between their behavior and the consequences and often develop resentment toward the teacher. The use of contrived consequences is not effective and not recommended by Levin and Nolan.

Teaching the Skills They Need

For many students, academic instruction is a negative event. Inappropriate behavior is displayed to escape the task. To illustrate Nu is a second-grade student who has difficulty with simple math concepts, adding and subtracting. Every time the teacher asks Nu to work at the board, he refuses and becomes angry. Nu's behavior is likely to be an atempt to avoid the math task. If avoiding the task is the purpose of Nu's behavior, the teacher needs to spend time teaching Nu math skills. Nu needs to experience some level of comfort and competence with the math concepts before being asked to work on the board.

Teaching is not just about eliminating or suppressing problem behavior. Teaching involves giving children the skills and knowledge they need to be successful socially and academically. Instructional approaches to management that teach appropriate behavior rather than punish misbehavior provide alternatives to exclusionary discipline. Darch, Miller, and Shippen (1998) observed that teaching appropriate behavior is instructional and proactive. They viewed student behavior problems as failures of learning rather than purposeful misconduct. Correcting a behavior after it has occurred is reactive not proactive. The authors encouraged teachers to strategically teach what is required so students have the skills necessary to behave appropriately. They suggested that teachers often respond to academic problems differently from behavior problems.

Darch et al. (1998) recommended the Instructional Classroom Management (ICM) approach to managing behavior. In this strategy, the teacher spends some time teaching children appropriate skills for behaving in a group (e.g. listening, taking turns, and giving appropriate feedback). An instructional approach helps the teacher determine whether students cannot do what they are being asked because they do not know how or they will not do what they are asked. When students make academic errors, we assume they do not know the answer. We assume they need further instruction. When students are disruptive, we assume the problem is a *won't* problem—that the student knows how to behave but chooses not to. The instructional approach may prevent teachers from punishing students inappropriately. Behavior management, like instruction, is a process that requires planning and reflection and takes place over time.

Kohn (1996) likened appropriate discipline to constructivist classrooms in which the process is just as important as the product. He argued for the value of conflict:

> In an important sense, the conflict is the lesson—or at least it can become one if the teacher doesn't take over and solve (or end) the problem. The wrestling with dilemmas, the clash of ideas, the need to take others' needs into account—these are ultimately more meaningful than any list of rules or guidelines that may ultimately result.
>
> (p. 74)

Glasser (1990) talked about the importance of students learning to take responsibility for their own behaviors. He commented, "The process of stating the problem, finding reasonable alternatives, and implementing what seems to be the best alternative is education" (p. 36).

Reflection

♦ **Develop your own management plan including your philosophy of behavior, strategies for preventing problem behaviors from occurring, and strategies to respond to minor disruptions.**

Summary

Numerous factors, such as teacher perception, student characteristics, and cultural and environmental influences, affect students' learning and behavior. Effective teachers are aware of their own beliefs and biases regarding students' academic and behavioral goals. They have an understanding of research and theory in classroom management and students' social and psychological needs. They provide a classroom environment that is safe, nurturing, and engaging and they utilize proactive strategies to minimize problem behavior. Classroom rules and procedures are developed by students and teachers and are clearly defined and consistently reinforced. Academic and social goals are developed according to individual students' learning styles and needs. Effective teachers use various teaching and assessment methods to engage students in learning and minimize problem behavior. When problems do occur, they are seen as opportunities for learning. Students are encouraged to take responsibility for their own behavior through guided instruction and self-management, not through teacher control. A goal, then, of classroom management is to create a community of learners in which students feel they belong, a place where they have opportunities to actively participate with peers and adults in the learning process.

Resources

Behavior Management
- Dr. Mac's
  http://www.behavioradvisor.com
- Teacher Vision
  http://www.teachervision.fen.com/classroom-discipline/resource/6283.html
- Positive Behavior Management for Teachers
  http://en.wikibooks.org/wiki/Positive Behavior Management For Teachers
- Intervention Central
  www.interventioncentral.org/
- Natural and logical consequences
  http://www.rpeurifoy.com/parentng/logiccon.htm
- Positive behavioral interventions and supports
  www.pbis.org/
  www.teachervision.fen.com/classroom-discipline/resource/6283.html
  www.teachervision.fen.com/classroom-discipline/resource/5806.html

Unit IV

Best Practices for Communication in Diverse Settings

The final unit reviews research examining best practices for the delivery and discovery of academic material. Chapter 9 begins with a discussion of the importance of planning. Two ways of planning are reviewed. First, we discuss a traditional lesson plan discussed by Hunter (1984). Second, we review literature on Differentiated Instruction and argue this framework is particularly effective in designing instruction for diverse learning contexts. The next part of the chapter discusses ways to use communication to put curriculum design into action. Ways to effectively use lectures, small groups, and cooperative learning are discussed. The chapter concludes with a review of communication practices used to enhance understanding of the academic material. The final chapter focuses on role of technology on learning. This chapter is divided into three sections. The first section reviews different ways to use technology. The second section explores problems with the use of technology and the final section provides guidelines on how to effectively use technology in the classroom.

Chapter 9

Instructional Strategies

Mr. Dullard peers over the top of his horn-rimmed glasses in a futile attempt to make eye contact with the blurry-eyed students trying to pay attention as he begins his lesson on the California Missions in the Unit on California History. His body seems frozen to the computer station where he reads the first slide on his PowerPoint presentation. His voice, deep, muffled, and monotone has a numbing affect on the students. Steven is in the back of class, eyes shut, with his head precariously perched on his hand. Several snickering students in the class are watching to see if his hand will slip causing his head to crash on the desk. Another student is sending a text message to his girlfriend in another class. Ana and Esperanza are flirting with Carlos, the star athlete at the school who is in the desk next to them. Desia is sitting straight up grinning and nodding, pretending to listen while he rehearses football plays for Friday's game. Once more, Mr. Dullard has not achieved his goal to engage his students in his lesson. In this chapter we will provide a framework for increasing teacher efficacy in diverse classrooms.

This chapter focuses on ways to use effective communication to accomplish instructional goal in diverse classrooms. We begin the discussion by identifying ways to plan and organize lessons. This is followed with a review of specific communication strategies that are at the center of instructional discourse. The final section focuses on the instructional strategies that promote understanding.

Orlich, Harder, Callahan and Gibson (2001) argued that planning is key to effective teaching. They contended that the teaching of master teachers is characterized by well-organized lesson plans, clear communication, and high expectations for all students. Lesson plans can vary by the experience of the teacher, grade level, the content being discussed, and the characteristics of the learner. Orlich et al. (2001) also noted that some teachers, especially experienced ones, may not write out formal lesson plans, but after teaching many years of constructing plans they may have them etched in their head or stored on teaching files in their computers. We believe that it is essential for teachers to formalize their plans and continually adapt them to better meet the needs of their students. Figure 9.1 contains one format that is commonly used.

Component	Description
Objective	The explicit purpose for the lesson. The objective specifies what students are expected to demonstrate after the lesson is completed
Standards	The state-adopted curriculum standards which align subject matter and grade level requirements
Anticipatory set	A strategy for grabbing interest and focusing on what is supposed to be learned?
Presentation/communication	Input: The teacher provides the information needed to accomplish the objective Modeling: the teacher uses the new information to illustrate what students are expected to demonstrate Checking for Understanding: Determining if the students are clear on what they are expected to do
Guided practice	Under the supervision of the teacher, students practice their new knowledge or skill
Closure	Communication strategies which bring the lesson to an appropriate conclusion
Independent practice	Strategies for reinforcing or "hard wiring" the new skill or knowledge. The may be accomplished through homework, group work, or a subsequent project
Adaptations	Identify an accommodations or modifications needed for students with disabilities, diverse learning styles, and or English learners

Figure 9.1 Components of a Lesson Plan.

Note: Adapted from Hunter (1984).

Differentiated Instruction is another way to plan with student diversity in mind. Tomlinson and McTighe (2006) stated that the "primary goal is ensuring that teachers focus on processes and procedures that ensure effective learning for varied individuals" (p. 3). Tomlinson (2003) indicated that differentiated instruction requires a teacher to proactively plan varied approaches that students need to learn, how they will learn it, and/or how they can express what they have learned in order to increase the likelihood that each student will learn as much as he or she can as efficiently as possible (p. 151).

Differentiated instruction is characterized by the modification of three key concepts of a lesson plan: content, process, and product. Modifying "one-size-fits-all" lesson plan is necessary to meet the diverse learning styles and abilities of all students. *Content* refers to what the student needs to learn or how they might access the information they need. Content is principle and concept focused. All classes have state-mandated content standards that must be met. Tomlinson and McTighe (2006) ask teachers to consider ways to meet standards and be responsive to individual students (p. 24).

Process refers to what activities the student is involved in to make sense of the content or to master the content presented. Process concerns the instructional communication strategies used to put the learning into action. Teacher and student communication strategies are central to differentiated Instruction and Culturally Responsive Teaching. These communication strategies range from teacher-centered such as lecturing to student-centered such as cooperative learning groups. As we have emphasized throughout this text, effective communication is central to academic engagement. We will discuss these strategies in more detail later in the chapter.

The final concept defining Differentiated Instruction is *product*—the learning outcomes. This includes initial and on-going assessments. Pre-assessment is critical because it gives teachers and students a sense of where they are with the instructional material and where they need to go to meet the state standards. Assessment is a central feature of differentiated instruction.

Experts recommend that teachers follow five guidelines for incorporating Differentiated Instruction into instructional practice (Gregory & Chapman, 2002; Tomlinson, 1999; 2001; Tomlinson & Kalbfeisch, 1998):

- Clarify and focus on key concepts.
- Use assessments as teaching tools before, during and after the learning takes place.
- Emphasize critical and creative thinking.
- Utilize a variety of learning tasks to engage the learners.
- Balance teacher and student selected tasks.

Tomlinson and McTighe (2006) argued that teachers need to understand the relationship between curriculum design (Understanding by Design) and Differentiated instruction. Understanding by design focuses on what to teach and what assessments to use. An elegant curriculum design or a clearly organized lesson plan that does not account for student diversity will not lead to effective learning for all students. Figure 9.2 is a planning template that can be used when designing lessons.

Stage 1 – Desired Results

Established Goal(s)
What relevant goals (e.g. or content standards, course program objectives, learning outcomes) will this design address?

Understanding(s)	**Essential Question(s)**
Student will understand that …	What provocative questions will foster inquiry, understanding, and transfer of learning?
What are the big ideas?	
What specific understandings about them are desired?	
What misunderstandings are predictable?	

Students will know...   Students will be able to …
What key knowledge and skills will students acquire as a result of this unit?
What should they eventually be able to do as a result of such knowledge and skill?

Stage 2 – Assessment Evidence

Performance Task(s)	**Other Evidence**
Through what authentic performance task(s) will students demonstrate the desired understandings?	Through what other evidence (e.g. quizzes, tests, academic prompts, observations, homework, journals) will students demonstrate achievement of the desired results?
By what criteria will "performances of understanding" be judged?	How will students reflect upon and self-assess their learning?

Stage 3 – Learning Plan

Learning Activities:
What learning experiences and instruction will enable students to achieve desired results? How will the design:

W = Help students know **Where** the unit is going and **What** is expected? Help the teacher know Where the students are coming from (prior knowledge interests)?

H = **Hook** all students and **Hold** their interest?

E = **Equip** students, help them **Experience** the key ideas, and **Explore** the issues?

R = Provide opportunities to **Rethink** and **Revise** their understandings and work?

E = Allow students to **Evaluate** their work and its implications?

T = Be **Tailored** (personalized) to the different needs, interests, and abilities of learners?

O = Be **Organized** to maximize initial and sustained engagement as well as effective learning.

Source: From *Understanding by Design Professional Development Workbook* (p. 30) by J. McTighe and G. Wiggins (2004), Alexandra, VA: Association for Supervision and Curriculum Development.

Figure 9.2 Planning Template.

Source: McTighe & Wiggins (2004).

Santamaria (2009) argued that differentiated instruction can also be used to accomplish culturally responsive teaching. Her research is grounded in the work of Ladson-Billings (1994) and Gay (2000). She argued that Differentiated Instruction is a way to modify instruction based on the knowledge, prior experiences, and performance styles of students from diverse backgrounds. She conducted a qualitative study on two culturally and linguistically diverse elementary schools in San Diego County. She collected data over five years from teachers, administrators, and parents. She developed codes for evidence of Differentiated and Culturally Responsive Teaching. She concluded from her analysis that academic gains occurred when teachers attended to differences in the academic, cultural, linguistic and socio-economic status. As a result of her analysis she argued that blending Differentiated and Cultural Responsive Teaching provides a framework for meeting the academic needs of all students.

The preceding discussion provides important information on how to plan lessons for culturally diverse classes. The next section discusses ways to put these plans into action through effective communication.

Classroom Communication in Diverse Classrooms: The Lecture

The instructional strategy with the longest history is the lecture and its derivative the lecture/discussion. Unfortunately, many teachers lecture like Mr. Dullard. They stand up in front of the class and impart information with little concern about making the content interesting or exciting. Book (1999) stated that people learn best when they: "(a) actively participate in the learning, (b) have knowledge (or specified feedback of the results of learning, (c) know what they are expected to learn, (d) know the purpose of what they are learning, and (e) find the learning to be meaningful to them." Incorporating these concerns into the lecture format is challenging but necessary.

One of the first decisions a teacher should make is when to lecture. Not all instructional goals are suited to this instructional strategy. McKeachie (1986) contended that lecturing is not appropriate when the information is available in printed form. Too many teachers lecture on material students have already read. Mr. Dullard could have taken the time to distribute handouts for the students to read, thus leaving time in class for other learning activities. Lecturing is most appropriate when it is used to give students the most up-to-date information or unique insight from a teacher. There frequently is a lag in time between the information that is in textbooks and new developments in an academic area. Lectures can help bridge these gaps. Lectures are also appropriate for synthesizing material collected from a wide range of sources. Finally, lectures can be used to adapt material to a particular audience. Instructors can take information that is written for one type of audience and adapt it to another.

Book (1999) outlined other practical reasons for using the lecture method. Lectures require few materials or equipment, thus giving the teacher a great deal of flexibility. A teacher can go from room to room or place to place to deliver the information. A lecture is not dependent on the size of room or size of class. A good lecture can be presented to two or 102 students. Studies investigating the effects of lectures indicate that when measures of knowledge are used, lectures appear to be as effective as other modes of instruction. When the measures are concerned with problem solving, delayed recall of information, transfer of learning, or attitude change, then discussion methods are more effective (McKeachie, 1986).

According to Book (1999), an effective lecture arouses student interest about the content, organizes key concepts, and provides an opportunity for students to apply the information to their own experiences. The centerpiece of the lecture is the instructor's knowledge and understanding of the content. The inability to provide explanations, examples, and illustrations are reflective of an instructor who does not have a good working knowledge of the content and does not know how to adapt the information to the students.

An effective lecture does not attempt to cover too much information. Book (1999) stated that a good lecture covers two or three main points with appropriate elaboration to make them meaningful and memorable. One way to highlight important points is to provide an organizational pattern that complements the lecture material. Table 9.1 contains examples of frequently used organizational patterns. Teachers should select the pattern that matches their goals and objectives.

According to Book (1999), an effective lecture will establish a learning set which helps students focus on important concepts and principles. Several strategies can be used to create a learning set. One strategy is to use the techniques for starting a speech such as posing a significant problem, telling a story, or using an activity that brings focus to the content. Another strategy is to use an advance organizer. Orlich, Harder, Callahan, and Gibson (2001) stated that an advance organizer is a frame of reference that presents the main facts, concepts or ideas to be learned. The advance organizer can be a study guide, a chart, or a list of ideas students have prior to the lesson. Teachers and students are better able to focus on relevant information when the main ideas are known in advance. Consider the following example:

In this lesson we will focus on:

- ways to organize a lecture;
- strategies for making lectures more exciting;
- how to write an advance organizer.

Table 9.1 Organizational Patterns

Topical. The lecture is divided into discrete topics that are developed and explained. A topical organizational pattern works well when the goal is to explain the components of a topic.

   I. The First Continental Congress was convened in Philadelphia.

      A. Twelve Colonies were represented.

      B. The representatives produced the Declaration of Rights and Grievances.

Chronological: This pattern follows a time sequence. History lessons frequently report on the sequence of events that occurred. This pattern can also be used to explain how to do or make something.

   I. Two meetings were convened to deal with grievances against England.

      A. On Sept 5, 1774, the Continental Congress was convened in Philadelphia.

      B. On Oct 26, 1774, a second meeting was convened.

Problem–Solution Organization: In this pattern a particular problem is posed and then the solutions are identified and discussed.

   I. The colonies believed that the British policies were unacceptable.

      A. The British created the Intolerable Acts.

      B. The British levied inappropriate taxes.

  II. Several solutions were implemented.

      A. Boycott trade with England.

      B. Committees of Safety were created to enforce actions against England.

Cause and Effect/Effect to Cause: In this pattern, the causes of certain conditions are proposed and explained.

   I. The British tax on tea created several problems.

      A. The Boston Government refused to pay for tea that was shipped from England.

      B. Several Bostonians, dressed as Native Americans, dumped the tea into Boston Harbor.

Instructors can also reinforce the learning set by using strategies to emphasize important points. Statements such as "Think about this," or "This is very important to understand," help frame important concepts and ideas.

A good lecturer must also attempt to actively engage students in the learning. Unlike Mr. Dullard, the effective lecturer checks for student understanding of the new material that has been provided in the lecture. Book (1999) stated that teachers should engage students by asking them to summarize the content in their own words.

Sitler (1997) advocated the use of the "spaced lecture" to increase student comprehension of material. In the spaced lecture the instructor pauses for two to three minutes throughout the lecture and gives the students an opportunity to write information in their own words. The instructor can collect this material to check student learning, or use pauses to give students an opportunity to ask for clarification or further explanation. This strategy is designed to connect listening, note taking, and learning.

The final feature of effective lecturing discussed by Book (1999) is delivering the information in a stimulating fashion. McKeachie (1986) argued that teacher enthusiasm is an important component of effective teaching. Recently Patrick, Hisley, and Kempler (2000) demonstrated that enthusiasm positively influences student intrinsic motivation. Their findings indicated that a lesson delivered with high energy leads students to experience greater interest in and enjoyment of the instructional material.

Studies examining communication style indicate that dramatic teaching is related to judgments of effective teaching. Norton and Nussbaum (1980) tested the proposition that effective teachers are optimally dramatic. They found that effective teachers were entertaining, told good stories, were humorous, and used double takes. Javidi, Downs and Nussbaum (1988) studied the classroom behaviors of award-winning teachers. They found that award-winning high-school and mid-high school teachers used humor, self-disclosure and narratives during lectures, primarily in relation to course content. These teachers, however, tend to use humor less frequently than award-winning college teachers.

Dramatic teachers do more than entertain; they increase arousal and interest in the content being discussed. A humorous story or the use of expressive and animated nonverbal behavior reinforces and complements content. One professor used a puppet named Ceceilia to explain the processes involved in relationship development. Another professor taught an entire lesson dressed as Mrs. Doubtfire, a character Robin Williams played in a popular film. Although there are instructional benefits to a dramatic teaching style, we don't equate good instructional practice with entertainment. Our goal is for teachers to consider ways to help students attend to and remember important concepts. In the context of the lecture, teacher enthusiasm and expressiveness facilitate learning.

Technology can also complement and enhance lecture materials. More and more teachers are using PowerPoint or other software programs to outline and highlight important lecture content. Some teachers integrate video clips, web sites and other graphics into the lecture material. An over dependence on technological tricks and gimmicks can work against learning goals. We explore technology further in Chapter 10.

Before writing a lecture, a teacher needs to consider the background information the students have about the intellectual material. The teacher must consider what the students know and what they need to know. Based on this, the teacher can determine the most appropriate organizational structure.

Reflection

♦ **Describe the characteristics of an effective lecturer you have had.**

♦ **How can a teacher use a lecture to accomplish culturally responsive teaching?**

♦ **Can a teacher be too dramatic? Explain.**

Small Groups

In our judgment, the use of small group discussion is an underemployed teaching strategy. One of the principal reasons is that a teacher must feel comfortable in shifting responsibility to students. Teachers who have a high need for control and believe that a good class is quiet and attentive have a difficult time assigning group projects. The research, however, suggests that small groups are an effective instructional tool (McKeachie, 1986; Orlich, Harder, Callahan & Gibson, 2001; Stahl & Clark, 1987). Group discussion moves students from passive to active modes of learning. In addition, as we indicated in Chapter 3, groups are a preferred mode of learning for females, Native Americans, African-Americans, and Latino(s).

Throughout this text, we have advocated building on the competencies that students bring to the learning situation. Students come to classes with a good deal of experience in groups. They belong to primary groups where the fundamental goal is to provide for basic needs and emotional and social support. Families, clans, cliques, gangs, are examples of these types of groups. Students also belong to secondary groups, whose purpose is to complete a task or solve a problem or to participate on some function. Church, community, and classroom groups are examples of secondary groups.

Schutz (1966) identified three basic needs that individuals have and each of these needs is connected to group participation. One need is inclusion. Group participation helps individuals feel that they are a part of something. Students who are isolated and disconnected are less likely to be interested in school and are more likely to experience failure. A second need is affection. Care, concern, and support are frequently expressed in group settings. Being liked and loved is a fundamental need and individuals feel better about themselves when they are in a context where this need is communicated. The final need is control. This need is concerned with the degree to which individuals have some power over themselves, others, and tasks. Many students feel that no amount of classroom effort will make any difference so they stop trying. These same students, however, may exercise a great deal of control and power on the playground or in other contexts where their skills matter. Clearly, academic success can be better accomplished when educators build upon the natural needs that students desire and seek out.

Why Small Groups are Successful

Small group instructional practices are effective because they engage the learner in active learning processes. As the old adage goes, "Two heads are better than one." The act of talking about a topic or issue engages the student in cognitive processes that are not stimulated in passive learning situations. Students must articulate, defend, plan, criticize, and analyze issues and problems. Some research suggests that through the process of collaboration, students are able to solve difficult problems that they would be incapable of solving alone (Forman & Cazden, 1985). Using groups is considered a best practice for Differentiated Instruction and Culturally Responsive Teaching. Following are some positive outcomes for using groups.

- increased problem solving;
- creative thinking;
- critical thinking;
- social skill development;
- increased cultural sensitivity.

There are two primary ways to use small groups in the classroom. The first is small group discussion and the second is cooperative learning groups. In small group discussion, groups are created and given a topic or issue to discuss. The topic should be related to classroom content, and be able to hold student interest. (Orlich et al. 2001). It is important for teachers to give groups an essential or provocative question for their deliberation. For example, one teacher designed a lesson to meet the state standard on visual and performance arts by asking students to discuss how television and film have influenced the perception of people of color. This assignment resonates with the indicator of Socio-Political Consciousness discussed by Ladson-Billings (2001). Orlich, Harder, Callahan, and Gibson (2001) provided a taxonomy of discussion groups varying in the amount of control required of the teacher. These discussion groups are: *brainstorming, tutorial, task group, role playing, simulation, and inquiry group.*

Brainstorming groups are designed to stimulate creative thinking. The purpose of brainstorming is to generate many ideas on a topic. Discussion and criticism of the ideas generated are discouraged. Brainstorming is usually an initiating activity. The information obtained can be used in other discussion formats or classroom activities. For example, brainstorming is an effective way to identify topics for research projects.

A second type of group, the *tutorial*, is utilized to help students who are having difficulty mastering or understanding certain subject material.

The tutorial leader assumes a great deal of control by identifying the learning problems, providing feedback on the skills needed to achieve mastery, and encouraging students to use other students as resources.

The use of tutorials can be an effective way to remediate learning problems. Cohen, Kulik, and Kulik (1992) found that students can learn as much from other students as they learn from teachers. Students share experiences and language forms that teachers may not know or understand. New insight and understanding can be obtained by drawing upon the expertise of peers.

The third type of group is the *task* group. Each participant in a task group is expected to make a specific contribution to the group. For example, one student may be responsible for computer graphics, another for library research, a third for typing a final report. Task groups can be effective in facilitating student cooperation and accountability. It is important to make students responsible for the tasks they have been assigned. Teachers should also discourage students from taking over the tasks assigned to other members. In our experience, some students have strong control needs and as a consequence can literally take over the group. The behavior of autocratic participants can be very divisive and counterproductive. Teachers need to help students understand that there is always more than one way to complete a task.

The fourth type of group involves *role-playing*. In role-playing groups, students are asked to simulate real-life situations. An elementary school teacher in Nebraska can ask students to play the roles of J. Sterling and Caroline Morton, who moved to Nebraska from Michigan. They missed the trees and shrubs of the northeast and started planting them each year. When he was in the state legislature, he proposed that one day be set aside to plant trees in the barren plains. This was the beginning of Arbor Day. The focus of role-playing is to dramatize the behaviors or symbols under investigation. Teachers should provide clear instructions on the roles students are supposed to play, discuss how the roles were played and reflect on what was learned as a result of the exercise.

The fifth type of group involves *simulation*. The purpose of a simulation is to re-create a real object, problem, or event. Business organizations and the military have used simulations as a central feature of their training programs. Teachers can also take advantage of this instructional strategy. For example, a fifth-grade history teacher in Madera, California, annually takes his students on a covered wagon trip to complement their study of California history. This activity gives students a genuine feeling and understanding of frontier life.

The final type of group format is *inquiry-centered* discussion. The purpose of the inquiry group is to simulate scientific thinking, develop problem-solving ability and promote the discovery of new perspectives and insights. Students are given a problem or question to examine. They collect and analyze data and then draw conclusions or make recommendations based on their efforts. This format is appropriate for the investigation of civil rights or other social issues. One of the values of this approach is to give students an opportunity to challenge and test their implicit theories and beliefs.

Teachers need to also be aware of how their own ideology can influence their response to this type of assignment. Teachers sometimes develop assignments to promote their own beliefs. Although difficult, teachers must maintain a facilitative role and help students make their own connections.

Cooperative Learning

Cooperative learning is an extension of the discussion methods discussed above. The research on cooperative learning is extremely positive (e.g. Johnson, & Johnson, 1999; Johnson, Johnson, & Holubec, 1993; Kagan, 1994; Morton, 1998; Sharan, 1994; Sharan, Kussell, Hertz-Lazarowitz, Bejarano, Raviv, & Sharan; 1984; Stevens & Slavin, 1995). Kagan (1994) identified three benefits of cooperative learning: (1) academic gains, especially for minority and low achieving students; (2) improved race relations among students in integrated classrooms; and (3) improved social and affective development among all students. Teachers genuinely interested in culturally reflective teaching should give serious attention to cooperative learning methods.

Johnson, Johnson and Holubec (1993) identified six essential features of cooperative learning.

1   *Positive interdependence.* The success of the group is dependent upon the cooperative activities of the members. Positive interdependence is achieved when students believe that one cannot succeed unless all succeed. Without positive interdependence cooperation is impossible.

2   *Individual and group accountability.* There are two types of accountability. At one level, the group must be held accountable for achieving its goal and each individual must be held accountable for his or her contribution to the group goal. Individual accountability achieved when the performance of each individual is assessed and the results are given to the group. Cooperative learning strengthens individual performance through continuous feedback and the opportunity to take corrective action.

3   *Face-to-face interaction.* Students need to do real work in which they promote each other's achievements, share resources, and encourage learning. The importance of face-to-face communication cannot be understated. Learning and understanding are facilitated when students

orally explain, correct, and re-explain ideas, processes, and concepts. In cooperative learning situations, students interact; assist one another in learning tasks, share diverse ideas, and beliefs and work as a team to accomplish instructional goals.

4   *Interpersonal and small group skills.* In cooperative learning, students are not only required to learn academic subject matter but also learn the social skills necessary to work in a group. Cooperative learning requires students to simultaneously engage in task work and teamwork. Among the skills necessary for successful group participation are leadership, decision-making, conflict management, and trust building. These skills must be taught as precisely as academic skills.

5   *Group processing.* Group processing exists when group members monitor their progress on task and working relationships. Improvement requires an analysis of what works and what creates problems in the group. Each student is held accountable for his or her academic work. The final evaluations come from teachers, peers, and self.

6   *Development of social skills.* Cooperative learning helps students develop the types of interpersonal skills necessary to succeed in work, school, and home. Students enhance interpersonal skills, develop conflict management skills, and increase critical thinking.

Cooperative learning groups should be comprised of students from different academic, social, ethnic, physical, religious, sexual, and attitudinal orientations. The benefits of peer interaction are increased in heterogeneous groups. Cooperative groups provide an excellent opportunity to celebrate diversity, so instructors must be willing to create diverse groups. Our experience is that some teachers don't want to take the risk and contend that "the students can't handle it, " so they create homogenous groups.

Depending on the instructional goals, several types of cooperative groups can be structured. There are several excellent texts available on ways to use cooperative learning in the classroom (Kagan, 1994; Johnson & Johnson, 1984; Johnson, Johnson, & Holubec, 1993).

One type of cooperative procedure is called Student Teams-Achievement Divisions (STAD). First, the instructor presents a lesson, frequently using the lecture mode we discussed earlier. Second, student teams are created and designed to prepare them for quizzes or other evaluation procedures. Third, students take individual quizzes. The content for the quizzes comes from the course content the students studied in the groups. Fourth, students receive a team score on how much each improved over their previous score. Fifth, team scores are publicized in a newsletter or other publication.

Another type of cooperative group is called Teams Games-Tournament (TGT). This procedure is very similar to STAD. In TGT, quizzes are replaced with a system of academic game tournaments in which teams of students compete against other teams of students. Odyssey of the mind, and academic decathlon are some examples of this type of group. Kagan (1994) cautioned against this type of cooperative format for classes that have a great deal of ethnic and academic diversity. There is a danger that these competitive scenarios may provide a structure where students from individualistic value orientations will excel. Students from cooperative value orientations are less likely to be successful in this type of format. Academic tasks can play an important role in how academic ability is displayed and measured and teachers need to give attention to these issues.

Teams-Assisted Individualization (TAI) combines cooperative teams with individualized instruction. Students work in four-to-five member teams on self-instructed materials at their own rate and level. Students are responsible for checking and managing the assignments. Teams are rewarded if they achieve preset standards.

In the original Jigsaw procedure (Aronson, Blaney, Stephan, Sikes, & Snapp, 1978), students were assigned to heterogeneous teams. Each member was given a unique set of information to discuss in expert groups made up of students from different teams who were also given the same information. The experts returned to their teams and taught the new information to the other members. At the end of instruction, students are assessed.

Slavin (1995a) modified the Jigsaw procedure to more closely match the Student Team Learning Format. In Jigsaw II, students work in four-to-five member teams. All students are assigned some material but each member is assigned a subtopic to master. Students discuss their topics in expert groups and then teach their teammates. Quiz scores are summed to form team scores, rather than individual scores. Kagan (1994) provided a number of ways to adapt Jigsaw procedures.

For group investigation, students are placed into small groups and select a topic from a unit being investigated by the class. The group reports to the class the findings of its investigation. Among the skills reinforced in this group are cooperative inquiry, group discussion, and cooperative planning.

Teachers can adapt any of the methods we have described to a cooperative learning context. Educators have applied cooperative learning to mathematics, language arts, social studies, critical thinking, history, and physical education. In order to gain maximum rewards, however, it is crucial that students be held accountable for the product the team produces. Cooperative learning does not work if teachers choose to place students in groups and grade them only on individual achievement or participation. Teachers interested in cooperative learning are encouraged to consult a number of the texts dedicated to this pedagogical practice and develop cooperative learning activities for their classrooms.

The previous section outlines different ways that teachers can organize and present instructional material. Lectures are appropriate for some instructional goals and cooperative learning groups are best for others. There are some communication practices that must be understood regardless of the approach. Teachers must explain material and ask questions in lectures and in group settings. In the next section, we will examine these communication practices.

Teacher Clarity

Because students want to understand a lesson, teacher clarity is essential to effective teaching. Clarity is concerned with the message strategies used to increase the fidelity of instructional messages. As we stated in Chapter 2, there are several characteristics of teacher clarity. Hines, Cruickshank, and Kennedy (1985) argued that clarity behaviors consist of: (1) stressing important aspects of content; (2) explaining by the use of examples; and (3) assessing and responding to perceived deficiencies in understanding.

Book and McCaleb (1985) characterized teacher clarity as the quality of being comprehensible. They argued that teacher clarity entails the use of the following types of communication behaviors: (1) definition of major concepts; (2) accuracy of examples; (3) sufficiency of examples; (4) sufficiency of explanation; (5) checking student understanding; (6) connective discourse; and (7) specific examples. Powell and Harville (1990) stated that the behaviors detracting from clarity include ambiguous terms, vagueness, hedging, bluffing, insufficient examples, mazes, and vague language. Other behaviors used to define the lack of clarity are nonfluencies, false starts, and vocal fillers.

Enhancing Explanations

Rowen (1999) provided a useful framework for examining teacher explanations, a central feature of teacher clarity. She stated that one of the principal responsibilities of teachers is to provide explanations that promote the understanding of subject matter. There are typically three areas where confusion occurs in instructional discourse. One source of confusion involves explaining unfamiliar concepts or using language in unfamiliar ways. A second source of confusion involves difficult-to-picture processes. The final sources of confusion involve counterintuitive explanations.

Rowen discussed three types of explanations that can be used to facilitate understanding. The first is called elucidating explanations. These explanations are designed to help students understand the meaning of a term or concept. According to Rowen, good elucidating statements contain "(a) each concept's critical features, (b) an array of examples, and (c) opportunities to practice distinguishing examples from nonexamples by looking for critical features."

The second type of explanation is quasi-scientific. When teachers try to help students understand complex processes such as osmosis, evolution, open systems theory, life cycles, or math formulae, they are engaging in quasi-scientific explanations. Several strategies can be used to facilitate the discussion of quasi-scientific discussions. Signaling devices, which focus on main points, figurative language, analogies (the San Joaquin Valley is California's bathtub) and graphics are effective strategies for bringing focus to important points.

Rowen recommended an instructional technique known as *elaborative interrogation* for quasi-scientific explanations. Students are asked to read an explanatory passage about how some phenomenon occurs and then explain it in their own words. This process requires students to construct their own mental models for difficult to understand processes. In lectures, elaborative interrogation could be used in a number of ways to engage students in the material under investigation.

The third type of explanation Rowen discussed is *transformative explanations*. These types of explanations help students deal with circumstances or events that do not resonate with their personal theories. Rowen stated that the best transformative explanations: (1) state the "implicit" or "lay" theory about the phenomenon; (2) acknowledge the plausibility of this theory; (3) demonstrate its inadequacy; (4) state the more accepted account; and (5) demonstrate the greater adequacy of the alternative theory. Engaging students in these alternative views promotes critical thinking and shapes new insights and understandings.

In Chapter 2 we emphasized that clarity does not occur simply because a teacher uses examples or illustrations. If the examples do not relate to the student's experiences, they are not likely to have much of an effect. We also explained the different ways that students signal their lack of understanding. Darling (1989) and Kendrick and Darling (1990) observed that student clarifying tactics vary according to the point the teacher is trying to make. We also believe that the relationship between the teacher and student influences clarity and the way it is managed. For example, the teacher who criticizes students for asking dumb questions, or nonverbally is impatient (rolling eyes, sighing) sends a clear message to students—don't ask questions. On the other hand, the teacher who is open and willing to address their lack of understanding sends a different message—let's stay with this idea until we get it. The relationship between the teacher and student also is related to clarity. As teachers develop an understanding of their students, they are more attentive to language and nonverbal cues that indicate understanding. Just as intimates grow more competent in assessing implicit messages, teachers and students grow more able to understand each other as their relationship develops. A look, a glance, a smile may say a great deal about student understanding. Finally, the culture of the student will influence how students signal their lack of understanding. Students from high-context, collectivistic cultures (Japanese, Hmong, Chinese) are unlikely to signal their lack of understanding because such a behavior would threaten the face of the instructor (he or she did a bad job of explaining the idea) and self (I am embarrassed because I don't understand). Students from these orientations may ask for clarification after class or may ask another student for an explanation.

Reflection

♦ **In what ways do you signal that you don't understand a teacher?**
♦ **How do teachers indicate that they do not want to clarify information?**

Questions

Asking and managing questions are an essential component of classroom interaction. Questions play an important role in both lectures and in small discussions. Research suggests that teachers spend a tremendous amount of time asking and processing student questions (Cleg, 1987; Hoetker & Ahlbrand, 1969). Effective discussions and lecture discussions require thoughtful attention to questions. However, many teachers often fall into a pattern of asking the same type of questions over and over again. Teachers could better manage questions if they possessed an understanding of what they want a question to accomplish and how the question is related to learning.

There are a variety of ways to use questions. Some are used to glean unknown information while others are used to check student knowledge. Pseudo questions, for example, are used to determine if students understand concepts or know certain facts. During a discussion of the Puritans, a teacher may ask, "Who gave the sermon, 'Sinners in the Hands of an Angry God?'" The teacher knows that the answer is Jonathon Edwards and is using the pseudo question to get students to recall this fact. Questions may also serve as directives. A misbehaving student may be asked a question to get him or her back on task. A teacher may ask a student who is not paying attention to an instructional task, "Johnny, have you finished your worksheet?" Upon hearing this question, Johnny is likely to stop what he was doing and get back to work.

Table 9.2 Bloom's Cognitive Domain of Learning

Level of Learning	Example
Knowledge: Recall of factual information.	Who developed the teacher immediacy scale?
Comprehension: Understands meanings.	What are the major components of teacher immediacy?
Application: Problem solving, applying information to produce a result.	How can teachers increase the perception of immediacy in their students?
Analysis: Breaking ideas or problems down into their relevant parts.	What other communication behaviors are related to teacher immediacy?
Synthesis: Creating a unique or original product.	Use three types of immediacy behavior in a five-minute micro lesson.
Evaluation: Using criteria to produce a judgment.	How well did the teacher in your previous class communicate non-verbal immediacy?

Research by Gall (1984) indicated that teachers seldom ask questions, which require higher levels of thinking (application, analysis, synthesis or evaluation). Teachers tend to ask questions requiring students to recall facts. This is unfortunate because higher order questions stimulate critical thinking. Recall that a central aspect of differentiated instruction is asking essential questions that require high levels of thinking.

Bloom, Englehart, Furst, Hill, and Krathwohl's (1956) Taxonomy of learning is a classic framework for conceptualizing cognitive questions. The Taxonomy (see Table 9.2) consists of a hierarchy of objectives that represent different levels of thinking. The six classes of objectives are knowledge, comprehension, application, analysis, synthesis and evaluation.

Cunningham argued, "For every cognitive operation, there is a complementary affective operation." 1987, (p. 69). In the cognitive area, Cunningham identified three levels of questions (Figure 9.3). The first level consists of *factual recall* questions. These questions are concerned with student recall and recognition. Key processes are naming, recalling, identifying, writing, listing, and distinguishing.

The second level consists of conceptualization questions. According to Cunningham (1987), convergent and divergent questions characterize this level. Questions vary on how open-ended they are. Low-convergent questions are used when the teacher is looking for the "right" answer but they are more complex than questions about the recall of facts. For example, the question "What type of state government is used in Nebraska?" requires students to sort through the various definitions of state government and select the one that applies to Nebraska.

Table 9.3 Key Words for Divergent and Convergent Questions

Convergent

Understand	comprehend
Translate	explain in your own words
State the problem	what are the main points?
Identify the thesis	what is the explicit theme?

Example: Donny, what is the main idea of the story?

Divergent

Apply	use	relate
Utilize	employ	assume
Hypothesis	manipulate	build
Construct	predict	compose
Formulate	create	design
Operate	make	wonder
Find another way	invent	try

Example: Anita, predict what will happen next in the story.

Key words for value questions

Rate	determine	assess
Appraise	critique	award
Criticize	prioritize	weigh
Accept/reject	critique	explain why
Grade	judge	censure

Example: Shen, do think this was a well-written story?

High-order convergent questions require students to demonstrate their comprehension of a concept or principle. These types of questions require students to provide evidence and reasons for their responses. At this level students must be able to differentiate facts from opinions. Here is an example of this type of question: "Does exposure to media violence cause viewers to act violently?" To adequately answer this question, students must understand causal reasoning.

Divergent questions give students the freedom to wrestle with a variety of issues without the constraint of searching for a correct answer. In order to respond to divergent questions, students should have a reasonable information base for their responses. Low-divergent questions require students to create new or different ideas. An example of a low-divergent question is "What are the ways of dealing with school overcrowding?" High-divergent questions call for creative thinking. Students are expected to think in new and novel ways. Cunningham (1987) contended that only 5% of classroom questions are of this type. An example of a high divergent question is "What role should schools play in fighting racism?" Table 9.3 shows the key words for divergent and convergent questions.

The third level concerns evaluative questions. These questions are based upon the other levels. This level of question requires students to judge the validity of materials, ask and argue a position. Reponses to these types of questions allow the teacher to probe for additional support and reasoning. The following is an example of an evaluative question, "What are the problems with the death penalty?"

Affective Domain

Students do not process information neutrally; therefore, questions have affective consequences. Some ideas connect and resonate with their experiences while others seem distant and irrelevant. Frequently, teachers miss the affective implications for the questions they ask, however. Cunningham (1987) discussed three levels of questions that are influenced by the affective domain.

The first level is *perceiving and initiating action*. This level of question is concerned with perceptual awareness. This level is concerned with how much attention a student needs to dedicate to the situation. For example, in a history class, a teacher may simply ask who in the class is aware of Cesar Chavez, the founder and leader of the United Farm Workers Union. Questions at this level are not designed to make assessments or evaluations but simply to note awareness.

The second level, *valuing questions,* addresses the worth or merit to the objects under examination. One role of the teacher is to help the students scrutinize and assess the values they hold. On some issues, students are aware of the topic under consideration but hold no strong attitudes about it, while others feel a great sense of commitment and ego involvement in the topic. As values become more internalized, students are more likely to seek out information that is affirming. Questions can be used to facilitate an examination of the value. Let's go back to our example of Cesar Chavez and consider the following question: Did Cesar Chavez act in a heroic fashion? Students viewing Chavez, as a champion of the rights of farm workers will respond one way and students viewing him as a threat to agribusiness will view him in another. Teachers facilitating a discussion on this topic might face a lively debate that would increase student awareness on both sides of the issue. Unfortunately, many teachers avoid such discussions because they perceive them as too controversial.

The third level, *actualizing questions*, are designed to challenge existing values and consider the merit of competing ones. At this level, students are exposed for what they believe in and stand for. Through this exploration, the total development of the learner is exposed. Teachers attending to the affective domain must remember that unlike cognitive questions, the teacher's role is not to direct the responses but to help students understand how they view the world (Cunningham, 1987).

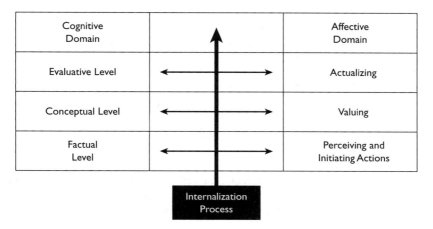

Figure 9.3 Question Types.

After discussing the civil rights movement, students might be asked the following: "Who had the greatest impact on the civil rights movement, Martin Luther King or Malcom X?" This type of question taps into student's ideas about racism, non-violence, religion, justice, and communication style.

Teachers need practice and guidance on asking a variety of questions. Effective questions engage students in the learning and help them shape the direction of classroom discourse. Further, it is through the management and negotiation of questions that important meanings emerge.

Another dynamic that is related to teacher questions involves wait time. Teachers seldom wait more than one second to answer their own questions. Students quickly learn that if they sit quietly, then the teacher will provide the necessary information. One rule for teachers to follow is to wait three seconds before answering a question or calling on a student to respond. The extra time will help students formulate better answers and give teachers an opportunity to connect student responses to important content. Competency in using questions takes time and effort. Other theorists offer important insight on questions in the classroom (Andersen, Nussbaum, Pecchioni, & Grant, 1999; Brophy and Good, 1986; Hunkins, 1976).

Reflection

♦ **What type of questions do you prefer that teachers ask?**
♦ **Which type of questions lead to class discussion?**

Summary

The purpose of this chapter was to overview a number of teaching strategies that can be used in diverse classrooms. We began the chapter with a framework for integrating Differentiated and Culturally Responsive Teaching. The research viewed in this chapter indicates academic performance is enhanced when teachers connect with and build on the lived experiences of students. The framework we discussed provides a template for identifying the essential learning that students are expected to demonstrate. We also discussed specific instructional communication strategies that put the framework into action. There is no perfect method. The selection of a strategy should be based on the goals of the instructor, the teaching strengths of the instructor, student strengths, and the availability of resources. The greater the repertoire of strategies available to a teacher, however, the greater the opportunity to adapt to the needs of the students.

Learning Activities

- Write a 5–7-minute lecture on a cultural artifact from your cultural background. Use the lesson plan discussed in the chapter to plan your lecture.
- Based on the lecture, write a question reflecting each part of Bloom's Taxonomy of learning.
- Use brainstorming groups to generate a list of famous people to investigate for a group project. After identifying the person, the groups will develop a way to present their information, such as oral presentations, role-playing skits, a musical.
- Conduct an analysis of a class. Draw upon an understanding of the concepts discussed in the class and address the following:

  - How effective was the physical space used?
  - In what ways was student diversity addressed?
  - Describe the student–teacher relationship and the classroom climate.
  - What behavioral management strategies were used?

Resources

- Effective lecturing
  www.reproline.jhu.edu/english/6read/6training/lecture/delivering_lecture.htm

- Eight steps to effective lectures
  www.ferris.edu/Htmls/academics/center/Teaching_and_
  Learning_Tips/Developing%20Effective%20Lectures/8step-
  stoactive.htm
- Using small groups and student teams
  http://depts.washington.edu/cidrweb/resources/grouptools.html
- The essential elements of cooperative learning in the classroom.
  ERIC.Digest
  www.ericdigests.org/1995-1/elements.htm
- Effective use of questions
  www.uab.edu/uasomume/cdm/questioning.htm

Chapter 10

Technology and Instructional Communication

Lee Harrison, a seventh-grade teacher at Kennedy Middle School, is on his way to the special meeting for all faculty and staff. Rumors have been flying around the school, about a major curriculum change that was about to take place. After everyone is seated, the Principal, Mrs. Dorothy Knight, steps to the microphone and makes the following announcement.

"Today I am happy to announce that we are creating a partnership with Hyperspeed Learning systems to create an integrated technological learning community here at Kennedy. We will begin by offering a laptop for learners program in our advanced classes, and in the next five years we will phase in several additional programs until we are fully integrated. Hyperspeed will create and manage the infrastructure, provide the computers the students will purchase, and train all teachers. We believe that this new partnership move takes us to where we need to go in the new millennium."

The hands of several faculty members shoot into the sky as they bombard the principal with questions: "Why was this decision made?" "How do we know it will positively affect learning?" "What is Hyperspeed and what's in this for us?" "What's going to happen to the kids who can't afford laptops or don't have computers at home?" "Why weren't we consulted?" Other teachers seem rather content and smug. One was heard to say, "Its about time. Technology is revolutionizing education and it is time to jump on board or stay in the dark ages."

Mr. Harrison leaves the meeting a bit overwhelmed. He is unsure about how this technological revolution will impact him, his teaching, and his students. No single educational development is more dramatic than the technological advancements of the last decade. Because these developments occur so quickly, there is little data to determine their educational consequences. Some educators are blindly committed to the benefits of technology. Others resist technology and believe that it threatens the human core of the educational enterprise. We can say this, technology will continue to be a significant force and education will be served best by understanding the way in which the teaching learning process is influenced by it. The focus of this chapter is how technology influences the communication process and learning in the classroom.

Technology and Education

It is an understatement to claim that technology is pervasive. Many students use cell phones to talk, text, take pictures, and send e-mails. Many students have myspace.com accounts on their home computers and most schools have computers and access to the Internet. In some ways, student competency in the use of technology exceeds the competency of teachers. Technology has become an important part of the social fabric and is having a profound effect on education.

Technology includes the mechanisms that are used to facilitate or mediate the teaching learning process. While teachers have used videos, TV programs, films, audiotapes, and filmstrips for a number of years, it is the computer that has had the most substantial impact. No other "teaching" tool has been mandated to become a central part of the educational process. In 1996, the Clinton Administration issued an initiative to make all students computer literate by the 21st century (*Getting America's Students Ready*). Literally millions of dollars have been committed to this goal. Let's turn our attention to the ways computer technology influences instructional practice.

Whenever technologies are employed, the roles of teachers and students change. According to Chizmar and Walbert (1999), technology allows the teacher to move from the "sage on the stage" to the "guide at the side." When technologies become infused into the curriculum, the teacher's role shifts from being primarily an information source to a facilitator, a coach, a guide, and a co-learner. Jones, Valdez, Nowakowski, and Rasmussen (1995) outlined the way in which these teacher roles are enacted in technologically rich classrooms. They contended that teachers are facilitators when they provide environments and opportunities for students to work collaboratively and solve authentic problems. When they act as a guide, teachers mediate, model, and coach. Teachers model when they competently demonstrate the use of technology. They coach by giving hints and encourage students to refocus and practice their skills. Finally, teachers are co-learners when they participate with students in the discovery and management of new information and insight.

Clearly, the technological developments in the last few years have dramatically influenced classroom interaction patterns. Computers and Internet access has increased substantially. Public school access to computers and the internet has increased from 65% in 1996 to 100% in 2005 (U.S. Department of Education, 2008). The computer and its ability to provide access to the information highway have the potential to alter the type of assignments that are developed, the form in which the assignments are presented, the competencies the students must possess to complete the assignments, the type of learning that will occur, the kinds of problems, both behavioral and technological, that will be remediated, and the way teachers will respond. Even though the increase in access appears impressive, it is unclear how these technologies are being used. A school may have one computer with Internet access, computer labs, and/or computers in each classroom.

Some advocate that technological developments offer limitless opportunities but teachers need a clear idea of how to use technology to extend their instructional goals. Bransford, Brown, and Cocking (2000) argued that technology is not an educational panacea:

> Technologies do not guarantee learning but ineffective use of technologies can hinder learning—for example students may spend most of their time picking fonts and colors for multimedia reports instead of planning writing and revising ideas. And everybody knows how much time students can waste on surfing the Internet.
>
> (p. 206)

The authors go on to offer five ways to effectively use technology:

- Bringing real-world problems into the classroom.
- Providing scaffolds and tools to enhance learning.
- Giving students and teachers more opportunity for feedback, reflection and revision.
- Building local and global communities that include teachers, administrators, students, parents, practicing scientists and other interested people.
- Expanding opportunities for teacher learning.

A brief discussion of these areas may help teachers and prospective teachers develop a working paradigm for instructional technology.

Real-World Learning

There are several ways to utilize technology to provide new types of learning opportunities for students. Utilizing a problem-solving orientation is not a new concept, but technology does offer the potential to change the boundaries of the typical classroom. Computer software can be used to simulate problems and give students a variety of ways to work through them. Bransford, Brown, and Cocking (2000) described two such programs: The Voyage of Mimi and the Jasper Woodbury Problem solving Series. In the Voyage of Mimi, students use video and the computer to "go to sea" and learn about whales and the Mayan culture of the Yucatan (Char and Hawkins, 1987). The goal of this instructional package is to help students refine their problem-solving skills in a real world (albeit simulated) environment. The Jasper Woodbury problem-solving series developed at Vanderbilt includes 12 videodisk adventures that focus on mathematical problem solving. Each adventure provides opportunities for problem solving, reasoning, and making connections to other areas such as science, social studies, literature, and history. Students are able to explore specific parts of a lesson and receive immediate feedback. They can revisit parts they do not understand, and probe deeper into more challenging environments (Cognition and Technology Group at Vanderbilt, 1997). Another popular program is the Oregon Trail. This software program was developed by Rawitsch, Heinemann, and Dillenberger (1974) for students 10 years or older. Students take on the roles of members of the families who traveled to the Oregon Territory in the 1840s. In the simulation, students interact with other families, work through difficult problems facing the pioneers and make decisions on how to survive the journey to the Willamette Valley.

A second way to use technology to facilitate real-world problem solving is to connect students with practicing scientists. In some schools, student–scientist partnerships are created. Students identify a significant problem and consult with professionals examining it. Through the Internet, they share tools, curricula, methods, and data with a goal of pooling their knowledge and publishing their findings. O'Neil, Wagner, and Gomez (1996) advocated the use of tele-mentoring to link students with professionals. In these programs, students are connected with practicing professionals, university faculty, or graduate students. Through e-mail, these mentors help the students as they investigate a significant problem. Bransford, Brown, and Cocking (2000) reported other projects that successfully utilized these interconnected learning communities.

Providing Scaffolds

Vygotsky (1978, 1981) argued that learning is facilitated when learners are provided models and guidance until they are able to perform tasks alone. Without this help, which he called scaffolding, students are often overwhelmed and do not know how to determine what is important and what is not. Computer-aided instruction can provide valuable scaffolding tools (Oliver, Omari, & Herrington, 1998). Bransford, Brown, and Cocking (2000) likened computer scaffolding with using training wheels to teach someone to ride a bike. The training wheels help the learner master some of the mechanics of bike riding without falling. Similarly, computer scaffolding allows learners to perform tasks and solve problems they could not do without the computer. With a coach or tutor, the learner receives hints and guidance in solving problems. Once this competency is established, the learner has a foundation to move on to solve tasks without help.

There are several ways to develop scaffolded experiences. One option is to use an apprenticeship model. In this approach, an expert (such as the teacher) models a learning function, and guides learners in practice until they can perform the task alone. Another approach is to allow individuals to work collaboratively because in most real-world applications, individuals frequently work with others.

Even though there is potential for scaffolding technologies, there are some potential pitfalls. Because of time constraints and a lack of patience, teachers and mentors may be inclined to do the work for the novice. The goal of scaffolding is to teach new skills, however; the new skill is not taught when the teacher or mentors lose sight of their roles—to help the novice use the skill independently. Over time, a pattern can unfold where the novice sits back and waits for someone else to take over the task.

Feedback, Reflection, and Revision

Feedback to students can be facilitated with the use of internet technology. In addition to traditional e-mail and web sites, new software allows for a more interactive educational environment. Blackboard, for example, is a web-based program with a number of interactive features which allow teachers to post course outlines, announcements, assignments, provide feedback to students on projects, answer questions from parents, and use interactive tests. Traditional web pages provide information and a certain amount of interactivity but students cannot receive immediate feedback on their work. Innovations such as Blackboard were developed to meet this need. Several other programs are also available.

Tele-Web integrates server side software and plug-ins with a Web server. Zhao, Englert, Chen, Jones, and Ferdig (2000) discussed the way this tool can be used to teach literacy. With this technology, teachers develop multimedia learning materials, and conduct collaborative learning projects. Teachers can use this tool to archive student assignments and track performance. Students are encouraged to explore independent ideas and collaborate with others. The curriculum focuses on four primary environments: Writing Room, Reading Room, Library, and Publishing Room. Each environment allows teachers and students to create projects and comment on progress.

Not only do these technological developments have the potential to link students with teachers, they also provide a way for students to connect with peers and tutors. Technologies such as Blackboard and Tele-WEB provide the opportunity for creating learning communities. Say, for example, student teams are asked to do a problem-solving activity. Each team member is required to investigate the different aspects of the problem. Information can be shared by e-mailing attachments with the different information that has been obtained. Through this process of information exchange and revision, the problem/question can be explored and solutions can be devised.

Finally, technology provides tutorial opportunities. For example, tutorial software is available in algebra, and writing. In algebra, the computer software program guides students through simple to more complex tasks and the writing software provides students with guidance on grammar, and style.

Connecting the Classroom to the Community

There are numerous ways technologies can link the school to the home and the larger community. For example, every school in Clovis Unified School district in California has a home page web site with links to extracurricular and curricular activities. Some faculty members have a web site with course assignments and grading criteria. The old student response "I don't have any homework tonight dad," can be verified by connecting to the web site and checking the assignments that are posted.

One common complaint from parents is that they do not know what is going on in the school. This is particularly problematic for divorced families where announcements may only go to one household. Many schools provide announcements on telephone message systems so that a parent can find out the time of a Frosh football game or open house. The same system can be used to leave voice mail with an instructor or administrator. The time has passed when the school newsletter was the primary tool for disseminating information.

Teacher Learning

The final area that Bransford, Brown, and Cocking (2000) addressed is teacher learning. Technology has dramatically changed the teaching and learning process. The authors contended that technology influences classroom instructional practices and affects the professional development of the teacher.

Teachers effectively using technology in the classroom model ways to use these tools to advance learning. For example, when teachers guide students through an instructional task, they may explore and experiment with different ways to solve a problem. This collaborative process helps students and teachers discover new insights and perspectives. Also, there may be occasions when a student understands more about the use of a particular technology than the teacher. In these occasions, the learning event unfolds into a collaborative venture where the roles of teacher and student are blurred or redefined. The student takes the lead as "instructor" and the teacher becomes "student."

Obtaining access to new teaching strategies and sharing information with other teachers can also be facilitated because of new technological developments. Teachers can explore teaching web sites, read articles in virtual libraries, and download information pertaining to teaching standards. The traditional role of teacher as expert is changed to teacher as facilitator.

One of the more exciting developments is the way in which technology can be used to help teachers prepare for their teaching responsibilities. CD ROMs with segments illustrating the use of different behavioral management approaches and video disks illustrating reading or math instruction are also available (i.e. Duffy, 1997; Risko and Kinzer, 1998).

Reflection
♦ **How does technology facilitate learning?**
♦ **Select a web site from the back of this chapter and discuss the way it influences learning.**

Concerns about Technology

The research reviewed above suggests that technology impacts education in a number of positive ways. But before we accept all of these benefits on face value, we must also understand that many of these benefits do not reach all students and are not applicable to all educational goals. Narrative arguments may exceed the objective data on the positive effects of technology on learning (Selfe, 1999). Healy (1998) observed, "Unfortunately, the political pressures to toss computers into classrooms and to get internet connections before people even know what to do with them is an attempt to run around the teaching profession" (p. 8). We want to emphasize that technology will not be a substitute for an effective teacher.

In this next section we will explore the problems that are associated with the infusion of technology. We will frame this discussion in terms of the daily practices of a teacher such as Mr. Harrison that we described in opening this chapter.

Access to and the Use of Technology

Several years ago access to computers and internet was considered a significant problem. The digital divide was the metaphor used to describe the disparity between those who had access to the computer and the

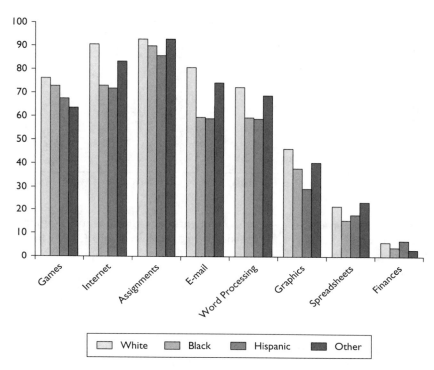

Figure 10.1 Computer Access by Ethnicity.

Source: U.S. Department of Education (2006).

internet to those who did not. In 1997, for example, 42.8% of elementary and secondary students had access to a home computer. In 2003, this number increased to 79% (U.S. Department of Education, 2006). There have also been changes in access to schools. In 1997, 78% of all public schools had internet access but by 2003, 100% of schools had internet access (U.S. Department of Education, 2006). Even though these data indicate that internet access has increased it is not clear how it has been incorporated into classroom practice. We do not know if the schools have access in all classrooms and grade levels.

Access continues to be influenced by ethnicity. According to the U.S. Department of Education (2006), for students 15 years of age and older, 84% of Whites, 49% of Blacks, 55% of Hispanics and 83% of others used a computer in the home. The type of application was also identified. Figure 10.1 contains the results of this analysis.

These data indicate that the greatest differences appear to be in areas of internet use, e-mail, and word processing. Blacks and Hispanics do

Table 10.1 Family Income, Age and Computer Access, 2003

Family income	5–9 years old	10–14 years old	15 or over
$15,000–$19,000	33.4	49.1	48.4
$20,000–$24,000	41.1	52.5	53.9
$25,000–$29,000	47.7	59.5	61.9
$30,000–$34,000	54.7	64.9	72.9
$35,000–$39,000	63	71	74
$40,000–$49,000	68.9	77.5	78.2
$50,000–$74,000	74.9	83.8	86.5
$75,000 or more	85	91	94

Source: U.S. Department of Education (2006).

not use the internet and e-mail as frequently as other groups. Similarly, Jackson, von Eye, Biocca, Barbatsis, Yong, and Fitzgerald (2005) found that that low income children primarily used their computers to play games and search the web for information.

A second factor that influences access is income. As income increases access to computers and high speed internet also increases. Table 10.1 shows how computer access increases according to family income in 2003.

Clearly, income plays a dominant role in access to home computers. What is not described in these data is that the number of computers that are accessible also increases with income. Families with income in the $20,000 range my have one computer that is shared among family members while wealthier families may have two or three computers.

Family occupation is a third factor that influences computer and internet access (Fairlie et al., 2006). Individuals who work in occupations that do not require a computer are less likely to own one. Families who work in agriculture, construction, service, or transportation may be less likely to own a computer. Families who work in education, law, own farms, or construction companies may be more likely to have computers.

The fourth factor, which is related to occupation and income, is education. As family education levels increase, the amount of access to computers increases. More educated families have careers that require computer access, have the skills to manage and use computers, and see their value. This is true for immigrant and non-immigrant families. Thus an immigrant from India or Mexico who went to college or graduated from high school is much more likely to have a computer than an immigrant or non-immigrant who had little education (Fairlie, London, Rosner, & Pastor, 2006).

The final factor influencing computer and internet access is language. Fairlie et al. (2006) reported that the majority of Web pages are in

English. Even when accounting for education and family income, Spanish-speaking Latino immigrants have very low access rates. Language also influences the content of internet sites and software programs. Unfortunately, little data are available on language and its role in computer access and use.

The data we have reviewed indicate that substantial portions of society have limited access to computers and internet. This creates a larger burden on educators to address this issue. Teachers from K-12 will have students who come from low-income families who do have computers at home. Because schools have increased their access, teachers need to think carefully about the ways they will provide technological access and opportunity for these students.

According to Brown, Higgins, and Hartley (2001), questions of access reveal themselves in different ways. Schools with diverse student bodies restrict access to technology. In many schools, computer stations are placed in labs with restricted access. By placing computers in labs, schools are sending two messages: one, the computer is not an integral part of the learning process, and two, students from poor or diverse backgrounds cannot be trusted with computers in the classroom. Together these messages indicate that technology is not central to the learning experiences of students from diverse cultural backgrounds (Swain & Pearson, 2001).

The type of computer instruction is different for students from diverse backgrounds. Research indicates that culturally diverse students receive instruction where the computer directed the learning, while white students receive instruction that encourages problem solving and student initiative (Anderson et al., 1984; Crist-Whitzel, 1985; Kozma & Croninger, 1992). Technology for some students is considered a tool to facilitate and explore learning and for others it is a tool to complete repetitive tasks, such as word processing or data entry. One type of student is given freedom to use the computer to explore ideas another is limited to developing remedial competencies.

Brown, Higgiens, and Hartley (2001) pointed out an additional pedagogical facet of the digital divide. The software does not reflect the concerns and interests of a diverse population of students. The authors observed that sound software is not available for students from diverse ethnic backgrounds, students with disabilities, students who are female, and students who have been identified as at risk. Software companies, like textbook companies have been inattentive to the interests and concerns of certain groups.

Access therefore presents difficult problems for teachers, especially for those in lower socio-economic areas. The first obstacle is financial. Teachers don't have the power to change the financial circumstances of families. They can, however, think through the ways in which they teach about the use of technology.

Brown, Higgins, and Hartley offered an extensive list of recommendations. Following are ones that we believe teachers should consider:

- Have roving computer stations that stay in classrooms for extended periods of time.
- Offer and allow typically underserved students opportunities to take technology courses and earn extra credit for graduation.
- Have girls' technology day, use female students, and students from diverse ethnic backgrounds as technology monitors, and have more sign-up slots for female students during free time.
- Lend laptop computers to students, much as band students receive musical instruments.
- Ensure equal technology use, regardless of gender, ethnicity, or achievement level by removing some of the biases and stereotypes associated with technology use.
- Consider summer school courses that meet at atypical times to accommodate students who work after school.
- Blend technology into the daily routine to promote learner-center.
- Make computers available to the public through schools, libraries, and community centers.
- Encourage students to use public library technology for after-school homework assistance and to take advantage of mentoring and tutoring programs.

The recommendations above can help teachers reduce the gaps between the technological have and have-nots. Other researchers offer recommendations on the digital divide (e.g. Becker & Sterling, 1987; Crist-Whitzel, 1985; Kozma & Croninger, 1992; Swain & Pearson, 2001; Yoder, 2001).

Reflection

- What are additional ways to narrow the digital divide?
- Should educational programs such as laptops for learners be implemented in public schools?

Technology and Learning

The significance of the digital divide is predicated on the strong belief that technology positively influences learning. Many people don't even question its value as they search for a bigger, faster, and more sophisticated machine. The objective data showing the effects of technology on learning, however, are less than straightforward. Some theorists go as far to claim that technology has a minimal effect on learning (Cuban, 2001; Roschelle, Pea, Hoadley, Gordon, & Means, 2000). Other research has been more positive.

Park (2008) conducted an extensive study on the role of technology on the mathematics achievement scores for English- and Spanish-speaking Hispanics. The author analyzed data from the Education Longitudinal Study (ES: 2002/2004). Individual computer use positively influenced mathematics performance, after controlling for external factors that impact academic performance i.e. family SES, parental support, attendance, delinquency). This effect was even larger for the Spanish-speaking Hispanics.

Boster, Meyer, Roberto, Inge, and Strom (2006) studied the effects of video streaming on learning outcomes. The authors conducted a series of studies on third and eighth graders from three school districts in the Southeast. Students were randomly assigned to either an experimental group that was exposed to video streaming or a control group that did not receive exposure to video streaming. Students took standardized tests to determine if video streaming had an impact on learning. The results indicated that video streaming had a positive effect on third grade science, and social studies performance. For the eighth grade experiment, video streaming did not affect science performance but did affect social studies performance. While the data generally supported the proposition that video streaming positively impacts learning, however, the authors identify a number of factors that may have affected the outcomes and they recommend that additional research on other grade levels and content areas needs to be conducted.

Researchers have also examined if computer technology can be used to effectively teach about diversity. Lee and Bertera (2007) designed a study to determine if participation in an on line diversity forum (ODF) would influence students, perception of their cultural competency, and positively influence their relationships with students, family members, and neighbors. They also wanted to identify the specific benefits of using instructional technology to support a multicultural course. The authors surveyed students who took a multicultural course in their masters of social work program. The participants completed a survey that assessed how the instructional technology influenced their cultural competency. The researchers also conducted a content analysis of student on-line postings.

Based on the postings, two groups were identified. The positive group believed that they appreciated the opportunity to share with other students and reported that they learned from the experience. The negative group criticized the appropriateness of the on-line forum and felt it was a nuisance. Interestingly the negative group posted more anonymous messages on the forum. The results, while generally positive, did not support the claim that instructional technology always enhances learning. It may be that the participants' initial attitude about multicultural education and beliefs about on-line instruction may have clouded the results. Students who are open to multicultural issues and competent in the use of on-line instruction may have responded differently than students who are negative about multicultural education and do not feel competent in on-line instruction.

Another extensive study was conducted by Kulik (1994) who conducted a meta-analysis on a set of 97 studies examining the effects of technology on learning. A meta-analysis is procedure that compares the effects of a relevant variable across a range of studies. Kulik argued that in order to understand the effects of computers it is necessary to identify how they are used. For example, a computer can be used as a tutor, to manage information, simulations, or for programming. Each of these uses may influence learning in a different way. The results indicated that the most positive and consistent effect concerned tutoring. Elementary and high school students generally learned more in classes that used computer tutoring. No other computer application had a consistent effect. In another meta-analysis, Bayraktar (2001) investigated the effects of computer-aided instruction on science achievement. The results indicated that the effect of the computer varied by the way it was used. The most effective mode of instruction was simulation, followed by tutorial. The findings of Kulik (1994) and Bayraktar (2001) suggest that the computer may be best used for some instructional goals and not for others.

Student Learning Style and Technology

Student learning style may also influence the effects of computer technology on learning. Ross, Drysdale, and Schulz (2001) examined learning style and performance in a computer applications class. Students were measured on the Gregorc Style Delineator (Gregorc, 1982). This assessment categorizes learning in four ways: Concrete Sequential (practical, thorough, well organized, analytical); Abstract Sequential (evaluative, analytical, logical, and orderly); Abstract Random (focus on the world of feeling and emotion), and Concrete Random (organize information in three-dimensional patterns, think intuitively and impulsively). The authors assessed whether learning style influenced the grades obtained in the class. The results indicated that Abstract Sequential and Concrete Sequential learners performed better in the computer course than Abstract Random and Concrete Random students. The authors argued that students with CS and AS learning styles are suited to computer tasks such as programming because these activities require linear processing and logical reasoning skills. These findings suggest that the learning style mediates the positive effects of computer-aided instruction. The positive effects of computer application are not equivalent for all learners.

Research has also identified differences between males and females on attitudes about computer use. Weber and Custer (2005) studied the preferences of male and female middle and high school students enrolled in technology classes. The results indicated that females preferred designing activities that involved a focus on problem solving or to use technology for communication. Males preferred utilizing activities where they could build or construct items. These findings suggest that gender mediates the way in which technology is used.

Healy (1998), a more vocal critic, explicated other problems with computer technology and education. One problem is that computers will not turn bad teachers into good ones. A teacher's philosophy and orientation are not likely to be changed as a result of technology. Teachers are likely to select software and assignments that fit into their existing ideologies. If teachers believe they should feed facts to students, then the technology will be used to collect and categorize facts. If teachers believe that they should facilitate problem solving and collaboration, they will use technology to accomplish these goals.

Additionally, teachers may not be adequately trained to take full advantage of technological opportunities. Selfe (1999) stated that when teachers are not adequately trained, they resort to commercial programs written by programmers who do not have substantial educational training. Programs designed to teach composition, for example, may be little more than electronic versions of a printed grammar textbook. Prepackaged programs simply do what has always been part of the curriculum: drill, memorization, and word processing. How these tasks prepare students for the 21st century is not clear.

One argument that is often advanced in support of technology is that it makes learning fun. Healy (1998) countered that just because something is fun does not mean that it has educational value. Learning can be fun but it also is hard work. Technology can short circuit the process of cultivating a work ethic that is vital to academic and "real-world success." Advocates may contend that technological competence helps individuals work smarter not harder. Yet there is a rather compelling data base on the positive effects of diligence and effort on academic success (e.g. Covington, 2000; Dweck, 1986). Much computer software, however, allows students to develop impulsive and trial and error responses that simply do not facilitate higher order thinking.

Healy (1998) also observed that newer technologies emphasize rapid processing of visual symbols such as computer icons and minimize verbal fluency fostered through reading, interaction, and argument. Westby and Atencio (2002) raise similar concerns. They observed that printed texts require readers to read left to right and up and down. Computers, on the other hand may use hypertext that includes graphics, animation, video, and digitized sound. With this medium, readers, move rapidly from one text chunk to another, non-sequentially. Visual and aural texts have taken the place of the written and spoken word. Watch how students "surf" through different web sites. They may be drawn to images that are aesthetically appealing rather than cognitively challenging.

The computer may be more that just a tool to promote decision making and problem solving. A shovel, a lawnmower, or a broom are tools we use to complete certain tasks, but they do not have much of an effect on the way the brain processes information. Westby and Atencio (2002) observed: "The ways that children access information on a computer, the manner of its presentation, and the ways it can be manipulated all alter children's perceptions of knowing and doing" (p. 74).

Technology influences socio-emotional development and relational competency. Think for a moment about students who are labeled the "computer geeks." These students may be viewed as socially awkward, isolated, and immature. The computer does not tell these students to blow their noses when they run, how to take turns in conversation, to "get a grip" when they don't get their way or feel shame when they hurt someone's feelings. These competencies are only developed and refined through face-to-face communication with significant others. Think about the way these students react when their computer "goes down," or freezes. Do they become agitated, unsure of what to do, unable to decide on alternative activities?

Authors such as Goleman (1995) and Gardner (1993; 1999) contended that emotional and interpersonal skills are extremely important to academic and personal success but are often neglected in the instructional process. The emotionally mature individual can take the perspectives of others, and read emotional states, and can suspend immediate gratification. Excessive time watching television or connected to a computer limits the amount of time a child is engaged in meaningful social interaction. Technology, according to Healy (1998), can not develop "feeling" centers of the brain.

Mobile Phones and Instructional Communication

Mobile technology, specifically cell phones. is dramatically influencing the instructional landscape. More and more students bring cell phones or personal digital assistants into the classrooms. Some school districts view cell phones as a problem and ban their use but these policies are difficult to enforce. After the school shootings in Columbine Colorado, and the terrorist attacks in New York, Pennsylvania, and Washington, D.C., parents have pressured schools to permit students to have cell phones.

There is a growing trend to use mobile technology to meet academic goals. Katz (2005), for example, discussed various uses of cell phone technology. He stated that cell phones could be used for tutoring. Cell phones can be used to access Internet experts who can provide help on definitions and reference information. They can also be used to connect students with faculty, students, administrators, and coaches to find out about assignments, adjust schedules, and get help on academic and personal matters.

Administrators can use cell phones to manage attendance and adjust schedules set up meetings. Parents can use cell phones to monitor the activities of their children, to e-mail teachers, and to stay connected to their students.

Even though there are some positives, there are also a number of problems with cell phone use. Katz (2005) identified four specific problems: class disruption, delinquency, chicanery, and teacher autonomy.

There are several ways that cell phones cause class disruption. It is not uncommon for students to receive and respond to phone calls or text messages during class. Students will also use their phones to send text messages, play games, or to participate in other non-academic activities. Katz reported a case where a student who missed lunch used his phone to order a pizza.

A second problem is delinquency. Katz observed that mobile phones might be the targets of theft or phone piracy (demanding to use someone else's cell phone for personal use). Perhaps one of the most disturbing problem is the use of cyberbullying. Smith, Mahdavi, Carvalho, Fisher, Russell, and Tippett (2008) defined cyberbulling as "An aggressive, intentional act carried out by a group or individual, using electronic forms of contact, repeatedly and over time against a victim who cannot easily defend him or herself" (p. 376). Smith et al. state that cyberbullying may include phone calls, text messages, video clip bullying, and e-mails. There are no clear boundaries when these events occur. A student can receive a bullying message at home, in class or on the playground.

A third problem identified by Katz (2005) is chicanery such as truancy and cheating. Students who "skip school" use cell phones to contact friends and find out when it is safe to return to school without being detected. Cell phones can also be used to cheat. Pictures of a test can be taken and sent to other students who will take the test later in the day. It's also possible for a student in class to text an answer to another student in the same class.

The final problem is the erosion of teacher autonomy. More and more schools are implementing policy about cell phones. Some schools want to ban them altogether. Some require students to turn off the phones before coming to class, others penalize students by lowering their grade if their cell phone rings, vibrates, or plays a song during class. Monitoring these policies takes teachers and students away from academic engagement.

Mobile phone technology will continue to challenge educators. The number of functions a cell phone will perform will increase. It is unlikely that school authorities will be successful in banning cell phones. Not having any policy, however, allows the student who may not like what is happening in a given instructional moment to surf the web, text friends, or play games. Rather than viewing cell phones only as a source of irritation, crime and disruption, teachers can consider thoughtful ways to utilize them to support instructional goals.

> ### Reflection
> ♦ Identify three ways to use cell phones to meet academic goals.
> ♦ What would you do if a student told you that he/she was receiving harassing text messages?

Technology will continue to be an ubiquitous force in education. It is unreasonable to believe that technology will not have an important place in education. Moreover, education will always lag behind technological innovations. Postman (1995) make an insightful observation about technology and teaching when he stated:

> To be against technology makes no more sense than to be against food. We can't live without either. But to observe that it is dangerous to eat too much food, or to eat food that has no nutritional value is not to be "anti-food." It is to suggest what may be the uses of food. Technology education aims at students' learning about what technology helps us do and what it hinders us from doing; it is about how technology uses us, for good or ill, and about how it has used people in the past, for good or ill. It is about how technology creates new worlds, for good or ill.
>
> (p. 192)

Attributes of Meaningful Learning Using Technology

In order to deal effectively with technology in its many forms, teachers have a clear idea on what they want to accomplish. Ashburn (2006) discusses six attributes of meaningful learning using technology (MLT). The first is *intentionality*. Teachers and students should be directed toward achieving specific learning objectives. Teachers provide the context for learning by identifying the curriculum standards and by designing learning activities that facilitate the accomplishment of the outcomes. This attribute presupposes that teachers are able to design the learning activities or have access to support providers who can help the teacher create the experiences.

The second attribute is *content*. The goal here is to use technology to foster the exploration of "big ideas," or essential questions. Ashburn contends that challenging students to examine big ideas provides the "connective tissue" that binds classroom learning to their personal lives. For example, we might ask future teachers to examine how technology impacts literacy. What does someone need to know to be a literate user of technology? This question can take students in several directions. They can explore different types of technologies, or they can categorize different competencies that are needed.

Authentic work is the third attribute discussed by Ashburn. Students must be challenged to engage in tasks that require complex thinking and problem solving. This is a major departure from an orientation that encourages students to memorize facts or work on worksheets. For example, students may be challenged to closely investigate the effects of immigration patterns, legal and illegal, on the economy. This requires students to move past personal bias and examine sources and evaluate them on their relevance and credibility. Authentic work makes students use technology to do the work that historians, and scientists do. Teachers must be willing to design learning tasks that are "real" to students and as a result may challenge the teacher's belief systems. They also need to understand the orientations of students. Our discussion of culturally responsive teaching is an essential criterion for developing authentic work for students.

The fourth attribute identified by Ashburn is *active inquiry*. The feature of MLT encourages students to think deeply and purposefully about the types of questions they want to answer, to analyze the information used to answer the questions, and to think critically about the degree to which the evidence they collect appropriately answers their questions. Let's return to the example about examining the question, "How does immigration, legal and illegal, impact the economy? The students need to consider where they will obtain information on this question. Will the "data" come from U.S. Government Statistics that are available on Web pages? Will they collect reports from "independent agencies," local and state? What criteria will the students use to assess the value of the information they collect. Once they analyze the data, they must draw conclusions from their analysis and communicate their findings.

Ashburn identifies five obligations that teachers must meet. First, teachers need to know how to create a "culture of inquiry," where learning units are connected to relevant standards. Second, teachers need to be skillful in using student questions to connect to the curriculum standards. For example, the teacher must know how to link the student questions to an appropriate Web-based resource. This presupposes that the teacher is competent in navigating the Web. Third, the teachers must model the inquiry method and assess student understanding of the process. Teachers cannot just turn them loose and expect them to locate information that solves the problem. Teachers must be skillful in helping students generate questions they will own and connect them to the standards they are trying to meet. Teachers need to model the inquiry process by showing students how to use the appropriate technologies to work through the inquiry process. Fourth, teachers need to help transform student identity. Students must see themselves as principled investigators, rather than as passive regurgitators of what the teacher deems important. Finally, teachers need skills in using the technological tools that undergird the inquiry process.

Mental model construction is the fifth attribute discussed by Ashburn. Mental models are the constructions of how the world works. Ashburn contends that teaching for meaningful learning requires the teacher to help students unpack or make visible their implicit theories. All students come to class with notions about the way the world works. Teachers can help students to understand the way they make sense out of instructional material by cognitive mapping, metaphor analysis, or idea webbing. In the technology classroom, software programs can be used to identify student constructions. Ashburn suggests that the MLToolbox Inquiry Station can be used to scaffold the development of student constructions of the content they are exploring. Technology can be used, therefore, to help students understand how they think and organize material. Think about the way a PowerPoint presentation illustrates how students make connections among important ideas. We stressed in Chapter 3 that different cultures have preferred ways of organizing and sequencing information, technology can be used to help students and teachers understand how material is stored, organized, and retrieved.

The final attribute discussed by Ashburn is *collaborative work*. Within this approach, students work collaboratively on common tasks to accomplish common goals. In Chapter 9 we discussed the importance of collaboration and cooperative learning. Teachers need to design learning tasks that take advantage of technology and fulfill the obligations of collaborative learning. For example, student investigative teams can be developed to explore an important question. In these groups, students need to discuss, argue, deliberate, reflect, and share their ideas on the question under consideration.

The recommendations discussed above may seem complex and difficult, but technology is here to stay. We challenge teachers to learn as much as they can so that they can make the most out of it. We would like to close this discussion by referring to Postman (1995) who offered the following:

1   All technological change is a Faustian bargain. For every advantage a new technology offers, there is always a corresponding disadvantage.
2   The advantages and disadvantages of new technologies are never distributed evenly among the population. This means that every new technology benefits some and harms others.

3 Embedded in every technology there is a powerful idea, sometimes two or three powerful ideas. Like language itself, a technology predisposes us to favor and value certain perspectives and accomplishments and to subordinate others. Every technology has a philosophy, which is given expression in how the technology makes people use their minds, in what it makes us do with our bodies, in how it codifies the world, in which senses it amplifies, and in which of our emotional and intellectual tendencies it disregards.

4 A new technology usually makes war against an old technology. It competes with it for time, attention, money prestige, and a "world-view."

5 Technological change is not additive, it is ecological. A new technology does not merely add something; it changes everything.

6 Because of the symbolic forms in which information is encoded, different technologies have different intellectual and emotional biases.

7 Because of the accessibility and speed of their information, different technologies have different political biases.

8 Because of the physical form, different technologies have different sensory biases.

9 Because of the conditions in which we attend to them, different technologies have different social biases.

10 Because of their technical and economic structure, different technologies have different content biases. (pp. 192–193)

In this chapter, we have explored the conundrum evolving around educational practice and technological development. Mr. Harrison, the teacher in the opening of this chapter faces and will continue to face some very difficult decisions. New technologies will continually be developed. Just as one is mastered, a new one will come along. Some of these developments will contribute to classroom goals, others will amount to bells and whistles that on the surface look good but don't have much of a direct influence on learning. Sorting out these differences will not be easy. School districts, publishing houses, and families will put pressure on Mr. Harrison to make the right choice.

The digital divide will not go away but will continue. Students from privilege will continue to have increased access that may or may not prepare them academically. Access to some of the exciting developments we reviewed earlier in this chapter will not be equal for all students. Yet, Mr. Harrison has an obligation to teach all the students assigned to his class. He will be well aware of the substantial role that interpersonal communication plays in the classroom, and that technology will not help him create empathy, caring, and character. The way in which he will balance and manage these differences will have a major impact on the learning and the student affective orientations to learning.

Reflection

- How would you advise Mr. Harrison to best use technology?
- How should schools accommodate students who cannot afford computers?
- What type of training will help Mr. Harrison accomplish his goals?

Learning Activities

- Design a research assignment around an essential question (e.g. What is the impact of global warming on the environment?; What are the effects, social and economic, of illegal immigration?). Ask students to contact experts who are studying these problems. Once the research is completed, ask students to develop a PowerPoint presentation to report their findings to the class.
- Design a problem-solving task that requires students to participate in "virtual groups" through the use of mobile technology. Upon completion of the assignment have students write a reflection paper on the quality of the solution and the challenges of working in virtual groups.
- Design a cyberbullying policy. What consequences will you impose on students who use the computer to harass other students?
- Identify a contemporary controversial topic. Ask students to create a "blog" on Twitter. Select a group of students to content analyze the blogs. What were the common themes or perspectives that were posted by the students?

Resources: Sources for Providing Online Safeguards

- The International Society for Technology in Education
  http://cnets.iste.org
- I-Safe
  www.isafe.org
- Parents guide to the internet
  www.ed.gov/pubs/parents/internet
- CyberSmart! Education Company
  www.cybersmart.org
- NetSmartz
  www.netsmartz.org
- Stop cyberbullying
  www.stopcyberbullying.org

Bibliography

Albert, L. (1996). *Cooperative discipline.* Circle Pines, MN: American Guidance Service.

Alberto, P. A., & Troutman, C. A. (2006). *Applied behavior analysis for teachers* (7th ed.). Upper Saddle River, NJ: Merrill/Prentice Hall.

Algozzine, B., Browder, D., Karvonen, M., Test, D. W., & Wood, W. M. (2001). Effects of interventions to promote self-determination for individuals with disabilities. *Review of Educational Research, 71*(2), 219–277.

Altman, I., & Taylor, D. (1973). *Social penetration.* New York: Holt.

American Association of University Women (AAUW) (1991). *Shortchanging girls, shortchanging America.* Washington, DC: Greenberg–Lake Analysis Group.

American Association of University Women (AAUW) (1999). *Gender gaps: Where schools still fail our children.* New York: Marlow & Company.

American Psychiatric Association (1994). *Diagnostic and statistical manual of mental disorders* (4th ed.). Washington, DC: Author.

American Speech-Language-Hearing Association (1993). Definitions of communication disorders and variations. *AHSA, 35*(Suppl. 10), 40–41.

Andersen, J. F. (1979). Teacher immediacy as a predictor of teaching effectiveness. In D. Nimmo (Ed.) *Communication yearbook 3* (pp. 543–559). New Brunswick, NJ: Transaction Books.

Andersen, J., Nussbaum, J., Pecchioni, L., & Grant, J. A. (1999). Interaction skills in instructional settings. In A. Vangelisti, J. Daly, & G. W. Friedrich (Eds.), *Teaching communication* (2nd ed.) (pp. 359–374). Mahwah, NJ: Lawrence Erlbaum.

Anderson, R., Welch, W., & Harris, L. (1984). Inequities in opportunities for computer literacy. *The Computer Teacher, 11,* 10–12.

Arends, R. I., Winitzky, N. E., & Tannenbaum, M. D. (2001). *Exploring teaching* (2nd ed.). Boston: McGraw-Hill.

Armstrong, T. (2000) *Multiple intelligences in the classroom* (2nd ed.). Alexandria, VA: Association for Supervision and Curriculum Development.

Aronson, E., Blaney, N., Stephan, C., Sikes, J., & Snapp, M. (1978). *The jigsaw classroom.* Beverly Hills, CA: Sage.

Ashburn, E. (2006). *Meaningful learning using technology: What educators need to know.* New York: Teachers College Press.

Azmitia, M. (1998). Peer interactive minds: Developmental, theoretical, and methodological issues. In D. Faulkner, K. Littleton, & M. Woodhead (Eds.), *Learning relationships in the classroom* (pp. 207–234). New York: Routledge.

Baca, L. M., & Cervantes, H. T. (2004). *The bilingual special education interface* (4th ed.). Upper Saddle River, NJ: Merrill/Prentice Hall.

Bandura, A. (1977a). *Social learning theory*. Morristown, NJ: General Learning Press.

Bandura, A. (1977b). Self-efficacy: Toward a unifying theory of behavioral change. *Psychological Review, 84,* 191–215.

Bandura, A. (1981). Self-referent thought: A developmental analysis of self-efficacy. In J. H. Flavell & L. Ross (Eds.), *Social cognitive development: Frontiers and possible futures*. Cambridge: Cambridge University Press.

Bandura, A. (1986). *Social foundations of thought and action: A social cognitive theory*. Englewood Cliffs, NJ: Prentice Hall.

Bandura, A. (1991). Social cognitive theory of self-regulation. *Organizational Behavior and Human Decision Processes, 50,* 248–287.

Bandura, A. (1997). *Self-efficacy: The exercise of control*. New York: W.H. Freeman.

Banks, J. A. (1994). *Multiethnic education: Theory and practice*. Needham Heights, MA: Allyn & Bacon.

Banks, J. A. (1999). *An introduction to multicultural education* (2nd ed.). Boston: Allyn & Bacon.

Banks, J. A., & Banks, C. M. (1989). *Multicultural education: Issues and perspectives*. Boston: Allyn & Bacon.

Baringer, D. K., & McCroskey, J. C. (2000). Immediacy in the classroom: Student immediacy. *Communication Education, 49,* 178–186.

Barnlund, D. C. (Ed.) (1968). *Interpersonal communication*. Boston: Houghton-Mifflin.

Barone, F. J. (1997). Bullying in school. *Phi Delta Kappan, 79,* 80–82.

Bate, B. (1992). *Communication and the sexes*. Prospect Heights, IL: Waveland Press.

Batsche, G. M., & Knoff, H. M. (1994). Bullies and their victims: Understanding pervasive problem in the school. *School Psychology Review, 23,* 165–174.

Battistich, V., & Hom, A. (1997). The relationship between students' sense of their school as a community and their involvement in problem behaviors. *American Journal of Public Health, 87*(12), 1997–2001.

Battistich, V., Solomon, D., Kim, D., Watson, M., & Schaps, E. (1995). Schools, communities, poverty levels of student populations, and students' attitudes, motives, and performance: A multilevel analysis. *American Educational Research Journal, 32*(3), 627–658.

Baumeister, R. F., & Leary, M. R. (1995). The need to belong: Desire for interpersonal attachments as a fundamental human motivation. *Psychological Bulletin, 117*(3), 497–529.

Baxter, L. (1987) Symbols of relationship identity in relationship cultures. *Journal of Social and Personal Relationships, 4,* 261–279.

Baxter, L. (1988) A dialectical perspective on communication strategies in relationship development. In S. W. Duck, D. F. Hay, S. E. Hobfoll, W. Iches, & B. Montgomery (Eds.), *Handbook of personal relationships* (pp. 257–273). London: John Wiley.

Baxter, L. (1990). Dialectical contradictions in relationship development. *Journal of Social and Personal Relationships, 7,* 69–88.

Baxter, L. (1992) Forms and functions of intimate play in personal relationships. *Human Communication Research, 18,* 336–363.

Baxter, L. (1993). The social side of personal relationships: A dialectical perspective. In S. Duck (Ed.), *Understanding relationship processes, 3: Social context and relationships* (pp. 139–165). Newbury Park, CA: Sage.

Bayraktar, S. (2001). A meta-analysis of the effectiveness of computer-assisted instruction in science education. *Journal of Research on Technology in Education, 34,* 173–189.

Beatty, M., McCroskey, J. C., & Heisel, J. (1998). Communication apprehension as temperamental expression: A communibiological paradigm. *Communication Monographs, 65,* 197–219.

Beatty, M., McCroskey, J. C., & Valencic, K. (2001). *The biology of communication: A communibiological perspective.* Cresskill, NJ: Hampton Press.

Becker, B. J. (1989). Gender and science achievement: A reanalysis of studies from two meta-analyses. *Journal of Research in Science Teaching, 26,* 141–169.

Becker, H., & Sterling, C. (1987). Equity in school computer use: National data and neglected considerations. *Journal of Educational Computing Research, 3,* 289–311.

Belinky, M., Clinchy, B., Goldberger, N., & Tarule, J. (1986). *Woman's ways of knowing.* New York: Basic Books.

Bell, R. A., & Daly, J. A. (1984). The affinity-seeking function of communication. *Communication Monographs, 51,* 91–115.

Belleck, A., Kliebard, H., Hyman, R., & Smith, F. (1966). *The language of the classroom.* New York: Columbia Teachers College Press.

Bennett, C. (1995). Preparing teachers for cultural diversity and national standards of academic excellence. *Journal of Teacher Education, 46,* 259–266.

Berlo, D. (1960). *The process of communication.* New York: Holt, Rinehart and Winston.

Bernard, B. (1993). Fostering resiliency in kids. *Educational Leadership, 51,* 44–48.

Bernstein, B. (1990). *The structuring of pedagogic discourse.* London: Routledge.

Block, J. H. (1984). *Sex role identity and ego development.* San Francisco, CA: Jossey-Bass.

Bloom, B. S. (1976). *Human characteristics of school learning.* New York: McGraw-Hill.

Bloom, B., Englehart, M., Furst, E., Hill, W., & Krathwohl, D. (1956). *Taxonomy of educational objectives: Cognitive domain.* New York: Longmans, Green.

Book, C. (1999). Lecturing. In A. Vangelisti, J. Daly, & G. Friedrich (Eds.), *Teaching communication* (2nd ed.) (pp. 333–347). Mahwah, NJ: Lawrence Erlbaum.

Book, C., & McCaleb, J. (1985). Teacher clarity and student awareness and achievement. Paper presented at the annual meeting of the Speech Communication Association, Denver.

Boster, F. J., Meyer, G. S., Roberto, A. J., Inge, C. & Strom, R. (2006). Some effects of videostreaming on educational achievement. *Communication Education, 55,* 46–62.

Bostrom, R. (1983). *Persuasion.* Englewood Cliffs, NJ: Prentice Hall.

Bosworth, K. (1995). Caring for others and being cared for: Students talk caring in school. *Phi Delta Kappan, 77,* 686–693.

Boutte, G. (1999). *Multicultural education: Raising consciousness.* Belmont, CA: Wadsworth.

Boyatzis, C. J., Baloff, P., & Durieux, C. (1998). Effects of perceived attractiveness and academic success on early adolescent peer popularity. *Journal of Genetic Psychology, 159,* 337–345.

Bransford, J. D., Brown, A. L., & Cocking, R. R. (2000). *How people learn: Brain, mind, experience, and school.* Washington, DC: National Academy Press.

Brendtro, L., Brokenleg, M., & Van Brokern, S. (1990). *Reclaiming youth at risk: Our hope for the future.* Bloomington, IN: National Educational Service.

Brewster, A. B., & Bowen, G. L. (2004). Teacher support and the school engagement of Latino middle and high school students at risk of school failure. *Child and Adolescent Social Work Journal, 21,* 47–67.

Brill, C. L. (1994). The effects of participation in service learning on adolescents with disabilities. *The Association for Professionals in Service for Adolescents, 17*(4), 369–380.

Bronfenbrenner, U. (1979). *The ecology of human development.* Cambridge, MA: Harvard University Press.

Bronfenbrenner, U. (1986). Alienation and the four worlds of childhood. *Phi Delta Kappan, 7,* 430–436.

Brooks, J. G., & Brooks, M. G. (1993). *The case for constructivist classrooms.* Alexandria, VA: Association for Supervision and Curriculum Development.

Brophy, J. (1981). Teacher praise: A functional analysis. *Review of Educational Research, 51,* 5–32.

Brophy, J. (1998). *Motivating students to learn.* Boston: McGraw-Hill.

Brophy, J., & Good, T. L. (1986). Teacher behavior and student achievement. In M. C. Wittrock (Ed.), *Handbook of research on teaching.* New York: Macmillan.

Brophy, J., & Good, T. L. (2000). *Looking in classrooms* (8th ed.). New York: Harper & Row.

Brophy, J., & Rohrkemper, M. (1981). The influence of problem ownership on teachers' perceptions of and strategies for coping with problem students. *Journal of Educational Psychology, 73,* 295–311.

Brown, M. S., & Bauer, A. M. (1994). Acting out or acting together? Social community formation and behavior management. *Beyond Behavior, 5*(3), 15–18.

Brown, M., Higgins, K., & Hartley, K. (2001). Teachers and technology equity. *Teaching Exceptional Children, 33,* 32–39.

Brugh, M. (1997). Teaching character education through service learning. *Social Studies Review, 37*(1), 68–72.

Bryan, T., Pearl, R., & Herzog, A. (1989). Learning disabled adolescents' vulnerability to crime: Attitudes, anxieties, experiences. *Learning Disability Quarterly, 5,* 51–60.

Bryant, J., Comisky, P., & Zillmann, D. (1979). Teacher's humor in the college classroom. *Communication Education, 28,* 110–118.

Burgoon, J. K. (1985). Nonverbal signals. In M. L. Knapp, & G. R. Miller (Eds.), *Handbook of interpersonal communication* (pp. 344–390). Newbury Park, CA: Sage.

Burleson, B., & Sampter, W. (1990). Effects of cognitive complexity on the perceived importance of communication skills in friends. *Communication Research, 17*, 165–182.

Bush, A. (1977). An empirical investigation of teacher clarity. Paper presented at the annual meeting of the American Educational Research Association, April.

Bush, A. J., Kennedy, J. J., & Cruickshank, D. R. (1977). An empirical investigation of teacher clarity. *Journal of Teacher Education, 28*, 53–58.

Cairn, R. W., & Kielsmeier, J. (1991). *Growing hope: A sourcebook on integrating youth service into the school curriculum.* Roseville, MN: National Youth Leadership Council.

Caplin, P. J., Crawford, M. J. S., & Hyde, J. T. E. (1997). *Gender differences in human cognition.* New York: Oxford University Press.

Carrozza, C. (1996). Using learning styles and multiple intelligences to differentiate instruction and assessment. In R. W. Strong, & H. F. Silver (Eds.), *An introduction to thoughtful curriculum and assessment* (pp. 145–152). Woodbridge, NJ: The Thoughtful Education Press.

Carruthers, W. L., Sweeny, B., Kmitta, D., & Harris, G. (1996). Conflict resolution: An examination of the research literature. *The School Counselor, 44*, 5–17.

Cartledge, G., & Talbert-Johnson, C. (1998). African American males and serious emotional disturbance (SED): Genetic disposition versus social bias. Paper presented at the American Education Research Association, San Diego, CA.

CAST (2008). *Universal design for learning guidelines*, version 1.0. Wakefield, MA: Author. Center for Applied Special Technology, available at: www.cast.org/publications/UDLguidelines/version1.html. Accessed September 26, 2009

Cazden, C. (1988). *Classroom discourse: The language of teaching and learning.* Portsmouth, NH: Heinemann.

Chandler, L. K., & Dahlquist, C. M. (2010). *Functional assessment: Strategies to prevent and remediate challenging behaviors in school settings* (3rd ed.). Upper Saddle River, NJ: Merrill.

Char, C., & Hawkins, J. (1987). Charting the course: Involving teachers in the formative research and design of the Voyage of Mimi. In R. D. Pea, & K. Sheingold (Eds.), *Mirrors of the minds: Patterns of experience in educational computing.* Norwood, NJ: Ablex.

Chesebro, J. L., McCroskey, J. C., Atwater, D., Bahrenfuss, R., Cawelti, G., Gaudino, J., & Hodges, H. (1992). Communication apprehension and self-perceived communication competence of at-risk students. *Communication Education, 41*, 345–360.

Chizmar, J., & Walbert, M. (1999). Web-based learning environments guided by principles of good teaching practice. *The Journal of Economic Education, 30*, 248–259.

Christensen, L., & Menzel, K. (1998). The linear relationship between student reports of teacher immediacy behaviors and perceptions of state motivation and of cognitive, affective, and behavioral learning. *Communication Education, 47*, 82–91.

Christophel, D. M. (1990). The relationship among teacher immediacy behaviors, student motivation, and learning. *Communication Education, 39,* 323–340.

Civikly, J. M. (1992a). Clarity: Teachers and students making sense of instruction. *Communication Education, 41,* 138–152.

Civikly, J. M. (1992b). *Classroom communication: Principles and practices.* Dubuque, IA: Wm C. Brown.

Claxton, C. S. (1990) Learning styles, minority students and effective education. *Journal of Developmental Education, 14,* 6–8.

Cleary, L. M., & Peacock, T. D. (1998) *Collected wisdom: American Indian education.* Boston: Allyn & Bacon.

Cleg, A. (1987) Why questions? In W. W. Wilen (Ed.). *Questions, questioning, techniques, and effective teaching* (pp. 11–21). Washington, DC: National Education Association.

Cognition and Technology Group at Vanderbilt (1997). *The Jasper project: Lessons in curriculum instruction, assessment and professional development.* Mahwah, NJ: Lawrence Erlbaum.

Cohen, P. A., Kulik, J. A., & Kulik, C. C. (1992). Educational outcomes of tutoring: A meta-analysis of findings. *American Educational Research Journal, 19,* 237–248.

Coleman, J. M., McHam, L. A., & Minnett, A. M. (1992). Similarities in the social competencies of learning disabled and low achieving elementary school children. *Journal of Learning Disabilities, 25,* 671–677.

Coleman, J. S., Campbell, E. Q., Hobson, C. J., McParland, J., Mood, A. M., Weinfeld, F. D., & York, R. L. (1966). *Equality of educational opportunity.* Washington, DC: U.S. Government Printing Office.

Collier, M. J. (1994) Cultural identity and intercultural communication. In L. Samovar, & R. Porter (Eds.), *Intercultural communication: A reader* (7th ed.) (pp. 36–45). Belmont, CA: Wadsworth.

Collier, M. J., & Powell, R. G. (1990). Ethnicity, instructional communication and classroom systems. *Communication Quarterly, 38,* 334–349.

Comadena, M., & Prusank, D. (1988). Communication apprehension and academic achievement among elementary and middle school students. *Communication Education, 32,* 185–193.

Comstock, J., Rowell, E., & Bowers, J. W. (1995). Food for thought: Teacher nonverbal immediacy, student learning, and curvilinearity. *Communication Education, 44,* 251–266.

Conboy, S. M. (1994). *Peer mediation and anger control: Two ways to resolve conflict.* St. Paul, MN: University of St. Thomas.

Condit, C. M. (2000). Culture and biology in human communication: Toward a multi-causal model. *Communication Education, 49,* 7–24.

Condravy, J., Skirboll, E., & Taylor, R. (1988). Faculty perceptions of classroom gender dynamics. *Women and Language, 21,* 18–28.

Conrad, D., & Hedin, D. (1991). School-based community service: What we know from research and theory. *Phi Delta Kappan, 72*(10), 743–749.

Conroy, M. A., Sutherland, A. S., Snyder, K. S., Al-Hendawi, M., & Vo, A. (2009). Creating a positive classroom atmosphere: Teachers' use of effective praise and feedback. *Beyond Behavior, 18,* 18–26.

Cooper, P. J., & Simmonds, C. (1999) *Communication for the classroom teacher* (6th ed.). Boston: Allyn & Bacon.

Coopersmith, S. (1967). *The antecedents of self-esteem*. San Francisco, CA: W. H. Freeman.

Covington, M. V. (2000). Goal theory, motivation, and school achievement: An integrative review. *Annual Review of Psychology, 51*, 171–200.

Cox, B., & Ramirez, M. (1981). Cognitive styles: Implications for multiethnic education. In J. Banks (Ed.), *Education in the 80's*. Washington, DC: National Education Association.

Crist-Whitzel, J. (1985). *Computers for all children: A literature review of equity issues in computer utilization*. San Francisco: Far West Laboratory for Educational Research and Development (ERIC Document Reproduction Service No 419–512).

Cronin, C., & Jreisat, S. (1995). Effects of modeling on the use of nonsexist language among high school fresh persons and seniors. *Sex Roles: A Journal of Research, 33*, 819–831.

Croninger, R. G., & Lee, V. E. (in press). Social capital and dropping out of high school: Benefits to at-risk student of teachers' support and guidance. *Teachers College Record*.

Cuban, L. (2001). *Oversold and underused: Computers in the classroom*. Cambridge, MA: Harvard University Press.

Cullinan, D., Epstein, M. H., & Lloyd, J. W. (1991). Evaluation of conceptual models of behavior disorders. *Behavioral Disorders, 16*(2), 148–157.

Cunningham, R. (1987). What kind of question is that? In W. W. Wilen (Ed.). *Questions, questioning, techniques, and effective teaching* (pp. 67–93). Washington, DC: National Education Association.

Cupach, W. P., & Imahori, T. (1993). Managing social predicaments created by others: A comparison of Japanese and American facework. *Western Journal of Communication, 57*, 431–444.

Cupach, W. P., & Metts, S. (1990). Remedial processes in embarrassing predicaments. In J. A. Andersen (Ed.), *Communication yearbook 13* (pp. 353–364). Newbury Park, CA: Sage.

Cupach, W. P., & Metts, S. (1992). The effects of types of predicament and embarrassability on remedial responses to embarrassing situations. *Communication Quarterly, 40*, 149–161.

Curwin, R. L. (1993). The healing power of altruism. *Educational Leadership*, November, 36–39.

Daly, J. A., & Friedrich, G. (1981). The development of communication apprehension: A retrospective analysis of contributory correlates. *Communication Quarterly, 29*, 243–255.

Damon, W. (1995). *Greater expectations: Overcoming the culture of indulgence in America's homes and schools*. New York: Free Press.

Dance, F. E. X. (Ed.) (1982). *Human communication theory*. New York: Harper & Row.

Darch, C., Miller, A., & Shippen, P. (1998). Instructional classroom management: A proactive model for managing student behavior. *Beyond Behavior, 9*(3), 18–27.

Darling, A. (1989). Signaling non-comprehensions in the classroom: Toward a descriptive typology. *Communication Education, 38*, 34–40.

Davis, B., Clarke, A. R. B., Francis, J., Hughes, G., MacMillan, J., McNeil, J., & Weshaver, P. (1992). Dress for respect: The effect of teacher dress on student expectations of deference behavior. *The Alberta Journal of Educational Research, 38,* 27–31.

Davis, H. A. (2003. Conceptualizing the role and influence of student–teacher relationships on children's social and cognitive development. *Educational Psychologist, 38,* 207–234.

Deci, E. L., & Ryan, R. M. (1985). *Intrinsic motivation and self-determination in human behavior.* New York: Plenum.

Deci, E. L., Vallerand, R. J., Pelletier, L. G., & Ryan, R. M. (1991). Motivation and education: The self-determination perspective. *Educational Psychologist, 26*(3 & 4), 325–346.

Delpit, L. (1995). *Other people's children: Cultural conflict in the classroom.* New York: The New York Press.

Dewey, J. (1963). *Experience and education.* New York: Macmillan.

Dewey, J. (1971). *The child and the curriculum and the school and society.* Chicago: University of Chicago Press.

Diefendorf, A. O. (1996). Hearing loss and its effects. In T. E. C. Smith, E. A. Polloway, J. R. Patton, & C. A. Dowdy, *Teaching students with special needs in inclusive setting* (7th ed.). Boston: Allyn & Bacon.

Diller, A., Houston, B., Morgan, K. P., & Ayim, M. (1996). *The gender question in education: Theory, pedagogy, and politics.* Boulder, CO: Westview Press.

Dindia, K., & Baxter, L. A. (1987). Definitions and theoretical perspectives on maintaining relationships. *Journal of Social and Personal Relationships, 4,* 143–158.

Downs, V. C., Javidi, M., & Nussbaum, J. (1988). An analysis of teachers' verbal communication within the college classroom: Use of humor, self-disclosure, and narratives. *Communication Education, 37,* 127–141.

Dreikurs, R., & Cassel, P. (1972). *Discipline without tears: What to do with children who misbehave.* New York: Hawthorn.

Dreikurs, R., Grunwald, B. B., & Pepper, F. C. (1982). *Maintaining sanity in the classroom.* New York: HarperCollins.

Duffy, T. M. (1997). Strategic teaching framework: An instructional model for learning complex interactive skills. In C. Dills, & A. Romiszowski (Eds.), *Instructional development state of art: Paradigms and educational technology* (Vol. 3, pp. 571–592). Englewood Cliffs, NJ: Educational Technology Publications.

Duncan, B. B., Forness, S. R., & Hartsough, C. (1995). Students identified as seriously emotionally disturbed in day treatment: Cognitive, psychiatric, and special education characteristics. *Behavioral Disorders, 29,* 238–252.

Dundon, B. L. (1999). My voice: An advocacy approach to service learning. *Educational Leadership,* December, 34–37.

Dunn, R., & Griggs, S. A. (Eds.) (2000). *Practical approaches to using learning styles in higher education.* Westport, CT: Bergin & Garvey.

Dweck, C. (1986). Motivational processes affecting learning. *American Psychologist, 41,* 1040–1048.

Eder, D., & Sanford, S. (1986). The development and maintenance of interactional norms among early adolescents. In P. Adler, & P. Andler (Eds.), *Sociological studies of child development* (Vol. I, pp. 283–300). Greenwich, CT: JAI.

Eisenberg, E. M. (1984). Ambiguity as strategy in organizational communication. *Communication Monographs, 51*, 227–242.

Ekman, P., & Friesen, W. V. (1969). Nonverbal leakage and clues to deception. *Psychiatry, 32*, 88–108.

Elias, M. J., & Schwab, Y. (2006). From compliance to responsibility: Social and emotional learning and classroom management. In C. M. Evertson, & C. S. Weinstein (Eds.), *Handbook of classroom management: Research, practice and contemporary issues* (pp. 309–342). Mahwah, NJ: Lawrence Erlbaum.

Elias, M. J., & Tobias, S. E. (1996). *Social problem solving: Interventions in the schools.* New York: Guilford.

Elias, M. J., et al. (1997). *Promoting social and emotional learning: Guidelines for educators.* Alexandria, VA: Association for Supervision and Curriculum Development.

Fairlie, R. W., London, R. A. Rosner, R., & Pastor, M. (2006). *Crossing the divide: Immigrant youth and digital disparity in California.* Santa Cruz, CA: Center for Justice, Tolerance, and Community. University of California Santa Cruz.

Fisher, J., & Smith-Davis, J. (1990). *Children of the inner cities: A NASDSE seminar.* Washington, DC: National Association of State Directors of Special Education.

Fleming, M. L., & Malone, M. R. (1983). The relationship of student characteristics and student performance in science as viewed by meta-analysis research. *Journal of Research in Science Teaching, 20*, 481–495.

Fogel, H., & Ehri, L. C. (2000). Teaching elementary students who speak Black English Vernacular to write in Standard English: Effects of dialect transformation practice. *Contemporary Educational Psychology, 25*, 212–235.

Forman, E. A., & Cazden, C. (1985). Exploring Vygotskyian perspectives in education: The cognitive value of peer interaction. In J. V. Wertsch (Ed.), *Culture, communication and cognition: Vygotskian perspectives.* New York: Cambridge University Press.

Forman, E., & Cazden, C. (1998). Exploring Vygotskian perspectives in education: The cognitive value of peer interaction. In D. Faulkner, K. Littleton, & M. Woodhead (Eds.), *Learning relationships in the classroom* (pp. 189–206). New York: Routledge.

Forness, S. R., & Kavale, K. A. (1988). Planning for the needs of children with serious emotional disturbance: The National Mental Health and Special Education Coalition. *Behavior Disorders, 13*, 127–133.

Forness, S. R., & Kavale, K. A. (1999). Treating social skill deficits in children with learning disabilities: A meta-analysis of the research. *Learning Disability Quarterly, 19*, 2–13.

Fox, L., Carta, J., Strain, P., Dunlap, G., & Hemmeter, M. L. (2009). Response to intervention and the pyramid model. Tampa, FL: University of South Florida Technical Assistance Center on Social Emotional Intervention for Young Children.

Freud, S. (1935). *A general introduction to psychoanalysis.* New York: Liveright.

Friedrich, G. (1982). Classroom communication. In L. Barker (Ed.), *Communication in the classroom* (pp. 55–76). Englewood Cliffs, NJ: Prentice Hall.

Friedrich, G. W., & Cooper, P. (1999). The first day. In A. Vanglisti, J. A. Daly, & G. W. Friedrich (Eds.), *Teaching communication* (2nd ed.) (pp. 287–298). Mahwah, NJ: Lawrence Erlbaum.

Friedriksen, K., & Rhodes, J. (2004). The role of teacher relationships in the lives of students. *New Directions for Youth Development, 103*, 45–54.

Friend, M., & Cook, L. (1996). *Interactions: Collaboration skills for school professionals* (2nd ed.). White Plains, NY: Longman.

Frymier, A. B. (1994). The use of affinity-seeking in producing liking and learning in the classroom. *Applied Communication Research, 22*, 87–105.

Frymier, A. B., & Houser, M. L. (2000). The teacher student relationship as an interpersonal relationship. *Communication Education, 49*, 207–219.

Frymier, A. B., & Thompson, C. A. (1992). Perceived teacher affinity-seeking in relation to perceived teacher credibility. *Communication Education, 41*, 388–399.

Fuchs, D., & Fuchs, L. S. (1998). Researchers and teachers working together to adapt instruction for diverse learnings. *Learning Disabilities Research & Practice, 13*, 126–137.

Fuchs, D., & Fuchs, L. S. (2006). Introduction to response to intervention: What, why, and how valid is it? *Reading Research Quarterly, 41*, 93–99.

Fuchs, D., Fuchs, L. S., & Burish, P. (2000). Peer-assisted learning strategies: An evidence-based practice to promote reading achievement. *Learning Disabilities Research & Practice, 15*(2), 85–91.

Fulk, B. M., & King, K. (2001). Classwide peer tutoring at work. *Teaching Exceptional Children, 34*(2), 49–53.

Gall, M. (1984). Synthesis of research on teachers' questioning. *Educational Leadership, 2*, 40–47.

Garcia, E. (1999). *Student cultural diversity: Understanding and meeting the challenge* (2nd ed.). Boston: Houghton Mifflin.

Gardner, H. (1983). *Frames of mind: The theory of multiple of intelligences.* New York: Basic Books.

Gardner, H. (1993). *Multiple intelligences.* New York: Basic Books.

Gardner, H. (1999). *The disciplined mind.* New York: Simon & Schuster.

Gay, G. (2000). *Culturally responsive teaching: Theory, research and practice.* New York: Teachers College Press.

Gay, G. (2002). Preparing for culturally responsive teaching. *Journal of Teacher Education, 53*, 106–116.

Gettinger, M., & Stoiber, K. C. (1999). Excellence in teaching: Review of instructional and environmental variables. In C. R. Reynolds, & T. B. Gutkin (Eds.), *The handbook of school psychology* (3rd ed.) (pp. 993–958). New York: John Wiley & Sons.

Gibson, J. (1982). Do looks help children make the grade? *Family Weekly*, June 2, p. 9.

Gill, M. M. (1994). Accent and stereotypes: Their effect on perceptions of teachers and lecture comprehension. *Journal of Applied Communication Research, 22*, 348–362.

Gilligan, C. (1982). *In a different voice: Psychological theory and women's development.* Cambridge, MA: Harvard University Press.

Glasser, W. (1969). *Schools without failure.* New York: Harper & Row.

Glasser, W. (1990). *The quality school: Managing students without coercion.* New York: HarperCollins.

Godley, A. J., Sweetland, J., Wheeler, R. S., Minnici, A., & Carpenter, B. D. (2006). Preparing teachers for dialectically diverse classrooms. *Educational Researcher, 35,* 30–37.

Goffman, I. (1959). *The presentation of self in everyday life.* Garden City, NJ: Doubleday Anchor.

Goffman, I. (1963). *Behavior in public places.* New York: Free Press.

Goldstein, A. P., & McGinnis, E. (1977). *Skillstreaming the adolescent: New strategies and perspectives for teaching prosocial skills.* Champaign, IL: Research Press.

Goleman, C. (1995). *Emotional intelligence.* New York: Bantam.

Gollnick, D. M., & Chinn, P. C. (1994). *Multicultural education in a pluralistic society* (4th ed.). New York: Macmillan.

Good, T. (1983). Classroom research: A decade of progress. *Educational Psychologist, 18,* 127–144.

Good, T., & Brophy, J. E. (1973). *Looking in classrooms.* New York: Harper & Row.

Good, T., & Brophy, J. E. (1984). *Looking in classrooms* (3rd ed.). New York: Harper & Row.

Good, T., & Brophy, J. E. (1987). *Looking in classrooms* (4th ed.). New York: Harper & Row.

Good, T., & Brophy, J. E. (1991). *Looking in classrooms* (5th ed.). New York: Harper & Row.

Good, T., & Brophy, J. E. (1997). *Looking in classrooms.* (7th ed.). New York: Longman.

Goodenow, C. (1993). Classroom belonging among early adolescent students: Relationships to motivation and achievement. *Journal of Early Adolescence, 13,* 21–43.

Gordon, T. (1974). *Teacher effectiveness training.* New York: Peter H. Wyden.

Gordon, T. (1987). *T.E.T.: Teacher effectiveness training.* New York: David McKay.

Gorham, J. (1988). The relationship between verbal immediacy behaviors and student learning. *Communication Education, 37,* 40–53.

Gorham, J., & Christophel, D. M. (1990). The relationship of teachers' use of humor in the classroom to immediacy and student learning. *Communication Education, 39,* 46–62.

Gorham, J., Cohen, S. H., & Morris, T. L. (1997). Fashion in the classroom ii: Instructor immediacy and attire. *Communication Research Reports, 14,* 11–23.

Greenspan, S., & Granfield, J. M. (1992). Reconsidering the construct of mental retardation: Implications of a model of social competence. *American Journal of Mental Retardation, 96*(4), 442–453.

Gregorc, A. (1982). *Gregorc style delineator.* Columbia, CT: Gregorc Associates, Inc.

Gregory, G. H., & Chapman, C. (2002). *Differentiated instruction strategies: One size doesn't fit all.* Thousand Oaks, CA: Corwin Press.

Gresham, F. M. (1981). Social skills training with handicapped children: A review. *Review of Educational Research, 51,* 139–176.

Gresham, F. M. (2004). Current status and future direction of school-based behavioral interventions. *School Psychology Review, 33,* 326–343.

Gresham, F. M., & Elliott, S. N. (1989). Social skills deficits as a primary learning disability. *Learning Disability Quarterly, 22,* 120–124.

Grossman, H. (1991). Special education in a diverse society: Improving services for minority and working-class students. *Preventing School Failure, 36,* 19–27.

Grossman, H. (1995). *Special education in a diverse society.* Boston: Allyn & Bacon.

Guevremont, D. (1990). Social skills and peer relationship building. In R. A. Barkely (Ed.), *Attention deficit hyperactivity disorder: A handbook for diagnosis and treatment* (pp. 540–572). New York: The Guilford Press.

Guild, P. (1994). The culture/learning style connection. *Educational Leadership, 51*(8), 16–21.

Gurian, M., & Henley, P. (2001). *Boys and girls learn differently.* San Francisco, CA: Jossey-Bass.

Gurian, M., & Stevens, K. (2005). *The minds of boys: Saving our sons from falling behind in school and life.* San Francisco, CA: Jossey-Bass.

Hall, E. T. (1976). *Beyond culture.* New York: Doubleday.

Hall, R., & Sandler, B. (1982). *The classroom climate: A chilly one for women? Project on the status and education of women.* Washington, DC: Association of American Colleges.

Hallahan, D. P., & Kauffman, J. M. (1994). *Exceptional learners: Introduction to special education* (6th ed.). Boston: Allyn & Bacon.

Hallahan, D. P., & Kauffman, J. M. (2003). *Exceptional learners: Introduction to special education* (9th ed.). Boston: Allyn & Bacon.

Hardin, C. J. (2008). *Effective classroom management* (2nd ed.). Upper Saddle, NJ: Pearson Education.

Harville, B. A. R. (1990). A cross-cultural analysis of instructional immediacy. Unpublished master's thesis, California State University Los Angeles.

Harwell, J. M. (2002). *Complete learning disabilities handbook* (2nd ed.). Paramus, NJ: The Center for Applied Research in Education.

Haslett, B. (1987). *Communication, strategic action in context.* Hillsdale, NJ: Lawrence Erlbaum.

Head, J. (1996). Gender identity and cognitive style. In P. F. Murphy, & C. V. Gipps (Eds), *Equity in the classroom: Towards effective pedagogy for girls and boys* (pp. 59–70). London: Falmer Press.

Healy, J. (1998). *Failure to connect.* New York: Simon & Schuster.

Heath, R. W., & Nielson, M. A. (1974). The research basis for performance-based teacher education. *Review of Educational Research, 44,* 463–484.

Hecht, M., Collier, M. J., & Ribeau, S. (1993). *African American communication: Ethnic identity and cultural interpretation.* Newbury Park, CA: Sage.

Hedges, L. V., & Nowell, A. (1995). Sex differences in mental test scores, variability and numbers of high-scoring individuals. *Science, 269,* 41–45.

Heider, F. (1958). *The psychology of interpersonal relations.* New York: John Wiley.

Heidi, S., & Harackiewicz, J. M. (2000). Motivating the academically unmotivated: A critical issue for the 21st century. *Review of Educational Research, 70,* 151–180.

Helms, J. E. (1990). *Black and white racial identity: Theory, research and practice.* New York: Greenwood.

Helmstetter, E., Curry, C. A., Brennan, M., & Sampson-Saul, M. (1998). Comparison of general and special education classrooms of students with severe disabilities. *Education and Training in Mental Retardation and Developmental Disabilities, 33*(3), 216–227.

Hensley, W. E. (1981). The effects of attire, location, and sex on aiding behavior: A similarity explanation. *Journal of Nonverbal Behavior, 6*, 3–11.

Hess, J. A., & Smythe, M. J. (2001). Is teacher immediacy actually related to student cognitive learning? *Communication Studies, 52*, 197–220.

Heward, W. L. (2000). *Exceptional children: An introductory survey of special education* (7th ed.). Englewood Cliffs, NJ: Prentice Hall.

Hines, C. V., Cruickshank, D. R., & Kennedy, J. J. (1985). Teacher clarity and its relationship to student achievement and satisfaction. *American Educational Research Journal, 22*, 87–99.

Hoetker, J., & Ahlbrand, W. P. (1969). The persistence of recitation. *American Educational Research Journal, 6*, 145–167.

Hofstede, G. (1980). *Culture's consequences: International differences in work-related values*. Beverly Hills, CA: Sage.

Hofstede, G. (2001). *Culture's consequences: International differences in work-related values* (2nd ed.). Beverly Hills, CA: Sage.

Holland, D., Lachicotte, W. Jr., Skinner, D., & Cain, C. (1998). *Identity and agency in cultural worlds*. Cambridge, MA: Harvard University Press.

Hoover, J. J., & Collier, C. (1986). *Classroom management through curricular adaptations*. Lindale, TX: Hamilton.

Horne, A. M., & Socherman, R. (1996). Profile of a bully: Who would do such a thing? *Educational Horizons, 74*, 77–83.

Houston, B. (1996). Gender freedom and the subtleties of sexist education. In A. Diller, B. Houston, K. Morgan, & M. Ayim (Eds.), *The gender question in education: Theory, pedagogy, and politics* (pp. 50–63). Boulder, CO: Westview Press.

Howard, G. (2000). Whites in multicultural education: Rethinking our role. In J. Banks (Ed.), *Multicultural education: Transformative knowledge* (pp. 323–334). New York: Teachers College Press.

Hudson, L., & Jacot, B. (1991). *The way men think*. New Haven, CT: Yale University Press.

Hunkins, F. P. (1976). *Involving students in questioning*. Boston: Allyn & Bacon.

Hunter, M. (1984). Knowing, teaching, supervising. In P. Hosford (Ed.), *Using what we know about teaching* (pp. 169–192). Alexandra, VA: Association for Supervision and Curriculum Development.

Hyde, J. S. (2005) The gender similarities hypothesis. *American Psychologist, 60*, 581–592.

Hyde, J. S., Finnema, E., & Lamou, S. J. (1990). Gender differences in mathematics performance: A meta-analysis. *Psychological Bulletin, 107*, 139–155.

Hyde, J. S., & Linn, M. C. (1988). Gender differences in verbal ability: A meta-analysis. *Psychological Bulletin, 104*, 53–69.

Hyde, J. S., & McKinley, N. (1997). Gender differences in cognition: Results from meta-analysis. In P. J. Caplan, M. Crawford, J. S. Hyde, & J. T. E. Richardson (Eds.), *Gender differences in human cognition* (pp. 30–51). New York: Oxford University Press.

Ishii-Jordan, S. R. (2000). Behavioral interventions used with diverse students. *Behavioral Disorders, 25*(4), 299–309.

Ivy, D., & Backlund, P. (2000). *Exploring genderspeak: Personal effectiveness in gender communication.* San Francisco, CA: McGraw-Hill.

Jackson, L. A., von Eye, A., Biocca, F., Barbatsis, G., Yong, Z., & Fitzgerald, H. E. (2005). *Journal of Interactive Learning Research, 16,* 259–272.

Javidi, M., Downs, V., & Nussbaum, J. (1988). A comparative analysis of teachers' use of dramatic style behaviors at higher and secondary educational levels. *Communication Education, 37,* 278–288.

Jenkins, J., & Jenkins, L. (1985). Peer tutoring in elementary and secondary programs. *Focus on Exceptional Children, 17,* 1–12.

Jensen, E. (2000). *Brain-based learning.* San Diego, CA: The Brain Store.

Johnson, D. W., & Johnson, R. T. (1986). Mainstreaming and cooperative learning strategies. *Exceptional Children, 52,* 553–561.

Johnson, D. W., & Johnson, R. T. (1999). *Learning together and learning alone: Cooperative competitive and individualistic learning* (5th ed.). Boston: Allyn & Bacon.

Johnson, D. W., Johnson, R. T., & Holubec, E. J. (1993). *Circles of learning: Cooperation in the classroom.* Edina, MN: Interaction Book Company.

Johnson, R. T., & Johnson, D. W. (1996). Conflict resolution and peer mediation programs in elementary and secondary schools: A review of the research. *Review of Educational Research, 66,* 459–473.

Jones, B. F., Valdez, G., Nowakowski, J., & Rasmussen, C. (1995) *Plugging in: Choosing and using education technology.* Oak Brook, IL: North Central Regional Educational Laboratory.

Jones, E. E., & Davis, K. E. (1965). From acts to dispositions. In L. Berkowitz (Ed.), *Advances in experimental and social psychology,* Vol. 2. New York: Academic Press.

Jones, V. F., & Jones, L. S. (2001). *Comprehensive classroom management: Creating communities of support and solving problems* (6th ed.). Boston: Allyn & Bacon.

Jones, V. F., & Jones, L. S. (2007). *Comprehensive classroom management: Creating communities of support and solving problems* (8th ed.). Boston, MA: Allyn & Bacon.

Kagan, S. (1994). *Cooperative learning resources for teachers.* San Juan Capistrano: Resources for Teachers.

Katz, J. E. (2005) Mobile phones in educational settings. In K. Nyiri (Ed.), *A sense of place: The global and the local in mobile communication* (pp. 305–317). Vienna: Passagen.

Kauffman, J. M. (1997). *Characteristics of emotional and behavioral disorders of children and youth* (6th ed.). Upper Saddle River, NJ: Merrill.

Kauffman, J. M., Mostert, M. P., Trent, S. C., & Hallahan, D. P. (1998). *Managing classroom behavior: A reflective case-based approach* (2nd ed.), Needham Heights, MA: Allyn & Bacon.

Kauffman, J. M., Pullen, P. L., & Ackers, E. (1986). Classroom management: Teacher–child peer relationships. *Focus on Exceptional Children, 19*(1), 1–10.

Kavale, K. A., & Forness, S. R. (1996). Social skill deficits and learning disabilities: A meta-analysis. *Journal of Learning Disabilities, 29,* 226–237.

Kaye, C. B. (2000). *The service learning book shelf* (2nd ed.). Los Angeles, CA: Association of Supervision and Curriculum Development (ASCD) Books.

Kazdin, A. E. (2001). *Behavior modification in applied settings.* Belmont, CA: Wadsworth.

Kearney, P., Plax, T. G., Smith, V., & Sorensen, G. (1988). Effects of teacher immediacy and strategy type of college student resistance. *Communication Education, 37,* 54–67.

Kearney, P., Plax, T. G., & Wendt-Wasco, N. J. (1985). Teacher immediacy for affective learning in divergent college classes. *Communication Quarterly, 33,* 61–74.

Kelley, H. H. (1967). Attribution theory in social psychology. *Nebraska Symposium on Motivation, 15,* 192–240.

Kelly, D. H. E., & Gorham, P. (1988). Effects of immediacy on recall of information. *Communication Education, 37,* 198–207.

Kelly, G. (1955) *The psychology of personal constructs.* New York: North.

Kendrick, W. L., & Darling, A. L. (1990). Problems of understanding in classrooms: Students' use of clarifying tactics. *Communication Education, 39,* 15–29.

Kennedy, C. H., & Itkonen, T. (1994). Some effects of regular class participation on the social contacts and social networks of high school students with severe disabilities. *Journal of the Association for Persons with Severe Handicaps, 19*(1), 1–10.

Kennedy, C. H., Shukla, S., & Fryxell, D. (1997). Comparing the effects of educational placement on the social relationships of intermediate school students with severe disabilities. *Exceptional Children, 64,* 31–47.

Kennedy, D. M. (1995). Plain talk about creating a gifted-friendly classroom. In R. B. Lewis, & D. H. Doorlag (Eds.), *Teaching special students in general education classrooms* (pp. 379–380).Columbus, OH: Merrill/Prentice Hall.

Kindsvatter, R., Wilen, W., & Ishler, M. (1996). *Dynamics of effective teaching.* White Plains, NJ: Longman.

Kirtley, M. D., & Weaver III, J. B. (1999). Exploring the impact of gender role self-perception on communication style. *Women's Studies in Communication, 22,* 190–201.

Kleinke, C. L. (1977). Effects of dress on compliance to requests in a field setting. *The Journal of Social Psychology, 101,* 223–224.

Kluver, R. (1990). *A cross-cultural analysis of instructional immediacy.* Unpublished master's thesis, California State University Los Angeles.

Knapp, M. L. (1978). *Social intercourse: From greeting to goodbye.* Boston: Allyn & Bacon.

Knapp, M. L., Cody, M. J., & Reardon, K. K. (1987). Nonverbal signals. In C. Berger, & S. Chaffee (Eds.), *Handbook of communication science* (pp. 385–418). Beverly Hills, CA: Sage.

Knapp, M. L., & Hall J. A. (1992). *Nonverbal communication in human interaction* (3rd ed.). San Diego, CA: Holt Rinehart and Winston.

Knapp, M. L., & Vangelisti, A. (2000). *Interpersonal communication and human relationships* (4th ed.). Boston: Allyn & Bacon.

Knapp, M. L., Wiemann, J., & Daly, J. (1978). Nonverbal communication: Issues and appraisal. *Human Communication Research, 4,* 271–280.

Knitzer, J., Steinberg, Z., & Fleisch, F. (1990). *At the schoolhouse door: An examination of the programs and policies for children with behavioral and emotional problems.* New York: Bank Street College of Education.

Kohn, A. (1991). Caring kids: The role of the schools. *Phi Delta Kappan, 72,* 496–506.

Kohn, A. (1993). *Punished by rewards: The trouble with gold stars, incentive plans, A's, praise, and other bribes.* Boston: Houghton Mifflin.

Kohn, A. (1996). *Beyond discipline: From compliance to community.* Alexandra, VA: Association for Supervision and Curriculum Development.

Kohn, A. (1998). *What to look for in a classroom.* San Francisco, CA: Jossey-Bass.

Kolb, D. A. (1976). *Learning style inventory technical manual.* Boston: McBer and Co.

Kolb, D. A. (1985). *Learning style inventory.* Boston: McBer & Co.

Kozma, R., & Croninger, R. (1992). Technology and the fate of at-risk students. *Education and Urban Society, 24,* 440–453.

Kulik, J. (1994). Meta-analytic studies of findings on computer-based instruction. In E. L. Baker, & H. F. O'Neil Jr. (Eds.), *Technology assessment in education and training* (pp. 9–34). Hillsdale, NJ: Lawrence Erlbaum.

Kumashiro, D. (2000). Toward a theory of anti-oppressive education. *Review of Educational Research, 70,* 25–54.

Kuykendall, C. (1992). *From rage to hope: Strategies for reclaiming Black & Hispanic students.* Bloomington, IN: National Educational Service.

Ladd, G. W. (1990). Having friends, keeping friends, making friends, and being liked by peers in the classroom: Predictors of children's early school adjustment? *Child Development, 61,* 1081–1100.

Ladson-Billings, G. (1994). *The dreamkeepers: Successful teachers of African-American children.* San Francisco, CA: Jossey-Bass.

Ladson-Billings, G. (2001) *Crossing over to Canaan: The journey of new teachers in diverse classrooms.* San Francisco, CA: Jossey-Bass.

LaFrance, M., & Mayo, C. (1979). A review of nonverbal behaviors of women and men. *Western Journal of Speech Communication, 43,* 96–107.

LaFromboise, T. (1982). *Assertion training with American Indians: Cultural/behavioral issues for trainers.* New York: ERIC Clearinghouse on Rural Education and Small Schools.

Lam, S-F., Yim, P-S., & Ng, Y. I. (2008). Is effort praise motivational? The role of beliefs in the effort–ability relationship. *Contemporary Educational Psychology, 33,* 694–710.

Lane, D. A. (1989). Bullying in school. *School Psychology International, 10,* 211–215.

Lang, R. (1986). The hidden dress code dilemma. *Clearing House, 59,* 277–279.

Langer, S. (1942). *Philosophy in a new key.* Cambridge, MA: Harvard University Press.

Lee, O. E., & Bertera, E. (2007). Teaching diversity by using instructional technology: Application of self-efficacy and cultural competence. *Multicultural Education & Technology Journal, 1,* 112–125.

Levin, J., & Nolan, J. F. (2007). *Principles of classroom management: A professional decision-making mode* (5th ed.). Boston: Allyn & Bacon.

Linn, M. C., & Peterson, A. C. (1985). Emergence and characterization of sex differences in spatial ability: A meta-analysis. *Child Development, 56,* 1479–1498.

Liontos, L. B. (1992). *At risk families and schools: Becoming partners.* New York: ERIC Clearinghouse on Educational Management.

Little, S. S. (1993). Nonverbal learning disabilities. *Journal of Learning Disabilities, 24,* 439–446.

Lochman, J. E. (1992). Cognitive-behavioral intervention with aggressive boys: Three-year follow-up and prevention effects. *Journal of Consulting and Clinical Psychology, 60,* 426–432.

Loewen, J. (1995). *Lies my teacher told me: Everything your American history textbook got wrong.* New York: Touchstone.

Long, N. J., Morse, W. C., & Newman, R. G. (1965). *Conflict in the classroom: The education of emotionally disturbed children.* Belmont, CA: Wadsworth.

Luckasson, R., Coulter, D. L., Polloway, E. A., Reiss, S., Schalock, R. L., Snell, M. E., Spitalnik, D. M., & Stark, J. A. (1992). *Mental retardation: Definition, classification, and systems of supports.* Washington, DC: American Association on Mental Retardation.

Luftig, R. L. (1988). Assessment of the perceived school loneliness and isolation of mentally retarded and nonretarded students. *American Journal of Mental Retardation, 92*(5), 472–475.

Lukavsky, J., Butler, S., & Harden, A. (1995). Perceptions of an instructor: Dress and students' characteristics. *Perceptual and Motor Skills, 81,* 231–241.

Lustig, M. W., & Koester, J. (1999). *Intercultural competence* (3rd ed.). Menlo Park, CA: Longman.

Lustig, M. W., & Koester, J. (Eds.) (2000). *Among us: Essays on identity, belonging, and intercultural competence.* New York: Longman.

Maag, J. W. (2001). Rewarded by punishment: Reflections on the disuse of positive reinforcement in schools. *Exceptional Children, 67*(2), 173–186.

Maag, J. W. (2003). *Behavior management: From theoretical implications to practical applications* (2nd ed.). San Diego, CA: Singular.

Maag, J. W., & Katsiyannis, A. (1999). Teacher preparation in E/BD: A national survey. *Behavioral Disorders, 24,* 189–196.

Madden, N. A., & Slavin, R. E. (1983). Mainstreaming students with mild handicaps: Academic and social outcomes. *Review of Educational Research, 53,* 519–569.

Maehr, M. L., & Meyer, H. A. (1997). Understanding motivation and schooling: Where we've been, where we are and where we need to go. *Educational Psychology Review, 9,* 371–409.

Malian, I. M., & Love, L. (1998). Leaving high school: An ongoing transition study. *Teaching Exceptional Children, 30*(3), 4–10.

Malmgren, K., Abbott, R. D., & Hawkins, J. D. (1999). LD and delinquency: Rethinking the "link." *Journal of Learning Disabilities, 32*(3), 201–211.

Manning, M. L., & Baruth, L. G. (2000). *Multicultural education of children and adolescents* (3rd ed.). Boston: Allyn & Bacon.

Martin, C. L. (1989). Children's use of gender-related information in making social judgments. *Developmental Psychology, 25,* 80–88.

Maslow, A. (1968). *Toward a psychology of being.* New York: D. Van Nostrand.

Mathinos, D. A. (1991). Conversational engagement of children with learning disabilities. *Journal of Learning Disabilities, 24,* 439–446.

Mathur, S., Kavale, K., Quinn, M., Forness, S., & Rutherford, R. (1998). Social skills intervention with students with emotional and behavioral problems:

A quantitative synthesis of single subject research. *Behavioral Disorders, 23,* 193–202.

McAllister, G., & Irvine, J. J. (2000). Cultural competency and multicultural teacher education. *Review of Educational Research, 70,* 3–24.

McCroskey, J. C., & Andersen, J. (1976). The relationship between communication apprehension and academic achievement among college students. *Communication Research, 3,* 73–81.

McCroskey, J. C., Booth-Butterfield, S., & Payne, S. (1989). The impact of apprehension on college student retention and success. *Communication Quarterly, 37,* 100–107.

McCroskey, J. C., & McCroskey, L. L. (2002). Willingness to communicate and communication apprehension in the classroom. In J. L. Chesbro, & J. McCroskey (Eds.), *Communication for teachers* (pp. 19–34). Boston: Allyn & Bacon.

McCroskey, J. C., & Richmond, V. (1978). Community size as a predictor of development of communication apprehension: Replication and extension. *Communication Monographs, 27,* 212–219.

McKeachie, W. (1986). *Teaching tips: A guidebook for the beginning college teacher* (8th ed.). Lexington, MA: D. C. Heath and Company.

McLaughlin, B. (1995). *Fostering second language development in young children: Principles and practices.* Santa Cruz, CA: National Center for Research on Cultural Diversity and Second Language Learning.

McMillan, D. W., & Chavis, D. M. (1986). Sense of community: A definition and theory. *Journal of Community Psychology, 14,* 6–23.

McPherson, K. (1997) Service learning: Making a difference in the community. *Schools in the Middle,* Jan–Feb, 9–15.

McTighe, J., & Wiggins, G. (2004). *Understanding by design: Professional development workbook.* Alexandra: VA: ASCD.

Mead, G. H. (1934). *Mind, self, and society.* Chicago: University of Chicago Press.

Mehrabian, A. (1969a). Significance of posture and position in the communication of attitude and status relationships. *Psychological Bulletin, 71,* 359–372.

Mehrabian, A. (1969b). Some referents and measures of nonverbal behavior. *Behavioral Research Methods and Instruments, 1,* 213–217.

Mehrabian, A. (1970a). The development and validation of measures of affiliative tendency and sensitivity to rejection. *Educational and Psychological Measurement, 30,* 417–428.

Mehrabian, A. (1970b). A semantic space for nonverbal behavior. *Journal of Consulting and Clinical Psychology, 35,* 248–257.

Mehrabian, A. (1971). *Silent messages.* Belmont, CA: Wadsworth.

Mehrabian, A. (1981). *Silent messages* (2nd ed.). Belmont, CA: Wadsworth.

Meichenbaum, D. (1977). *Cognitive-behavior modification: An integrative approach.* New York: Plenum.

Meichenbaum, D. (1980). Cognitive-behavior modification: A promise yet unfulfilled. *Exceptional Education Quarterly, 1*(1), 83–88.

Meyer, J. C. (2000). Humor as a double-edged sword: Four functions of humor in communication. *Communication Theory, 10,* 310–331.

Miller, J. W. (2000). Exploring the source of self-regulated learning: The influence of internal and external comparisons. *Journal of Instructional Psychology, 27,* 47–52.

Miller, M. (1987). Argumentation and cognition. In M. Hickman (Ed.), *Social and functional approaches in language and thought* (pp. 225–249). San Diego, CA: Academic Press.

Miltenberger, R. G. (2007). *Behavior modification: Principles and procedures* (4th ed.). Belmont, CA: Wadsworth.

Minnett, A. M. (1992). Similarities in the social competencies of learning disabled and low achieving elementary school children. *Journal of Learning Disabilities, 25,* 671–677.

Molloy, J. T. (1975). *Dress for success.* New York: Warner Books.

Mongeau, P. A., & Blalock, J. (1994). Student evaluations of instructor immediacy and sexually harassing behaviors: An experimental investigation. *Journal of Applied Communication Research, 22,* 256–272.

Montagu, P., Mecham, M., & McLaughlin, T. F. (1991). Peer tutoring in special education: Effects on the academic achievement of secondary students with mild handicaps. *British Columbia Journal of Special Education, 15,* 47–63.

Montgomery, M. D., & Paul, J. L. (1982). Ecological theory and practice. In J. L. Paul, & B. C. Epanchin (Eds.), *Emotional disturbance in children: Theories and methods for teachers* (pp. 214–241). Columbus, OH: Merrill.

Moore, A., Masterson, J. T., Christophel, D., & Shea, K. (1996). College teacher immediacy and student ratings of instruction. *Communication Quarterly, 44,* 29–40.

Moos, R. H., & Moos, B. S. (1978). Classroom social climate and student absences and grades. *Journal of Educational Psychology, 70,* 263–269.

Morris, T. L., Gorham, J., Cohen, S. H., & Huffman, D. (1996). Fashion in the classroom: Effects of attire on student perceptions of instructors in college classes. *Communication Education, 36,* 1–12.

Morton, T. (1998). *Cooperative learning and social studies: Towards excellence to equity.* San Clemente, CA: Kagan Cooperative Learning.

Mosteller, F., & Moynihan, D. P. (1972). *On equality of educational opportunity.* New York: Vintage Books.

Mostert, M. P. (1998). *Interprofessional collaboration in schools.* Boston: Allyn & Bacon.

Murphy, P., & Gipps, C. V. (1996). *Equity in the classroom: Towards an effective pedagogy for girls and boys.* Washington, DC: Falmer Press.

Murrell, P. C. (2002). *African-centered pedagogy: Developing schools for African-American children.* Albany, NY: State University Press.

Muscott, H. S. (2000). A review and analysis of service-learning programs involving students with emotional/behavioral disorders. *Education and Treatment of Children, 23,* 346–368.

Muscott, H. S. (2001). An introduction to service-learning for students with emotional and behavioral disorders: Answers to frequently asked questions. *Beyond Behavior, 10*(3), 8–15.

Myrick, R. D., & Erney, T. (1984). *Caring and sharing: Becoming a peer facilitator.* Minneapolis, MN: Educational Media Corporation.

Myrick, R. D., & Erney, T. (1985). *Youth helping youth: A handbook for training peer facilitators.* Minneapolis, MN: Educational Media Corporation.

Nadler, L., & Nadler, M. (1990). Perceptions of sex differences in classroom communication. *Women's Studies in Communication, 13,* 46–65.

National Joint Committee on Learning Disabilities (1994). Learning disabilities: Issues on definition, a position paper of the National Joint Committee on Learning Disabilities. In *Collective perspectives on issues affecting learning disabilities: Position papers and statements* (pp. 3–8). Austin, TX: Pro-Ed.

Nelson, J., Lott, L., & Glenn, H. S. (1993). *Positive discipline in the classroom*. Rocklin, CA: Prima.

Neuliep, J. W. (1991). An examination of the content of high school teachers' humor in the classroom and the development of an inductively derived taxonomy of classroom humor. *Communication Education, 40*, 343–355.

Newhouse, R. C. (1984). Teacher appearance in cooperative initiation processes. *Journal of Instructional Psychology, 11*, 158–164.

Nieto, S. (2002). *Language, culture, and teaching: Critical perspectives for a new century*. Mahwah, NJ: Lawrence Erlbaum.

Noddings, N. (1995). Teaching themes of care. *Phi Delta Kappan, 76*, 675–679.

Noguera, P. (1995). Preventing and producing violence: A critical analysis of responses to school violence. *Harvard Educational Review, 65*, 189–212.

Norton, R., & Nussbaum, J. (1980). Dramatic behaviors of the effective teacher. In D. Nimmo (Ed.), *Communication yearbook 5* (pp. 565–582). New Brunswick, NJ: Transaction Books.

Nussbaum, J. (1992). Effective teacher behaviors. *Communication Education, 41*, 167–180.

Nussbaum, J., Comadena, M. E., & Holladay, S. J. (1985). Verbal communication within the college classroom. Paper presented at the annual meeting of the International Communication Association, Chicago, May.

Nussbaum, J., & Scott, M. (1979). The relationship among communicator style, perceived self-disclosure, and classroom learning. In D. Nimmo (Ed.), *Communication yearbook 3* (pp. 533–552). New Brunswick, NJ: Transaction Books.

Ogbu, J. U. (1999). Beyond language: ebonics, proper English, and identity in a Black-American speech community. *American Educational Research Journal, 36*, 147–186.

Oliver, R., Omari, A., & Herrington, J. (1998). Investigating implementation strategies for www-based learning environments. *International Journal of Instructional Media, 25*, 121.

O'Neil, D. K., Wagner, R., & Gomez, L. M. (1996). Online mentors: Experimenting in science class. *Educational Leadership, 54*, 39–42.

Opt, S. K., & Loffredo, D. (2000). Rethinking communication apprehension: A Meyers-Briggs perspective. *The Journal of Psychology, 134*, 556–568.

Orbe, M. P., & Harris, T. M. (2001). *Interracial communication: Theory into practice*. Belmont, CA: Wadsworth.

Orlich, D. C., Harder, R. J., Callahan, R. C., & Gibson, H. W. (2001). *Teaching strategies: A guide to better instruction* (6th ed.). Boston: Houghton Mifflin.

Osterman, K. F. (2000). Students' need for belonging in the school community. *Review of Educational Research, 70*(3), 323–367.

Paley, V. G. (1989). *White teacher*. Cambridge, MA: Harvard University Press.

Park, H. S. (2008). The impact of technology use on Hispanic students' mathematics achievement within family and school contexts: Subgroup analysis between English-and non-English speaking students. *Journal of Educational Computing Research, 38,* 453–468.

Parker, H. C. (1996). *Adapt: Accommodations help students with attention deficit disorders.* ADD Warehouse Articles on ADD [On-line]. Available at: www.addwarehouse.com.

Parks, J. B., & Roberton, M. A. (1998) Contemporary arguments against non-sexist language: Blaubergs (1980) revisited. *Sex Roles, 39,* 445–461.

Patrick, B., Hisley, J., & Kempler, T. (2000). "What everybody so excited about?": The effects of teacher enthusiasm on student intrinsic motivation and vitality. *The Journal of Experimental Education, 68,* 217–236.

Pavri, S., & Monda-Amaya, L. (2000). Loneliness and students with learning disabilities in inclusive classrooms: Self-perceptions, coping strategies, and preferred interventions. *Learning Disabilities Research & Practice, 15*(1), 22–33.

Perry, N. E., Vandekamp, K. O., Mercer, L. K., & Nordby, C. J. (2002). Investigating teacher–student interactions that foster self-regulated learning. *Educational Psychologist, 37,* 5–15.

Peterson, J. M., & Hittie, N. M. (2003). *Inclusive teaching: Creating effective schools for all learners.* Boston: Allyn & Bacon.

Philbin, M., Meier, E., Huffman, S., & Boverie, P. (1995). A survey of gender learning styles. *Sex Roles: A Journal of Research, 32,* 485–495.

Piaget, J. (1955). *Thought and language of the child.* Cleveland, OH: The World Publishing Company.

Piaget, J. (1965). *The moral judgment of the child.* New York: Basic Books.

Pianta, R. C., & Steinberg, M. (1992). Teacher–child relationships and the process of adjusting to school. In R. C. Pianta (Ed.), *Beyond parent: The role of other adults in children's lives* (pp. 61–80). San Francisco, CA: Jossey-Bass.

Pipher, M. (1994) *Reviving Ophelia: Saving the selves of adolescent girls.* New York: Ballantine.

Pollack, J. P., & Freda, P. D. (1997). Humor, learning, and socialization in middle level classrooms. *The Clearing House, 70,* 176–179.

Pollack, W. (1998). *Real boys: Rescuing our sons from the myths of boyhood.* New York: Henry Holt.

Postman, N. (1995). *The end of education.* New York: Vintage Books.

Powell, R., & Aston, W. (1994). Teacher classroom immediacy and time on task: An exploratory study. Paper presented at the annual meeting of the International Communication Association, Sidney, Australia, July.

Powell, R. G., & Avila, D. R. (1986). Ethnicity, communication competency and classroom success: A question of assessment. *Western Journal of Speech Communication, 50,* 269–278.

Powell, R. G., & Harville, B. (1990). The effects of teacher immediacy and clarity on instructional outcomes: An intercultural assessment. *Communication Education, 39,* 369–379.

Rawitsch, D., Heinemann, B., & Dillenberger, P. (1974). *The Oregon Trail.* San Francisco, CA: The Learning Company.

Rawlins, W. K. (1992). *Friendship matters: Communication, dialectics, and life course.* New York: Aldine de Gruyter.

Rawlins, W. K. (2000). Teaching as a mode of friendship. *Communication Theory, 10,* 5–26.

Reagan, T. (2002). *Language, education, and ideology: Mapping the linguistic landscape of U.S. schools.* Westport, CN: Praeger.

Redl, F., & Wineman, D. (1952). *Controls from within: Techniques for the treatment of the aggressive child.* New York: Free Press.

Report to the Nation on Technology and Education (1996). *Getting America's students ready for the twenty-first century: Meeting the technology literacy challenge.* Washington, DC: U.S. Department of Education.

Rex, L. A. (2003) Loss of the creature: The obscuring of inclusivity in classroom discourse. *Communication Education, 52,* 30–46.

Reyes, P., Scribner, J. D., & Scribner, A. P. (Eds.). (1999). *Lessons from high-performing Hispanic schools.* New York: Teachers College Press.

Rezmierski, V., & Kotre, J. (1974). A limited review of theory of the psychodynamic model. In W. C. Rhodes, & M. L. Tracy (Eds.), *A study of child variance* (Vol. 1). Ann Arbor, MI: University of Michigan Press.

Rhodes, W. C. (1967). The disturbing child: A problem of ecological management. *Exceptional Children, 33,* 449–455.

Rhodes, W. C. (1970). A community participation analysis of emotional disturbance. *Exceptional Children, 36,* 306–314.

Richmond, V. P. (1990) Communication in the classroom: Power and motivation. *Communication Education, 39,* 181–195.

Richmond, V. P. (2002). Teacher nonverbal immediacy: Use and outcomes. In J. L. Chesebro, & J. C. McCroskey (Eds.), *Communication for teachers* (pp. 65–82). Boston: Allyn & Bacon.

Richmond, V., & Dyba, P. (1982). The roots of sexual stereotyping: The teacher as model. *Communication Education, 31,* 265–274.

Richmond, V., McCroskey, J., & Payne, S. K. (1987). *Nonverbal behavior in interpersonal relations.* Englewood Cliffs, NJ: Prentice Hall.

Risko, V. J., & Kinzer, C. K. (1998). *Multimedia cases in reading education.* Boston: McGraw-Hill.

Roach, D. D. (1997). Effects of graduate teaching assistant attire on student learning, misbehaviors, and ratings of instruction. *Communication Quarterly, 45,* 125–141.

Rockwell, S. (2001). Service-learning: Barriers, benefits, and models of excellence. *Beyond Behavior, 10*(3), 16–21.

Rodriguez, J., Plax, T., & Kearney, P. (1996). Clarifying the relationship between teacher nonverbal immediacy and student cognitive learning: Affective learning as the central causal mediator. *Communication Education, 45,* 293–305.

Roschelle, J. M., Pea, R. D., Hoadley, C. M., Gordon, D. N., & Means, B. M. (2000). Changing how and what children learn in school with computer-based technologies. *Children and Computer Technology, 10,* 76–101. Available at: www.futureofchildren.org. Accessed June 1, 2009.

Rose, D. H., & Meyer, A. (2002). *Teaching every student in the Digital Age: Universal design for learning.* Alexandra, VA: Association for Supervision and Curriculum Development.

Rosenfeld, L. B., Grant, H., & McCroskey, J. C. (1995). Communication apprehension and self-perceived communication competence of academically gifted students. *Communication Education, 44,* 79–86.

Rosenfeld, L. B., & Richman, J. R. (1999). Supportive communication and school outcomes, part II: Academically "at-risk" low income high school students. *Communication Education, 48,* 294–306.

Ross, J. L., Drysdale, M.T. B., & Schulz, R. A. (2001). Cognitive learning styles and academic performance in two postsecondary computer application courses. *Journal of Research on Technology in Education, 33,* 400–411.

Rowen, K. (1999). Explanatory skills. In A. Vangelisti, J. Daly, & G. Friedrich (Eds.), *Teaching communication* (2nd ed.) (pp. 319–331). Mahwah, NJ: Lawrence Erlbaum.

Rubin, J. Z., Provensano, F., & Luria, Z. (1974). The eye of the beholder: Parents' views on sex of newborns. *American Journal of Orthopsychiatry, 44,* 312–319.

Ryan, A. (2001). The peer group as a context for the development of young adolescent motivation and achievement. *Child Development, 72,* 1135–1160.

Ryan, A. M., & Patrick, H. (2001). The classroom social environment and changes in adolescents' motivation and engagement during middle school. *American Educational Research Journal, 38*(2), 437–460.

Ryan, R. M. (1995). Psychological needs and the facilitation of integrative processes. *Journal of Personality, 63*(3), 397–427.

Ryan, R. M., Stiller, J. D., & Lynch, J. H. (1994). Representations of relationships to teachers, parents, and friends as predictors of academic motivation and self-esteem. *Journal of Early Adolescence, 14*(2), 226–249.

Sadker, M., & Sadker, D. (1994). *Failing at fairness: How America's schools cheat girls.* New York: Charles Scribner's Sons.

Sagor, R. (1996). Building resiliency in students. *Educational Leadership,* September, 38–43.

Sale, P., & Carey, D. M. (1995). The sociometric status of students with disabilities in a full-inclusion school. *Exceptional Children, 62,* 6–19.

Salend, J. S. (2001). *Creating inclusive classrooms: Effective and reflective practices* (4th ed.). Columbus, OH: Merrill.

Samovar, L., Porter, R., & Stefani, L. A. (2000). *Communication between cultures* (3rd ed.). Belmont, CA: Wadsworth.

Sanders, J., & Wiseman, W. R. (1990). The effects of verbal and nonverbal teacher immediacy on perceived cognitive, affective, and behavioral learning in the multicultural classroom. *Communication Education, 39,* 341–353.

Santamaria, L. J. (2009). Culturally responsive differentiated instruction: Narrowing gaps between best pedagogical practices benefiting all learners. *Teachers College Record, 111,* 214–247.

Sarafino, E. P. (2001). *Behavior modification* (2nd ed.). Mountain View, CA: Mayfield.

Scheuermann, B. K., & Hall, J. A. (2007). *Positive behavioral supports for the classroom.* Upper Saddle River NJ: Pearson Education.

Schierloh, J. M. (1991). Teaching standard English usage: A dialect-based approach. *Adult Learning, 2,* 20–22.

Schneider, D. J. (1974). Effects of dress on self-presentation. *Psychological Reports, 35,* 167–170.

Schonert-Reichl, K. A. (1993). Empathy and social relationships in adolescents with behavior disorders. *Behavioral Disorders, 18*(3), 189–204.

Schulte, A. C., Osborne, S. S., & McKinney, J. D. (1990). Academic outcomes for students with learning disabilities in consultation and resource programs. *Exceptional Children, 57,* 162–172.

Schutz, W. (1966). *The interpersonal underworld.* Palo Alto, CA: Science and Behavior Books.

Schwartz, W. (1996). *A guide to communicating with Asian American families.* New York: ERIC Clearinghouse on Urban Education.

Scruggs, T. E., & Mastropieri, M. A. (1996). *Advances in learning and behavioral disabilities.* Greenwich, CT: JAI Press.

Seidel, J. F., & Vaughn, S. (1991). Social alienation and the learning disabled school dropout. *Learning Disabilities Research & Practice, 6,* 152–157.

Seifert, T. L. (2004) Understanding student motivation. *Educational Research, 46,* 137–149.

Selfe, C. L. (1999). *Technology and literacy in the twenty-first century: The importance of paying attention.* Carbondale, IL: Southern Illinois University Press.

Shade, B. J. (1989). The influence of perceptual development on cognitive styles: Cross-ethnic comparisons. *Early Child Development and Care, 51,* 137–155.

Shannon, C., & Weaver, W. (1949). *The mathematical theory of communication.* Urbana, IL: University of Illinois Press.

Sharan, S. (1994). *Handbook of cooperative learning methods.* Westport, CT: Greenwood Press.

Sharan, S., Kussell, P., Hertz-Lazarowitz, R., Bejarano, Y., Raviv, S., & Sharan, Y. (1984). *Cooperative learning in the classroom: Research in desegregated schools.* Hillsdale, NJ: Lawrence Erlbaum.

Shinn, M. R., & Powell-Smith, K. A. (1997). The effects of reintegration into general education reading instruction for students with mild disabilities. *Exceptional Children, 64,* 59–79.

Silver, H. F., Strong, R. W., & Perini, M. J. (2000). *So each may learn: Integrating learning styles and multiple intelligences.* Alexandria, VA: Association for Supervision and Curriculum Development.

Simmons, B. J. (1996). Teachers should dress for success. *The Clearing House, 69,* 297–299.

Sine, C. (1995) Teacher immediacy and time on task. Unpublished master's thesis. California State University Fresno, Fresno, CA.

Sitler, H. C. (1997). The spaced lecture. *College Teaching, 45,* 108–111.

Skiba, R. J., & Peterson, R. L. (2000). School discipline at a crossroads: From zero tolerance to early response. *Exceptional Children, 66*(3), 335–347.

Skiba, R. J., Peterson, R. L., & Williams, T. (1997). Office referrals and suspension: Disciplinary interventions in middle schools. *Education and Treatment of Children, 20,* 295–315.

Skinner, B. F. (1971). *Beyond freedom and dignity.* New York: Alfred A. Knopf.

Skinner, E. A., & Belmont, M. J. (1993). Motivation in the classroom: Reciprocal effects of teacher behavior and student engagement across the school year. *Journal of Educational Psychology, 85,* 571–581.

Slavin, R. E. (1979). Effects of biracial learning teams on cross-racial friendships. *Journal of Educational Psychology, 71,* 381–387.

Slavin, R. E. (1995a). *Cooperative learning: Theory, research, and practice* (2nd ed.). Boston: Allyn & Bacon.

Slavin, R. E. (1995b). Cooperative learning and intergroup relations. In J. Banks, & C. M. Banks (Eds.), *Handbook of research on multicultural education* (pp. 628–634). New York: Macmillan.

Slavin, R. E., & Cooper, R. (1999). Improving intergroup relations: Lessons learned from cooperative learning programs. *Journal of Social Issues, 55,* 647–663.

Slee, P. T. (1994). Situational and interpersonal correlates of anxiety associated with peer victimization. *Child Psychology and Human Development, 25*(97), 1–7.

Smith, D. D. (2001). *Introduction to special education: Teaching in an age of opportunity* (4th ed.). Boston: Allyn & Bacon.

Smith, D. D., & Rivera, D. M. (1993). *Effective discipline* (2nd ed.). Austin, TX: Pro-Ed.

Smith, H. (1984). Nonverbal behavior aspects in teaching. In A. Wofgang (Ed.), *Nonverbal behavior: Perspectives, applications, intercultural insights* (pp. 171–202). New York: C.J. Hofgrefe.

Smith, P. K., Mahdavi, J., Carvalho, M., Fisher, S., Russell, S., & Tippett, N. (2008). Cyberbullying: Its nature and impact in secondary school pupils. *Journal of Child Psychology and Psychiatry, 49,* 376–385.

Smith, T. E. C., Polloway, E. A., Patton, J. R., & Dowdy, C. A. (2001). *Teaching students with special needs in inclusive settings* (3rd ed.). Boston: Allyn & Bacon.

Solomon, D., Battistich, V., Watson, M., Schaps, E., & Lewis, C. (2000). A six district study of educational change: Direct and mediated effects of the Child Development Project. *Social Psychology of Education, 41*(1), 3–51.

Solomon, D., Watson, M., Battistich, V., Schaps, E., & Delucchi, K. (1996). Creating classrooms that students experience as communities. *American Journal of Community Psychology, 24*(6), 719–748.

Sorensen, G. (1989). The relationships among teachers: Self-disclosive statements, students' perceptions, and affective learning. *Communication Education, 38,* 259–276.

Sprague, J. (1992). Expanding the research agenda for instructional communication: Raising some unasked questions. *Communication Education, 41,* 1–25.

Stahl, S. A., & Clark, C. H. (1987). The effects of participation expectations in classroom discussion on the learning of science vocabulary. *American Educational Research Journal, 24,* 541–351.

Stern, M., & Karrakar, K. H. (1989). Sex stereotyping in infants: A review of gender labeling studies. *Sex Roles, 20,* 501–522.

Stevens, R. J., & Slavin, R. E. (1995). The cooperative elementary school: Effects on students' achievement, attitudes and social relations. *American Educational Research Journal, 32,* 321–351.

Stewart, J. (1986). Speech and human being: A complement to semiotics. *Quarterly Journal of Speech, 72,* 55–73.

Stone, W. L., & LaGreca, A. M. (1983). Comprehension of nonverbal communication: A reexamination of the social competencies of learning-disabled children. *Journal of Abnormal Child Psychology, 12,* 505–518.

Strangeman, N., Hitchcock, C., Hall T., Meo, G., Gersten, R., & Dimino, J. A. (2006). *LD OnLine: Response-to-Instruction and Universal Design for Learning: How might they intersect in the general education classroom?* Available at: www.ldonline.org/article/13002. Accessed September 25, 2009.

Sugai, G. (2007). Responsiveness-to-intervention: Lessons learned and to be learned. Keynote presentation at the RTI Summit, U.S. Department of

Education, Washington, DC, December. Available at: www.rtinetwork.org/Learn/Behavior/ar/SchoolwideBehavior. Accessed September 26, 2009.

Sugai, G. (2009). *School-wide positive behavior support and response to intervention*. Available at: www.rtinetwork.org/Learn/Behavior/ar/SchoolwideBehavior. Accessed September 26, 2009.

Swain, C., & Pearson, T. (2001). Bridging the digital divide: A building block for teachers. *Learning & Leading with Technology, 28*, 10–13.

Swift, M. S., & Spivack, G. (1969). Achievement related classroom behavior of secondary school normal and disturbed students. *Exceptional Children, 35*, 677–684.

Sylwester, R. (1995). *A celebration of neurons: An educator's guide to the human brain*. Alexandria, VA: ASCD.

Tanno, D. (1997). Names, narratives, and the evolution of ethnic identity. In A. Gonzalez, M. Houston, & V. Chen (Eds.), *Our voices* (2nd ed.). Los Angeles, CA: Roxsbury.

Taylor, H. U. (1989). *Standard English, Black English, and bidialectalism*. New York: Peter Lang.

Teven, J. J., & Hanson, T. L. (2004). The impact of teacher immediacy and perceived caring on teacher competence and trustworthiness. *Communication Quarterly, 52*, 39–53.

Thompson, S. M. (1996). Peer mediation: A peaceful solution. *The School Counselor, 44*, 151–154.

Tomlinson, C. A. (1999). *The differentiated classroom: Responding to the needs of all learners*. Alexandra, VA: Association for Supervision and Curriculum Development.

Tomlinson, C. A. (2001). *How to differentiate instruction in mixed-ability classrooms* (2nd ed.). Alexandra, VA: Association for Supervision and Curriculum Development.

Tomlinson, C. A. (2003). *Fulfilling the promise of the differentiated classroom: Strategies and tools for responsive teaching*. Alexandra, VA: Association for Supervision and Curriculum Development.

Tomlinson, C. A., & Kalbfleisch, M. L. (1998). Teach me, teach my brain: A call for differentiated classrooms. *Educational Leadership, 56*, 52–55.

Tomlinson, C. A., & McTighe, J. (2006). *Integrating differentiated instruction + understanding by design*. Alexandra, VA: Association for Supervision and Curriculum Development.

Toro, P. A., Weissberg, R. P., Guare, J., & Liebenstein, N. L. (1990). A comparison of children with and without learning disabilities on social problem-solving skill, school behavior, and family background. *Journal of Learning Disabilities, 23*, 115–120.

Townsend, B. L. (2000). The disproportionate discipline of African American learners: Reducing school suspensions and expulsions. *Exceptional Children, 66(3)*, 381–391.

Turnbull, R., Turnbull, A., Shank, M., Smith, S., & Leal, D. (2002). *Exceptional lives: Special education in today's schools* (3rd ed.). Columbus, OH: Merrill.

Tyler, J. S., & Mira, M. P. (1999). *Traumatic brain injury in children and adolescents: A sourcebook for teachers and other school personnel*. Austin, TX: Pro-Ed.

U.S. Department of Education (1998). *Twentieth annual report to Congress on the implementation of the Individuals with Disabilities Education Act*. Washington, DC: U.S. Government Printing Office.

U.S. Department of Education (2000). *Twenty-second annual report to Congress on the implementation of the Individuals with Disabilities Education Act.* Washington, DC: U.S. Government Printing Office.

U.S. Department of Education, National Center for Education Statistics (2006). *Student use of computers by level of enrollment, age, and student characteristics.* Washington, DC: U.S. Government Printing Office.

U.S. Department of Education, National Center for Education Statistics (2008). *The condition of education, 2008.* Washington, DC: U.S. Government Printing Office.

Utley, C. A., Mortweet, S. L., & Greenwood, C. R. (1997). Peer-mediated instruction and interventions. *Focus on Exceptional Children, 29*(5), 1–23.

Utley, C. A., & Obiakor, F. E. (2001). *Special education, multicultural education, and school reform: Components of quality education for learners with mild disabilities.* Springfield, IL: Charles Thomas.

Vang, C. T. (2005). Hmong-American students stiff face multiple challenges in public schools. *Multicultural Education, 13*(1), 27–35.

Vasquez, J. A. (1991) Cognitive style and academic achievement. In J. Lyanch, C. Modgil, & S. Modgil (Eds.), *Cultural diversity and the schools: Consensus and controversy.* London: Falconer Press.

Vaughn, S., & Hogan, A. (1994). The social competence of students with learning disabilities over time: A within-individual examination. *Journal of Learning Disabilities, 27,* 292–303.

Villa, R. A., & Thousand, J. S. (1995). *Creating an inclusive school.* Alexandria, VA: Association for Supervision and Curriculum Development (ASCD) Books.

Vygotsky, L. ([1962] 1981), *Thought and language* (trans. A. Hanfmann, & G. Vakar). Cambridge, MA: MIT Press.

Vygotsky, L. (1978). *Mind in society.* Cambridge, MA: Harvard University Press.

Wade, R. C. (1994). Community service learning: Commitment through active citizenship. *Social Studies and the Young Learner, 6*(1), 1–4.

Waldron, N. L., & McLeskey, J. (1998). The effects of an inclusive school program on students with mild and severe learning disabilities. *Exceptional Children, 64,* 395–405.

Walker, D. W., & Leister, C. (1994). Recognition of facial affect cues by adolescents with emotional and behavioral disorders. *Behavioral Disorders, 19*(4), 269–276.

Walker, H. M., McConnell, S., Holmes, D., Todis, B., Walker, J., & Golden, N. (1983). The Walker social skills curriculum: The ACCEPTS program. Austin, TX: Pro-Ed.

Walker, H. M., Todis, B., Holmes, D., & Horton, G. (1988). *The Walker social skills curriculum: The ACCESS program.* Austin, TX: Pro-Ed.

Walker, J. E., & Shea, T. M. (1999). *Behavior management: A practical approach for educators* (7th ed.). Upper Saddle River, NJ: Merrill.

Wanzer, M. B. (1998). An exploratory investigation of student and teacher perceptions of student-generated affinity-seeking behaviors. *Communication Education, 47,* 373–382.

Watkins, C. (2005). *Classrooms as learning communities: What's in it for schools?* New York: Taylor & Francis. Retrieved 20 September, from http://myilibrary. com/

Weber, K., & Custer, R. (2005). Gender-based preferences toward technology education, content activities, and instructional methods. *Journal of Technology Education, 16,* 55–71.

Wehby, J. H., Symons, F. J., Canale, J. A., & Go, F. J. (1998). Teaching practices in classrooms for students with emotional and behavioral disorders: Discrepancies between recommendations and observations. *Behavioral Disorders, 24,* 51–56.

Wehmeyer, M. L., Argan, M., & Hughes, C. A. (1998). *Teaching self-determination to students with disabilities: Basic skills for successful transition.* Baltimore, MD: Brookes.

Wehmeyer, M. L., & Schwartz, M. (1997). Self-determination and positive adult outcomes: A follow up study of youth with mental retardation or learning disabilities. *Exceptional Children, 63,* 245–255.

Weiner, B. (1984). Principles for a theory of student motivation and their application with an attributional framework. *Research on motivation in education: Student motivation, 6,* 15–38.

Weiner, B. (1985). An attributional theory of achievement motivation and emotion. *Psychological Review, 92,* 548–573.

Weiner, J., & Harris, P. J. (1997). Evaluation of an individualized, context-based social skills training program for children with learning disabilities. *Learning Disabilities Research & Practice, 12,* 40–53.

Wenger, E. (1998). *Communities of practice: Learning, meaning, and identity.* Cambridge: Cambridge University Press.

Wentzel, K. B., & Asher, S. R. (1995). The academic lives of neglected, rejected, popular, and controversial children. *Child Development, 66,* 754–763.

Wentzel, K. B., & Caldwell, K. (1997). Friendships, peer acceptance, and group membership: Relations to academic achievement in middle school. *Child Development, 68,* 1198–1209.

Werner, E. E., & Smith, R. S. (1982). *Vulnerable to invincible: A longitudinal study of resilient children and youth.* New York: McGraw-Hill.

Westby, C., & Atencio, D. J. (2002). Computers, culture and learning. *Topics in Language Disorders, 22,* 70–98.

Wielkiewicz, R. M. (1995). *Behavior management in the schools: Principles and procedures* (2nd ed.). Boston: Allyn & Bacon.

Williams, P. A., Alley, R. D., & Hensen, K. T. (1999). Managing secondary classrooms. *Principles and strategies for effective management and instruction.* Boston: Allyn & Bacon.

Wlodkowski, R. J., & Ginsberg, M. B. (1995). *Diversity and motivation: Culturally responsive teaching.* San Francisco: Jossey-Bass.

Wolford, P. L., Heward, W. L., & Alber, S. R. (2001). Teaching middle school students with learning disabilities to recruit peer assistance during cooperative learning group activities. *Learning Disabilities Research & Practice, 16*(3), 161–173.

Wolpe, J. (1961). The systematic desensitization treatment of neuroses. *Journal of Nervous and Mental Disease, 132,* 189–203.

Wolvin, A. D., & Coakley, C. G. (1993). A listening typology. In A. D. Wolvin, & C. G. Coakley (Eds.), *Perspectives on listening* (pp. 15–22). Norwood, NJ: Ablex.

Wood, J. T. (2001). *Gendered lives: Communication, gender and culture* (4th ed.). Belmont, CA: Wadsworth.

Yeung, A. S., Marsh, H. W., & Suliman, R. (2000). Can two tongues live in harmony?: Analysis of the National Education longitudinal data on the maintenance of home language. *American Educational Research Journal, 37,* 1001–1026.

Yoder, D., Retish, E., & Wade, R. (1996). Service-learning: Meeting student and community needs. *Teaching Exceptional Children, 28*(4), 14–18.

Yoder, M. B. (2001). The digital divide. *Learning and Leading with Technology, 28,* 10.

Zhao, Y., Englert, C. S., Chen, J., Jones, S. C., & Ferdig, R. E. (2000). The development of a web-based literacy learning environment: A dialogue between innovation and established practices. *Journal of Research on Computing in Education, 32,* 435–454.

Zionts, P., & Fox, R. W. (1998). Facilitating group classroom meetings: Practical guidelines. *Beyond Behavior, 9*(2), 8–13.

Zirpoli, T. J., & Melloy, K. J. (2001). *Behavior management: Applications for teachers.* Upper Saddle River, NJ: Merrill.

Zirpoli, T. J., & Melloy, K. J. (2007). *Behavior management: Applications for teachers* (5th ed.). Upper Saddle River, NJ: Merrill.

Index